AF826385

Philine-Luise Pulst

The Copyright Law of the People's Republic of China

Deutsches und internationales Wirtschaftsrecht

herausgegeben von

Prof. Dr. Dr. h.c. Marian Paschke

(Universität Hamburg)

Band 62

LIT

Philine-Luise Pulst

The Copyright Law of the People's Republic of China

Understanding the Development and Functioning of the Chinese Copyright Law and the Ongoing Reform as well as the International Influences from the Early Ages until Now

LIT

Thank you to the China-EU School of Law (CESL) at the China University of Political Science and Law (CUPL) in Changping District, Beijing, China for the possibility of a research stay as a Visiting Ph.D. of Law Student.

This book is printed on acid-free paper.

Bibliographic information published by the Deutsche Nationalbibliothek
The Deutsche Nationalbibliothek lists this publication in the Deutsche Nationalbibliografie; detailed bibliographic data are available in the Internet at http://dnb.dnb.de.

ISBN 978-3-643-91396-8 (hc)
ISBN 978-3-643-96396-3 (PDF)
Zugl.: Göttingen, Univ., Diss., 2021

A catalogue record for this book is available from the British Library.

© LIT VERLAG GmbH & Co. KG Wien,
Zweigniederlassung Zürich 2021
Flössergasse 10
CH-8001 Zürich
Tel. +41 (0) 76-632 84 35
E-Mail: zuerich@lit-verlag.ch https://www.lit-verlag.ch
Distribution:
In the UK: Global Book Marketing, e-mail: mo@centralbooks.com
In North America: Independent Publishers Group, e-mail: orders@ipgbook.com
In Germany: LIT Verlag Fresnostr. 2, D-48159 Münster
Tel. +49 (0) 2 51-620 32 22, Fax +49 (0) 2 51-922 60 99, e-mail: vertrieb@lit-verlag.de

PREFACE

This doctoral thesis was accepted as a dissertation by the Faculty of Law at the Georg-August-Universität Göttingen in the summer semester of 2020. Literature is mostly up to date as of February/March 2021.

First and foremost, I would like to thank my doctoral advisor, Professor Dr. Andreas Wiebe. I would also like to thank Professor Dr. Peter-Tobias Stoll for taking over and quickly preparing the second opinion and Professor Dr. Gerald Spindler, who conducted the oral examination together with Professor Dr. Andreas Wiebe.

Furthermore, I would like to thank Professor Dr. Dr. h.c. Marian Paschke for the inclusion in this series of publications.

My greatest thanks, however, goes to my husband and my entire family, who have continuously supported me unconditionally and lovingly and have always given me the necessary backing. This work is dedicated to them in gratitude.

Hamburg, May 2021 Philine-Luise Pulst

TABLE OF CONTENTS (Overview)

TABLE OF CONTENTS (Detailed)

NOTES

The English versions of Chinese statutes, regulations, et cetera have no legal effect in China, even if they are translated and published by the legislative authorities. This dissertation works with translations provided by institutions such as the World Intellectual Property Organization, HFG Law & Intellectual Property, China Copyright and Media and the like. The source of the English translations is stated in the reference list. Where no reference is made to an English version of the legislation, the author worked with the Chinese version.

LIST OF ACRONYMS

ABA	American Bar Association
BCIA	Berne Convention Implementation Act
CAVCA	The China Audio-Video Copyright Association
CCP	Communist Party of China
CFCA	The China Film Copyright Association
CPPCC	Chinese People's Political Consultative Conference
CRL	Current Chinese Copyright Law (2010)
CSC	Copyright Society of China
CNIPA	China National Intellectual Property Office (formerly SIPO)
CWWCS	The China Written Works Copyright Society
DSB	Dispute Settlement Body (WTO)
DSU	Understanding in Rules and Procedures Governing the Settlement of Disputes
GATT	General Agreement on Tariffs and Trade
ICSC	The Images Copyright Society of China
IP	Intellectual Property
IR	Implementing Regulations
IPR	Intellectual Property Rights
KMT	Kuomintang
MCSC	The Music Copyright Society of China
MIIT	Ministry of Industry and Information Technology (China)
MoU	Memorandum of Understanding
MPS	Ministry of Public Security (China)
NPC	National People's Congress (China)

NCAC	National Copyright Administration of the People's Republic of China
PRC	People's Republic of China
RCCM	Regulations on Copyright Collective Administration
RSCP	Regulations on Computer Software Protection
RIN	Regulations on the Protection of Right of Dissemination via Information Network
SIPO	State Intellectual Property Office (now CNIPA)
SLCAO	State Council Legal Affairs Office (China)
SPC	Supreme Court of the People's Republic of China
SPP	Supreme People's Procuratorate
TRIPS	Agreement on Trade-Related Aspects of Intellectual Property Rights
UCC	Universal Copyright Convention
UrhG	Urheberrechtsgesetz (German Copyright Act)
UNESCO	UN Educational, Scientific and Cultural Organization
U.S.	United States of America
U.S.T.R.	United States Trade Representative
VARA	Visual Artists Rights Act
WCT	World Copyright Treaty
WIPO	World Intellectual Property Office
WPPT	WIPO Performances and Phonograms Treaty
WTO	World Trade Organization

CHAPTER 1 – INTRODUCTION

When one talks about China on the one hand and copyright protection on the other hand, many people say:

"Does this actually exist in China?"

This dissertation aims at showing that copying on a large scale is in fact not just tolerated in the People's Republic of China but that China has been and still is undergoing intensive efforts to improve the protection of copyright works.

I. Introduction to the Chinese Copyright System

The People's Republic of China is currently in the process of creating a new and long-awaited copyright law. Intellectual property in general arrived quite late in the People's Republic of China and can be regarded as a transplanted law that was forced onto China by the Western Powers.[1]

This can be explained by China's legal history as the Confucian theories were against individual property and rather focussed on the community as a whole.[2] Copying was not seen as an offense but rather as a compliment to the creator.[3] Due to such a different approach to the meaning of intellectual property it was very hard for China to adapt to internationally set standards – this argument can be supported by the lack of actual enforcement of copyrights.

---

[1] William P. Alford, *To Steal a Book Is an Elegant Offense: Intellectual Property Law in Chinese Civilization* (Stanford: Stanford University Press, 1995), 2; and Ling Li, "The Sky is High and the Emperor is Far Way: The Enforcement of Intellectual Property Law in China" *Bol Mex Derecho Comp* 36, 108 (2003), 954; see also Jonathan Ocko, "Copying, Culture, and Control: Chinese Intellectual Property Law in Historical Context" *Yale J.L.& Human.* 8, 2 - Article 10 (1996), 560.

[2] Mark A. Groombridge in Clarisa Long, *Intellectual Property Law in Emerging Markets* (Washington D.C.: The AEI Press, 2000), 13; see also Alford, *To Steal a Book Is an Elegant Offense: Intellectual Property Law in Chinese Civilization* (1995), 22, 25.

[3] Mark A. Groombridge in Long, *Intellectual Property Law in Emerging Markets* (2000), 13.

China accessed the World Trade Organization in 2001[4] and by that time all laws had to be compliant with the agreements of the WTO, in particular with the Agreement on Trade Related Aspects of Intellectual Property Law (TRIPS) with regard to intellectual property rights.[5]

Contrary to other developing countries, China was not given a transition period for its laws meaning that by the time of accession all laws had to be TRIPS-compliant. However, although at that time the Chinese Copyright Law was being referred to as the "most-up-to-date copyright law" that existed, this did not mean that the enforcement thereof was also assured. In fact, intellectual property right holders feared and still fear the lack of enforcement of their rights in China.

The Copyright Law of the People's Republic in China has been reformed many times during the last decades and a further amendment was promulgated in November 2020 and comes into force on 1 June 2021. This dissertation will focus on the development and function of copyright law in China and the major changes that have been made in the current reform.

Copyright belongs to the group of intellectual property rights and includes scientific, artistic and literary works in all expressional forms and modes.[6] Copyright law does not protect the idea itself but rather the expression of a mind creation[7] – such as the protection of a sheet of music instead of the song as such, the protection of a drawing not the subject of a drawing or the protection of a book rather than the unwritten story.[8]

At the 12th National People's Congress in March 2017, the Chief Justice Zhou Qiang held a speech on the importance of intellectual property rights and provided a work report of the Supreme People's Court. Justice Zhou

---

4 WTO "Accession of the People's Republic of China" Protocol WT/L/432.
5 *Agreement on Trade-Related Aspects of Intellectual Property Rights* (1994), 1869 UNTS 299; 33 ILM 1197 (Annex 1C of the Marrakesh Agreement establishing the World Trade Organization, signed in Marrakesh, Morocco on 15 April 1994, 33 I.L.M. 1125) (provided by WTO).
6 Article 2 (1) *Berne Convention for the Protection of Literary and Artistic Works* (1979), TRT/BERNE/001 (provided by WIPO).
7 Article 9 (2) *TRIPS Agreement* (1994), 1869 UNTS 299; 33 ILM 1197 (Annex 1C of the Marrakesh Agreement establishing the World Trade Organization, signed in Marrakesh, Morocco on 15 April 1994, 33 I.L.M. 1125).
8 See Alford, *To Steal a Book Is an Elegant Offense: Intellectual Property Law in Chinese Civilization* (1995), 1-2.

Qiang said, that China will increase the trials of intellectual property right cases to encourage entrepreneurship and innovation.[9] He also emphasized that China is improving the intellectual property protection and has issued many judiciary interpretations for certain cases, opened up four new IPR tribunals in Nanjing, Suzhou, Wuhan and Chengdu and established information sharing platforms on law enforcement in 29 regions.[10]

In a further speech at the 13th National People's Congress in March 2019, Chief Justice Zhou Qiang again emphasized that China intensified its efforts to protect intellectual property rights and highlights the establishment of the new intellectual property division at the Supreme People's Court.[11] Unfortunately, no reference to the process of the revision of the copyright legislation was made.

On 17 July 2019, the State Council held an executive meeting chaired by Premier Li Keqiang in which it was decided that China has to further strengthen the protection of intellectual property rights.[12] General Secretary and President Xi Jinping stated

> *"that stronger protection of intellectual property rights can best bolster the sharpening of China's economic competitiveness."*[13]

In April 2018, the National Copyright Administration of China (NCAC) held the "2018 National Conference on Copyright Protection in Digital Environment" in Beijing. Yan Xiahong, the Vice Chairman of Cultural, Historical Records and Study Committee of the 13th National Committee of

[9] Xinhua, "China to step up IPR trials to stimulate innovation", 12 March 2017 (http://www.shanghaidaily.com/nation/China-to-step-up-IPR-trials-to-stimulate-innovation/shdaily.shtml, accessed: 6 March 2021).
[10] Ibid.
[11] The Supreme People's Court of The People's Republic of China, "Nation strengthens IPR protections", 13 March 2019 (http://english.court.gov.cn/2019-03/13/content_37449349.htm, accessed: 6 March 2021).
[12] Yue Zhang, "China to enhance IPR protection to improve business climate, boost tech innovation", 17 July 2019 (http://english.www.gov.cn/premier/news/201907/17/content_WS5d2fdfb2c6d00d362f668704.html, accessed: 6 March 2021).
[13] Ibid.

the CPPCC and Chairman of the Copyright Society of China (CSC) also emphasized the importance of copyright protection by saying:

> *"Copyright should be rigorously protected and efforts should be made to establish a mechanism of social co-governance characterized by judicial protection, government supervision, industrial coordination and corporate self-discipline. Resources should be allocated in a scientific way to encourage more creations of quality."*[14]

Yu Cike, the Director General of Copyright Department of NCAC, underlined that a strong protection of copyright is an inevitable requirement of innovation and economic growth with high quality.[15]

In a further speech at the International Forum on Copyright and Creative Industries in the Digital Economy in December 2019, he stated:

> *"Advancing copyright cooperation along the Belt and Road, promoting the development of creative industries, creating a business environment that respects the value of knowledge and achieving common prosperity are the essential contents of and important measures in deepening international exchanges and cooperation and building a community of shared future for mankind"*[16]

Yu Cike further emphasized that the digitalisation is bringing about multiple challenges for the protection and development of copyright.

---

[14] NCAC, "2018 National Conference on Copyright Protection in Digital Environment Held in Beijing", 11 May 2018 (http://en.ncac.gov.cn/copyright/contents/10361/375811.shtml, accessed: 16 May 2020).

[15] Ibid.

[16] NCAC, "International Forum on Copyright and Creative Industries in the Digital Economy: New Challenges and Opportunities", 16 December 2019 (http://en.ncac.gov.cn/copyright/contents/10361/409566.shtml, accessed: 6 March 2021).

These speeches by high officials in China demonstrate that China wants to show the world that a high priority is given to the improvement of the protection of intellectual property rights in China in order for the country and its economy to stay attractive to foreign investors as well as to national entrepreneurs.

II. Content of the Dissertation

For the purpose of clarity, the main focus as well as the structure of the dissertation will be briefly outlined in the following paragraphs.

1. Main Focus of the Dissertation

This dissertation focuses mainly on the legal historical development of copyright law in China in order to understand the reformation of the copyright law and the problems China has been and still is facing.

The current Copyright Law will be discussed in great detail to understand the structure of the law and to show its strengths and weaknesses. This includes a comparison to U.S. and the German copyright systems to better understand how the Chinese Copyright Law can be classified. A significant part is also devoted to the actual enforcement of copyrights in China including an analysis of the two-channel system that China has opted for. The dissertation concludes with a critical discussion of the current reform of the legislation.

2. Structural Overview

In the following, the content of each chapter is summarized.

Chapter 1 introduces copyright and its challenges in China, depicts the most recent developments and outlines the structure of this dissertation.

In **Chapter 2**, to understand the whole development and functioning of the copyright law in China this dissertation first starts off with explaining the theories of the conception of law and describing the sources of law in China. Then, the whole historical background and development of intellectual property legislation, in particular copyright law, in China is analysed.

Further, focus is placed upon the international relations of China as well as the agreements and conventions China has acceded to. China's accession to various international agreements is important in order to understand the fast development of the Chinese intellectual property legislation and the problem China has been facing in adjusting to international standards.

Following that, in **Chapter 3**, the current Copyright Law of the People's Republic of China is discussed and analysed by focussing on its main elements. A subsection of this chapter is a comparative analysis of the Chinese copyright law to the copyright systems of the United States of America (Anglo-American system) and of the Federal Republic of Germany (European Droit d'Auteur system) to further understand the structure of the Chinese Copyright Law.

This chapter also includes an overview of the Chinese state authorities and the actual enforcement system when dealing with copyright infringements. An insight into the various problems/weaknesses of the current system is provided and critically discussed. The chapter ends with statistics of copyright cases in China showing the developments over the last years.

Chapter 4 starts with an overview of the legislative process in China and then deals with the reformation process of the Chinese Copyright Law. In a first step, the development of the drafts of the revised Copyright Law are discussed and in a second step, the comprehensive third draft from 2014 is analysed in greater detail by giving an overview of the planned changes compared to the current copyright law and critically discussing the most important changes of the law drafted in the first part of the reform between 2012 and 2014. Further, an overview of the current developments in China, in particular the negotiations between the U.S. and China, will be given. Following that, the second part of the reform, finally resurrected in 2020, is presented and the final promulgated law which comes into force in June 2021 is critically analysed and evaluated.

Chapter 5 summarizes the findings of the dissertation and shows the improvements as well as the still existing weaknesses of the promulgated amended Copyright Law in China. It further includes an outlook to the possible developments of the legal framework in the future.

CHAPTER 2 – THE CONCEPTION OF LAW IN CHINA AND THE DEVELOPMENT OF A COPYRIGHT LAW

In order to understand Chinese Copyright Law, it has to be discussed in a historical context before analysing the international relations and accessions to various agreements and conventions.

I. Introduction to the Legal History and Conception of Law in China

For the purpose of understanding the complexities of Chinese intellectual property laws and the problems China was facing when creating such, it is very important to look at the development of China as an economic power and the culture of law that has been influenced by old philosophies and has shaped the law as it is today.

1. Economic Background

The People's Republic of China was founded in 1949 and is a socialist state combining communism and capitalism in one regime. The state-directed economy on the one hand and the existence of private and foreign assets as well as the peaceful creation of a new social order on the other hand can explain this hybrid of communism and capitalism.[17] In general, it can be said that China moved from a centrally planned economy to a more market based economy. The People's Republic of China is still recognised as a developing country although it has a great economic power and an enormous growth rate. This is due to the fact that the status of being a developing country is measured on the per capita income which is still very low in China.[18] In fact, China can be regarded as one of the fastest emerging markets in the world. Under the leadership of Deng Xiaoping, China

---

[17] Xun Yu, *Schadensersatzanspruch im Urheberrecht - Eine vergleichende Betrachtung des chinesischen und deutschen Rechts*, 1. Auflage, Reihe Rechtswissenschaft (Göttingen: Sierke Verlag, 2005), 2.

[18] Although China has come a long way during the last decades, China's GDP per capita is just over $9,700 in 2018 (approx. 1/6 of the GDP per capita of the United States) – for a country to be considered developed based on GDP per capita it should be higher than $12,235, see Zhiming Xin, "Developed country status is still some distance away", 5 March 2020

has opened up its markets in 1978 (Open Door Policy) and since then, has attracted many foreign investors because of the low production costs and the high potential of the market.[19] However, without a functioning legal system, in which foreign investors feel protected, the investment will eventually decrease if nothing is done to protect their rights. Intellectual property right holders, in particular, fear piracy and therefore a stronger protection of their rights is needed. This is the reason, why China has started amending its intellectual property laws since the 1990s to reach international standards in order for China to remain attractive to foreign investors.

2. The Chinese Conception of Law and Governance

Traditionally, the Chinese society has never put much emphasis on legal rules. Nevertheless, first appearances of legal rules and regulations can be found as early as 2100 B.C. in the Xia dynasty (夏朝) and were concerned with the structuring of living together in one tribe; however, only some written evidence can be found for that era.[20] The further analysis of the Chinese history of law shows some codifications of law that date back to the sixth century B.C..[21]
It can be argued that the early laws of China were very penal in nature which meant that civil matters or the like were only partially dealt with whereas criminal acts or acts contrary to the customs and rites were enforced quite harshly – that kind of behaviour was seen as a disruption of the social order and hence, unacceptable.[22]

(http://global.chinadaily.com.cn/a/202003/05/WS5e605c3ba31012821727c7bd.html, accessed: 6 March 2021).

[19] Paul B. Birden, "Technology Transfers to China: An Outline of Chinese Law" *Loy. L.A. Int'l & Comp. L.J.* 16 (1994), 413; Chris Devonshire-Ellis, Andy Scott, and Sam Woollard, *Intellectual Property Rights in China*, 2 ed. (Berlin: Springer, 2011), 1.

[20] Jianqiang Nie, *The Enforcement of Intellectual Property Rights in China* (London, UK: Cameron May, 2006), 71.

[21] The first codified laws can be found in the era of the Chou dynasty, see Derk Bodde, "Basic Concepts of Chinese Law: The Genesis and Evolution of Legal Thought in Traditional China" *Proc. Ameri. Phil. Soc.* 107, 5 (1963), 375, 381.

[22] Ibid., 375.

Proper detailed written evidence of the early laws of China can only be found from the Qin dynasty (秦朝) – between 221-206 B.C. – onwards.[23] Three main philosophies have mainly shaped the emergence of legal rules in China – Confucianism, Legalism and Buddhism.[24] The foundation of the first Chinese empire – Qin – was assisted by the Legalist which shows that the conception of law was formed in a legalist way.[25] However, the succeeding Han dynasty (漢朝), which can be dated from 207 B.C. until 220 A.D., acknowledged the Confucian theories and it can be argued that the Confucian and Legalist theories fused during that time.[26] Another main legal construct can be found in Buddhism.[27] In order to understand these three approaches to law they are discussed further in the following paragraphs.

a) The Buddhist Theories

Contrary to the theories of the Confucians and the Legalists, who follow the opinion that law is given by men, the Buddhist followers believe that the law is God-given and is derived from the doctrines of Buddha.[28] The law of the Buddha is called Buddha-Dharma (佛法 fófǎ) and arrived in China during the first century A.D..[29] The most-known law of Buddha is 'karma'. 'Karma' can be described as the "law of action and reaction"[30]. Therefore, every act – being negative or positive – has a certain response – punishment or reward – to it, which demonstrates that 'karma' can be understood as the widest law of all.[31]

---

[23] Ibid., 377.

[24] Other philosophies that influenced the development of China were Taoism and the Ying and Yang doctrine. Nie, *The Enforcement of Intellectual Property Rights in China* (2006), 63; Luke T. Lee and Whalen W. Lai, "The Chinese Conceptions of Law: Confucian, Legalist, and Buddhist" *Hastings L.J.* 29 (1977-1978), 1307.

[25] Lee and Lai, "The Chinese Conceptions of Law" *Hastings L.J.* 29 (1977-1978), 1307.

[26] Ibid.

[27] Ibid.

[28] Ibid.

[29] Ibid., 1312, 1313.

[30] Ibid., 1315.

[31] Ibid.

Nowadays, the Buddhist principles are still present in the thinking of Chinese people. One good example is the principle of equality being one of the main theories of both communism and Buddhism.[32]

b) The Confucian-Legalist Theories

Much more important to the understanding of the Chinese governance of law are the Confucian and Legalist approaches to law. As discussed above, the foundation of the first empire in China – the Qin dynasty – was strongly assisted by the Legalist movement and, during that time, Legalism was adopted as a state ideology.[33] During the succeeding dynasties, Confucianism was favoured more than Legalism but nevertheless, the Legalist structure of governance remained in the system.[34]

In China, the recognition of these two different conceptions of law can be seen in the two different terms that are used for rules and regulations – 'lǐ' (理) and 'fǎ' (法).[35]

aa) The Meaning of 'Lǐ' (理) – Confucian Principle

Confucianism is not based on any religious motifs but constitutes a school of political and ethical thought, which was founded by Confucius himself together with his disciples.[36] Confucianism evolved during the periods of Spring and Autumn (770-476 B.C.) – a time when many people were dissatisfied with the situation and many schools of thought arose.[37] The reason why Confucianism prevailed over the other theories is that the main aim of the Confucian school of thought was to establish peace and harmony.[38] Confucian devotees believe that rules and regulations do not need to be created for a society to work but that they exist naturally.[39] Taking this into account, it can be said that Confucianists are in strong favour of the rule of

---

[32] Ibid., 1325.
[33] Nie, *The Enforcement of Intellectual Property Rights in China* (2006), 64.
[34] Ibid.
[35] Lee and Lai, "The Chinese Conceptions of Law" *Hastings L.J.* 29 (1977-1978), 1308.
[36] Zhaojie Li, "Traditional Chinese World Order" *Chinese JIL* 1, 1 (2002), 36.
[37] Ibid., 36, 37.
[38] Ibid., 37.
[39] Lee and Lai, "The Chinese Conceptions of Law" *Hastings L.J.* 29 (1977-1978), 1307.

propriety – which is understood to be the concept of 'lǐ' (理).[40] This school of thought was accepted as the state ideology during the Han dynasty and has permanently shaped the Chinese understanding of the world.[41]

'Lǐ' can be translated in several ways meaning reason, logic, inner principle, propriety or moral rules and constitutes the main term of defining the Confucian doctrine of the 'five relations' of men – "ruler and subject, father and son, husband and wife, elder and younger brother, and friend and friend".[42] A unified definition for the meaning of 'lǐ' in Chinese law has never been achieved since it is a very complex concept.[43] One of the key principles of the Confucian doctrine is that the hierarchy between the different subjects – i.e. father and son (seniority and juniority) or ruler and subject (superiority and inferiority) – cannot be changed under any circumstances because these are provided by nature itself; only the obedience to this concept is able to achieve fairness and hence, a social order.[44] According to the Confucian doctrine, a bad human could be changed through good education and the understanding of morals and not by punishing a person for the acts that have been committed.[45] People who follow 'lǐ' are willing to amend their opinion and give in when a conflict arises in order to maintain harmony in the society.[46] By this method of making concessions to one another, litigation of certain individual rights will not be needed.[47]

Compared to Western principles, 'lǐ' could be compared to the rules of good faith and the principle of 'pacta sunt servanda'.[48] It is very hard to find a single definition of law for these constructs. For defining the law of a state or society it is not possible to only look at the rules and regulations that have been created by the state (politics) but also to take into account

---

40 Nie, *The Enforcement of Intellectual Property Rights in China* (2006), 64.
41 Li, "Traditional Chinese World Order" *Chinese JIL* 1, 1 (2002), 36.
42 Lee and Lai, "The Chinese Conceptions of Law" *Hastings L.J.* 29 (1977-1978), 1307.
43 Nie, *The Enforcement of Intellectual Property Rights in China* (2006), 64.
44 Ibid., 67.
45 Ibid., 68.
46 Glenn R. Butterton, "Pirates, Dragons and U.S. Intellectual Property Rights in China: Problems and Prospects of Chinese Enforcement" *Arizona L.R.* 38 (1996), 1109.
47 Ibid.
48 Lee and Lai, "The Chinese Conceptions of Law" *Hastings L.J.* 29 (1977-1978), 1311, 1328.

the 'living law' of the people which is shaped by the family customs, religion or other institutions such as diplomatic, social, political or military organizations.[49] However, it needs to be noticed that 'lǐ' is not a fixed custom and can be changed over the years in order to become conform with the evolving life; similar to the definition of Western customary law, 'lǐ' becomes an enforceable rule once it is accepted as a rule by the society.[50] A good example for that is the transition from the Confucian 'lǐ' to the Maoist 'lǐ' because the communist party under the leadership of Mao Zedong aimed at changing the society's thinking to accept the Communist principles.[51]

bb) The Meaning of 'Fǎ' (法) – Legalist Principle

In contrast to the Confucian thinking that the social harmony is naturally given, the core idea of the Legalists is the position of the leader (in earlier times the king) to create the rules and regulations for a society to work.[52] In other words, Legalists based their system on the rule of law – the concept of 'fǎ' (法).[53]

The term 'fǎ' can be translated as 'law' being not as complex as 'lǐ' and is traced back to the doctrines of Han Fei-tze (韓非子, also Han Feizi) – a Legalist school that blossomed in the beginning of the Qin dynasty.[54] During the Qin dynasty the whole Chinese territory was consolidated into one great empire and the Qin ruled the society in a very penal and stern way and formulated a very harsh administrative law for the purpose of maintaining the empire.[55] Similar to the Confucians, the Legalists did not focus

[49] Eugen Ehrlich and Klaus A. Ziegert, *Fundamental Principles of the Sociology of Law (translated by Walter L. Moll)*, 4 ed., 5, Harvard Studies in Jurisprudence (New Brunswick, USA and London, UK: Transaction Publishers (1936), 2009), 493-494; Nie, *The Enforcement of Intellectual Property Rights in China* (2006), 66.
[50] Lee and Lai, "The Chinese Conceptions of Law" *Hastings L.J.* 29 (1977-1978), 1326.
[51] Ibid.
[52] Ibid., 1307.
[53] Nie, *The Enforcement of Intellectual Property Rights in China* (2006), 64.
[54] Lee and Lai, "The Chinese Conceptions of Law" *Hastings L.J.* 29 (1977-1978), 1309.
[55] Butterton, "Pirates, Dragons and U.S. Intellectual Property Rights in China" *Arizona L.R.* 38 (1996), 1110.

their laws on civil matters but more on criminal acts and improprieties that would have led to the distortion of social harmony when not pursued and enforced by law.[56] Also, the law was not enforced between two parties on an equal level but rather, the victims had to go to the state which would have dealt with the perpetrator.[57]

The main difference between the Confucian and Legalist approaches is that 'lǐ' is meant to teach men from the beginning that something is forbidden whereas 'fǎ' punishes people after an illegal act has been committed.[58] In other words, Legalist devotees aim for governance by law and Confucian devotees strive for the governance of a society by men themselves.[59] Also, it can be argued that the Legalists pursued an objective and prescribed governance, in contrast to the Confucianists who followed no specified scheme and decided based on the situation by taking into account the positions and the relations of the person in question.[60] Therefore, 'fǎ' treats every person alike whereas 'lǐ' recognizes different personal situations and decides differently based on each individual situation.[61] The Legalists were of the opinion that a good society can only be built by that objective method and certain standards needed to be set up to punish or reward certain actions.[62] One of the main goals of codification was the transparency for the population that was able to understand the prohibitions when reading the law.[63] However, although the Legalists codified many criminal rules, there is no proof that the public actually gained access to such and also, whether the common people were in fact able to read the law.[64]

The Confucianists overruled the Legalists by the end of the Qin dynasty but nevertheless the Legalist system of governance continued to influence

---

[56] Ibid.
[57] Ibid., 1111.
[58] Lee and Lai, "The Chinese Conceptions of Law" *Hastings L.J.* 29 (1977-1978), 1308-1309.
[59] Ibid., 1309.
[60] Ibid.
[61] Nie, *The Enforcement of Intellectual Property Rights in China* (2006), 72.
[62] Ibid.
[63] Wallace Johnson, "Status and Liability for Punishment in the T'ang Code" *Chi.-Kent. L. Rev.* 71, 1 Symposium on Ancient Law, Economics and Society Part II: Ancient Rights and Wrongs / Symposium on Ancient Law, Economics and Society Part II: Ancient Near Eastern Land Laws (1995), 220.
[64] Ibid.

the Confucian rules in the succeeding dynasties. Thus, the argument of a Confucian-Legalist fusion is strengthened by that fact.

cc) Interaction of 'Lǐ' and 'Fǎ'

As mentioned above, first appearances of regulations for the society – both 'lǐ' and 'fǎ' – can be found long before the Qin dynasty and it can be argued that these two different approaches originate from the same customs.[65] China experienced many profound changes during the eras of Spring and Autumn and the Warring States (770 B.C. – 222 B.C.) in which the rules of propriety ('lǐ') were not satisfactory on their own and a strong Legalist movement occurred when China unified to an empire during the Qin dynasty.[66] After the fall of the Qin dynasty, Legalism was not accepted as a state ideology anymore but nevertheless the well-structured Legalist system remained during the strong eras of Confucianism.[67]

Both doctrines centralized the supremacy of the ruler and concentrated on the capability of governance instead of having a legitimate way of ruling a state.[68] As it becomes clear from the former discussions, the ways to achieve the efficient governance differ between 'lǐ' and 'fǎ' where the former focuses on moral education whereas the latter focuses on the punishment after a certain act has been committed.[69]

The Tang Code of 624 A.D. (唐律) is one of the most important legislations in the history of Chinese law.[70] As previously discussed, the Confucianists emphasized the relationship of men and put huge emphasis on the hierarchy between the different subjects and hence, differing rules.[71]

---

[65] Nie, *The Enforcement of Intellectual Property Rights in China* (2006), 74.
[66] Ibid., 75.
[67] Ibid.
[68] Ibid.
[69] Ibid., 75-76.
[70] Wallace Johnson, *The T'ang Code. Volume 1, General Principles - Introduction and Translation* (Princeton, New Jersey: Princeton University Press, 1979), 5.
[71] Lee and Lai, "The Chinese Conceptions of Law" *Hastings L.J.* 29 (1977-1978), 1307; Nie, *The Enforcement of Intellectual Property Rights in China* (2006), 64.

In contrast, the Legalists aimed for a coded law that could be applied to everyone with the state being the highest authority.[72] These two very different views ('lǐ' and 'fǎ') were combined in the Tang Code by stipulating a law that was applicable to everyone with differing regulations for various classes; this law can be seen as the first comingling of 'lǐ' and 'fǎ' and constituted a compromise of these two different conceptions of law in one codification.[73]

For the Confucianists, 'lǐ' is superior to 'fǎ'.[74] If those two concepts stand in conflict to each other a saying from the Analects of Confucius can be used to show the supremacy of 'lǐ':

> *"If the people be led by laws ('fa'), and uniformity sought to be given them by punishments, they will try to avoid the punishment, but have no sense of shame. If they be led by virtue, and uniformity sought to be given them by the rules of propriety ('li'), they will have the sense of shame, and moreover will become good."*[75]

'Lǐ' and 'fǎ' still coexist in modern China and constitute two of the most influential approaches to the Chinese legal system.[76]

c) Understanding the Complexities of Chinese Law

Since the Chinese people have so many different approaches to law and the governance of the Chinese society, the law needs to be studied very widely, looking at all areas that touch the creation of law such as politics, economics, religion, philosophy, psychology, sociology and classics.[77] The essence of the Chinese law will only be found when trying to discover its origin.

---

[72] Johnson, *The T'ang Code. Volume 1, General Principles - Introduction and Translation* (1979), 12.
[73] Ibid.
[74] Nie, *The Enforcement of Intellectual Property Rights in China* (2006), 76.
[75] Book II Chapter III of Confucius, *The Analects of Confucius (English translation by James Legge)* (Auckland, NZ: The Floating Press, 2010), 11-12.
[76] Lee and Lai, "The Chinese Conceptions of Law" *Hastings L.J.* 29 (1977-1978), 1312.
[77] Ibid., 1329.

3. The Link to Copyright Protection

The construct of copyright and related rights belongs to the group of intellectual property rights and is a great achievement of society to protect the creations of authors and artists including works such as paintings, books, music, sculptures, computer programs et cetera.[78] Copyright protection plays a very important role in international negotiations, exchanges and agreements concerning economics, politics, technology and science as well as cultural aspects.[79]

Intellectual property rights are not the result of the long Chinese culture.[80] Intellectual property rights were adapted into Chinese law from other jurisdictions during the last decades and are still changing as the laws of the People's Republic of China evolve in order to be accepted internationally. As discussed in the previous section, the Chinese conception of law is very different to the conception of the Western countries and intellectual property law, in particular, is contrary to the Communist understanding of society.[81] This is one of the reasons why China faced and still faces many difficulties in implementing an effective legal system for intellectual property rights.

For the purpose of understanding the development of the intellectual property law – especially the copyright law – in China, it is necessary to look at the cultural and historical aspects of China's intellectual property law.[82]

[78] WIPO, "Copyright - What is copyright?" (http://www.wipo.int/copyright/en/, accessed: 6 March 2021).
[79] Sanqiang Qu, *Copyright in China* (Beijing: Foreign Languages Press 2002), i.
[80] Zhi Wei, *Der Urheberrechtsschutz in China mit Hinweisen auf das Deutsche Recht*, Band 462, Rechtswissenschaftliche Forschung und Entwicklung (München: Verlag V. Florentz, 1994), 3.
[81] Mark A. Groombridge in Long, *Intellectual Property Law in Emerging Markets* (2000), 13.
[82] Qingjiang Kong, *WTO, Internationalization and the Intellectual Property Rights Regime in China* (Singapore: Marshal Cavendish International, 2005), 15-16; Mark Sidel, "The Legal Protection of Copyright and the Rights of Authors in the People's Republic of China, 1949-1984: Prelude to the Chinese Copyright Law" *Colum.-VLA Art&L.* 9 (1984-1985), 477.

4. Sources of Law in the People's Republic of China

First, it is necessary to understand the various sources of law and the hierarchy of the laws in China.

The legal system in the People's Republic of China is a coded system following the legal tradition of the neo-Roman Law, also called the Continental Law, and all legal rules and regulations need to be codified and promulgated by the organs that are authorized to pass new laws by the constitution.[83] The system of codification remained in the Chinese legal practice, although all existing laws, including the statutes of the Kuomintang government, were invalidated when the People's Republic of China was founded in 1949.[84] It is very complex to define a distinct hierarchy of norms in the People's Republic of China. However, for the Chinese law, it can be structured as follows:

a) Constitution and NPC

The Constitution of the People's Republic of China of 1982 that has been passed by the National People's Congress is the highest law in China.[85] The Constitution establishes the structure of the Chinese government and stipulates the fundamental rights and obligations of the citizens of China. Also, the fundamental laws (法律 fǎlǜ) that are passed by the NPC are superior to other laws and regulations. Examples for "fundamental laws" are the Criminal Law, the Administrative Procedural Law, the Civil Procedural Law and the General Principles of Civil Law.[86]

---

[83] Chenguang Wang, "Law-making functions of the Chinese courts: Judicial activism in a county or rapid social changes" *Front. Law China* 1, 4 (2006), 527.
[84] Ibid., 527-528; Kong, *WTO, Internationalization and the Intellectual Property Rights Regime in China* (2005), 16; Mark Sidel, "Copyright, Trademark and Patent Law in the People's Republic of China" *Tex. Int'l L.J.* 21 (1985-1986), 261. - Sidel is referring to Shen Ren'Gan and Zhong Yingke "Banquanfa Qiantan" (A Discussion of Copyright Law) (1982) at 100-04.
[85] The legislative competence is given to the NPC by Article 62 (1), (3) *Constitution of the People's Republic of China* (1982/2018 version) (provided by NPC Observer).
[86] Qingjiang Kong, "Enforcement of WTO Agreements in China - Illusion or Reality?" *Journal of World Trade* 35, 6 (2001), 1198.

b) Standing Committee of the NPC

Since the NPC is only meeting once a year, the Standing Committee is the steady legislative organ in the PRC. Hence, the laws that are passed by the Standing Committee of the National People's Congress (also called 法律 fǎlǜ) stand inferior to the Constitution and the fundamental laws.[87]

The 1990 Copyright Law of the People's Republic of China and its amendments in 2001 and 2010 is one example of a law that has been passed by the Standing Committee of the NPC.

c) State Council and Ministries

The State Council is responsible for the administration of the state.[88] According to Article 89 (3) of the Constitution, the State Council has the duty to lead and supervise the ministries, commissions and local authorities. The State Council and its ministries and commissions have the duty to release administrative regulations (行政法规 xíngzhèng fǎguī) such as regulations, provisions and guidelines which can be placed directly under the laws of the Standing Committee in the hierarchy of law.[89]

These regulations are national and therefore binding in the whole PRC.

d) Provinces and Autonomous Regions

In consequence, the following norms are the laws and regulations created by the provincial governments and the regulations from the autonomous zones (地方性法规 dìfāngxìng fǎguī) that have to report such laws to the Standing Committee of the NPC for the record.[90]

These laws can only be enforced in the respective provincial jurisdictions.

---

[87] The legislative competence is given to the Standing Committee by Article 67 (2) *Constitution PRC* (1982/2018 version).

[88] Article 85 ibid.

[89] The legislative competence is given to the State Council by Article 89 (1) and to the ministries under the State Council by Article 90 (2) ibid.

[90] The legislative competence is given to the people's congresses of the provinces and municipalities by Article 100 ibid.

e) International and Bilateral Agreements

Historically, the Chinese saw international agreements as being harmful to the sovereignty of the state and causing national degradation.[91] International treaties only came into the focus of China after the reform and the open policy of 1978 because the acceptance of such was necessary for preparing the accession to the World Trade Organization (WTO).[92] According to Article 89 (9) of the PRC Constitution, the power of concluding international treaties (条约 tiáoyuē) and international agreements (协定 xiédìng) lies with the State Council. The place of international treaties and agreements in the hierarchy of Chinese law is very complicated but one rule in order to determine the status of an international agreement is, whether it had to be ratified by the Standing Committee of the NPC prior to taking effect or whether it is enough that the State Council agreed upon and promulgated it on its own. The former has the same rank as the laws of the Standing Committee, whereas the latter has the same rank as the administrative regulations that are passed by the State Council.[93]

Examples for international agreements concerning copyright are the Berne Convention and the Agreement on Trade-Related Aspects of Intellectual Property Rights. The international agreements relating to copyright law that China has acceded to are discussed in greater detail in the following.

f) Legislative and Administrative Interpretation

Article 67 of the PRC Constitution[94], as well as Article 45 of the PRC Legislation Law[95], stipulate that the Standing Committee of the National People's Congress can interpret the Constitution and the laws. Since the Standing Committee is the second highest law-making organ in China, it has the exclusive power of legislative interpretation as long as the National People's Congress has the legislative power for the respective area of law. The

---

[91] Björn Ahl, "Chinese Law and International Treaties" *HKLJ* 39, 3 (2009), 737.
[92] Ibid., 738; also see Kong, "Enforcement of WTO Agreements in China" *Journal of World Trade* 35, 6 (2001), 1181-1183, 1195-1996.
[93] Kong, "Enforcement of WTO Agreements in China" *Journal of World Trade* 35, 6 (2001), 1204.
[94] Article 67 (1), (4) *Constitution PRC* (1982/2018 version).
[95] *Legislation Law of the People's Republic of China* (2000/2015 version) (provided by npc.gov.cn).

authority to make requests for legislative interpretations is also stipulated in the Chinese Legislation Law:

> *"The State Council, the Central Military Commission, the Supreme People's Court, the Supreme People's Procuratorate, and the special committees of the National People's Congress and the standing committees of the people's congresses of each province, autonomous region, and directly governed municipality, may submit requests for legislative interpretation to the Standing Committee of the National People's Congress."*[96]

However, the standing committees of the local people's congresses can also provide legislative interpretations if an interpretation of their own local regulations is required.[97] This distinction between national laws and decrees and local rules and regulations and the authorities that are responsible for interpretation of such can be called "classification test".[98] The Chinese Legislation Law also stipulates when and under what circumstance a legislative interpretation is allowed, the so-called "circumstance test".[99]

Article 45 Chinese Legislation Law states:

> *"The power of legal interpretation belongs to the Standing Committee of the National People's Congress.*
>
> *If the law has one of the following circumstances, it shall be explained by the Standing Committee of the National People's Congress:*

[96] Article 46 ibid.

[97] Xiaonan Yang, "Legislative Interpretations by the Standing Committee of the National People's Congress in China" *Hong Kong L.J.* 38, 1 (2008), 263.

[98] Ibid.

[99] Ibid.

> *(1) The provisions of the law need to further clarify the specific meaning;*
>
> *(2) After the law is enacted, a new situation arises that requires the legal basis for their application."*[100]

If the needed interpretation of the law does not fall within these two categories and rather concerns the application of laws and decrees, the State Council can issue legislative interpretations as long as no judicial or procuratorial interpretation is needed.[101] The legislative interpretations by the Standing Committee of the National People's Congress are directly binding like laws.[102] Other administrative authorities such as ministries, commissions and local governments and their departments can also issue respective interpretations.[103] These interpretations by the State Council that mainly relate to regulations and rules of an administrative nature are formally called administrative interpretations.[104] Administrative regulations often stipulate that the legislative body drafting the regulation usually has the authority to issue its interpretations as well.[105] The State Council's interpretations are often not very specific and can be generally applied to different situations, whereas lower administrative authorities are more specific in their interpretations.[106]

g) Judicial and Procuratorial Interpretation

In general, if the application of law is unclear, the Supreme Court of the People's Republic of China (SPC) or the Supreme People's Procuratorate (SPP) interprets the law.[107] Article 104 paragraph 3 Chinese Legislation Law also states:

---

[100] Article 45 *Legislation Law PRC* (2000/2015 version).
[101] Yang, "Legislative Interpretations by the Standing Committee" *Hong Kong L.J.* 38, 1 (2008), 263.
[102] Article 50 *Legislation Law PRC* (2000/2015 version).
[103] Wang, "Law-making functions of the Chinese courts" *Front. Law China* 1, 4 (2006), 534.
[104] Ibid., 534-535.
[105] Ibid.
[106] Ibid.
[107] Article 104 *Legislation Law PRC* (2000/2015 version).

> *"The judicial organs and procuratorial organs other than the Supreme People's Court and the Supreme People's Procuratorate must not make interpretations on the specific application of law."*[108]

Although China does not have a separation of powers, the 'judicative' has many functions and powers. According to Article 18 of the Organic Law of the People's Courts, the SPC is authorized to interpret the law if the application of laws and decrees is unclear in judicial proceedings.[109] Judicial interpretations can be defined as the bridge between the legislation passed by the NPC and the local governments and the jurisdiction in the courts when hearing a case.[110] In contrast to other countries following the civil law system, the Chinese judges have a great discretion in the interpretation of law concerning the application of general rules to concrete cases and in some situations creative interpretation is crucial for the conclusion of a case.[111]

The judicial interpretations of the SPC and the SPP are necessary for filling in the loopholes in the legislation of the NPC and although they are usually not directly binding it can be argued that they have a 'semi-legislative character' and take effect as secondary law (再次立法 zàicì lìfǎ or 二次立法 èr cì lìfǎ).[112] This can be explained by the fact that the People's Republic of China follows the "German-style" Continental Law System and not the Common Law System, so that precedents decided in court cannot be legally binding to the lower courts; nevertheless, lower courts often follow the decisions made by the higher courts.[113]

---

[108] Article 104 ibid.

[109] *Organic Law of the People's Courts of the People's Republic of China* (1979/2018 version) (provided by npc.gov.cn).

[110] Wang, "Law-making functions of the Chinese courts" *Front. Law China* 1, 4 (2006), 533.

[111] Ibid., 528.

[112] Ronald C. Keith and Zhiqiu Lin, "Judicial Interpretation of China's Supreme People's Court as "Secondary Law" with Special Reference to Criminal Law" *China Information* 23 (2009), 224.

[113] Yang, "Legislative Interpretations by the Standing Committee" *Hong Kong L.J.* 38, 1 (2008), 263-264.

The judicial and procuratorial interpretations must be reported to the Standing Committee of the National People's Congress within 30 days after the SPC and/or the SPP have created such.[114]

h) Jurisdiction, Legal Doctrine and Politics

Jurisdiction, legal doctrine and the political ideologies of the CCP are not sources of law but are very important for the judicial practice.[115]

II. The History of Copyright Law in China

This section explores the history of copyright law in the People's Republic of China and the international agreements China has acceded to in order to be recognised by foreign investors and gain worldwide acceptance.

1. The Doctrine of Confucianism relating to Intellectual Property Rights

Intellectual property rights are rights that are granted to an individual for a creation of the mind such as '*inventions, literary and artistic works, and symbols, names, images, and designs used in commerce*'[116]. The understanding of rights being granted to an individual had not been common in China for centuries. It can be said that the construct of individual rights, especially intellectual property rights, is not 'indigenous' to the legal concept in the People's Republic of China.[117] This can be mainly explained by looking at the theories of Confucianism and the two main concepts drawn out of it.[118]

---

[114] Article 104 *Legislation Law PRC* (2000/2015 version).
[115] Wei, *Der Urheberrechtsschutz in China mit Hinweisen auf das Deutsche Recht* (1994), 25.
[116] WIPO, "What is Intellectual Property?" (http://www.wipo.int/about-ip/en/index.html, accessed: 6 March 2021).
[117] Alford, *To Steal a Book Is an Elegant Offense: Intellectual Property Law in Chinese Civilization* (1995), 2; and Li, "The Sky is High and the Emperor is Far Way" *Bol Mex Derecho Comp* 36, 108 (2003), 954; also see Ocko, "Copying, Culture, and Control" *Yale J.L.& Human.* 8, 2 - Article 10 (1996), 560.
[118] Mark A. Groombridge in Long, *Intellectual Property Law in Emerging Markets* (2000), 13.

First, social advancement was seen as learning the range of classical literature and becoming familiar with the Chinese history rather than studying new subjects (technical training)[119]; this can also be illustrated by Confucius' saying

> *"I transmit rather than create; I believe in and love the Ancients."*[120]

The copying of works created by others was seen as a form of 'flattery' because an imitation confirmed the worthiness of a creation and did not constitute an offence to the creator nor was the creation of something new seen to be worthy of receiving monetary credit for it.[121]

Secondly, a great antagonism to the Western understanding can be seen when looking at the correlation of the state and an individual – the Chinese word for individual '个人' (gérèn) contains egoistic aspects that are seen as negative.[122] Therefore, works created by an individual were seen to be the intellectual property of the whole community rather than being the intellectual achievement of the individual itself. The whole concept of property can be hardly found in the Chinese legal history.[123]

In relation to copyright and related rights, it is interesting to look at the printing habits during the early times in China. In China, printing started during the Sui- (隋) and Tang- (唐) Dynasty (618-907) when handwritten books could not satisfy the demand of the – at that time – prosperous Chinese citizens anymore.[124] The printing companies received protection by the state and a so-called 'privilege of printing' evolved which can be seen as the first kind of protection of literature.[125] However, this cannot be seen as a proper copyright as it is understood today because this 'privilege of

[119] Alford, *To Steal a Book Is an Elegant Offense: Intellectual Property Law in Chinese Civilization* (1995), 22,25.
[120] The Analects of Confucius, bk.7 ch.1 as qoted in ibid., 9.
[121] Mark A. Groombridge in Long, *Intellectual Property Law in Emerging Markets* (2000), 13.
[122] Ibid., 15.
[123] Ocko, "Copying, Culture, and Control" *Yale J.L.& Human.* 8, 2 - Article 10 (1996), 567.
[124] Wei, *Der Urheberrechtsschutz in China mit Hinweisen auf das Deutsche Recht* (1994), 1.
[125] Ibid., 2.

printing' protected the printer rather than the author/creator of the work.[126] The aim of such protection was not to remunerate the author and protect private interest but much more to control the publication of works for the purpose of retaining harmony in the Chinese feudal state.[127] Up until the early 20th century, no concept of copyright protection can be found that is – to some extent – similar to the understanding of copyright nowadays, meaning that the author has exclusive rights to a work and can prevent others from violating the work in any way.[128] The 'privilege of printing' existed for a long time and was only replaced by the first copyright law during the Qing- Dynasty (清朝) at the beginning of the 20th century.[129]

2. Copyright During the Qing Dynasty (1644-1911)

Literacy became more and more important during the Qing-Dynasty and hence, the need for a protection of copyright arose.[130] The rulers of the Qing-Dynasty were the Manchus who had overthrown the Ming Dynasty; however, in the late 19th century China had to suffer from intrusions by the Western countries (especially Britain) which led to a destabilisation of the Qing-Dynasty and resulted in some treaties with the Western powers[131]

[126] Ibid.
[127] Qu, *Copyright in China* (2002), 3.
[128] Ibid.
[129] Wei, *Der Urheberrechtsschutz in China mit Hinweisen auf das Deutsche Recht* (1994), 2.
[130] Li Yufeng and Catherine W. Ng, "Understanding the Great Qing Copyright Law of 1910" *J. Copyright Soc'y U.S.A.* 56 (2008-2009), 767.
[131] Example of treaties during that time are: The Treaty of Nanjing with Britain in 1842 (南京條約 Nánjīng tiáoyuē), the Treaty of Wangxia with the United States in 1844 (望廈條約 Wàngxià tiáoyuē) and the Treaty of Whampoa with France in 1844 (黃埔條約 Huángpǔ tiáoyuē); China: Inspector General of Customs, *Treaties, Conventions, Etc., Between China and Foreign States*, 2 ed., 1 - Russia, International Protocol, Great Britain, United States of America, France, Import Tariff Agreement, China. Imperial Maritime Customs. III.- Miscellaneous Series No. 30 (Shanghai, China: Statistical Department of the Inspectorate General of Customs, 1908), 159-164 (Nanjing), 473-486 (Wangxia), 559-578 (Whampoa).

which granted extra-territoriality within China[132] because the Chinese laws at the time were not sufficient to ensure their rights.[133]

In the late Qing-Dynasty, the government finally put emphasis on foreign policies that made it inevitable for the republic to introduce some kind of copyright protection.[134] Another trigger for the necessity of an own copyright law was the upswing of the book- and journal industry after the Wuxu-Reform at the end of the 19th century and the foundation of guilds and trade associations by the publishers.[135] After the Russo-Japanese War at the beginning of the 20th century, the education of China started to change and the long established Confucian systems were replaced with more improved 'Western-styled systems'.[136] At that time, more and more copyright material was brought into China and the owners/authors feared infringement of their rights. Also, the desire for journalism increased tremendously during the years after the Wuxu- Reform; both revolutionaries and constitutionalists used newspapers and magazines to spread and promote their political beliefs.[137] Eventually, the pressure from the outside was too high, so that China agreed to negotiate some sort of mutual protection for copyright eligible material.[138] This resulted in many commercial agreements between China and the United States, Japan and the United Kingdom.[139] Whereas the United Kingdom focussed more on trademarks, Japan and the United States put more emphasis on copyright protection; one example are the Chinese-American negotiations which resulted in the Sino-

---

[132] E.g. look at Articles 21, 25 and 33 of the Treaty of Wangxia and Articles 25-28 of the Treaty of Whampoa.
[133] Yufeng and Ng, "Understanding the Great Qing Copright Law" *J. Copyright Soc'y U.S.A.* 56 (2008-2009), 769.
[134] Ibid., 768,771.
[135] Look at Zhang Tao, "Protestant Missionary Publishing and the Birth of Chinese Elite Journalism" *Journalism Studies* 8, 6 (2007); see also Wei, *Der Urheberrechtsschutz in China mit Hinweisen auf das Deutsche Recht* (1994), 3.
[136] Yufeng and Ng, "Understanding the Great Qing Copright Law" *J. Copyright Soc'y U.S.A.* 56 (2008-2009), 771.
[137] Jinfan Zhang, *The Tradition and Modern Transition of Chinese Law* (Heidelberg: Springer-Verlag Berlin, 2014), 614.
[138] Yufeng and Ng, "Understanding the Great Qing Copright Law" *J. Copyright Soc'y U.S.A.* 56 (2008-2009), 777-779.
[139] Qu, *Copyright in China* (2002), 21; Yufeng and Ng, "Understanding the Great Qing Copright Law" *J. Copyright Soc'y U.S.A.* 56 (2008-2009), 779.

U.S. Commercial Treaty of 1903 (通商行船条约 Tōngshāng Xíng Chuán Tiáoyuē).[140]

From 1906 until 1910, the Qing government promulgated some laws concerning the newspapers and printing. In 1906, the imperial court promulgated orders to draft a law for printing[141] which mainly aimed at controlling the publication of newspapers and magazines by obligating publishers to register their works before publication so that its content could be reviewed.[142] In the same year, the Regulations for Newspapers and Provisional Press Regulations were issued.[143] In 1907-08, a Press Law[144] mainly dealing with the registration and 'pre-publication-review', was issued but most of the publishing houses did not adhere to it so that a revision was needed; however, the revision in 1910 did not lead to a success because the Qing-Dynasty was abolished at that time and with it all the regulations.[145] Although laws finally existed for the publishers of magazines and newspapers, they did not aim at protecting the authors and theirs rights but merely aimed at controlling the printing and bringing public opinion under control.[146] Hence, this system can be compared to the former 'privilege of printing'.

In 1908, China participated in a Berne Convention meeting, which led to the first copyright legislation that was based on an international convention.[147] Due to the enormous pressure from the industrialized countries[148]

---

[140] Yufeng and Ng, "Understanding the Great Qing Copright Law" *J. Copyright Soc'y U.S.A.* 56 (2008-2009), 779-781.
[141] The Great Qing Specialised Law on Printing (大清印刷物专律 Dà Qīng Yìnshuā Wù Zhuānlǜ).
[142] Zhang, *The Tradition and Modern Transition of Chinese Law* (2014), 614-615.
[143] Joan Judge, *Print and Politics - 'Shibao' and the Culture of Reform in Late Qing China* (Stanford, California: Stanford University Press, 1996), 145.
[144] The Great Qing Press Law (大清报律 Dà Qīng Bàolǜ).
[145] Zhang, *The Tradition and Modern Transition of Chinese Law* (2014), 615.
[146] See Judge, *Print and Politics - 'Shibao' and the Culture of Reform in Late Qing China* (1996), 145; Zhang, *The Tradition and Modern Transition of Chinese Law* (2014), 615.
[147] Deli Yang, "The Development of Intellectual Property in China" *World Pat. Inf.* 25, 2 (2003), 133.
[148] Also called 'Western powers'.

in the 19th century, the government enacted the Great Qing Copyright Law[149] in 1910.[150] This can be seen as a milestone in the development of Chinese copyright law.[151] The Great Qing Copyright Law can be seen as the real starting point of intellectual property laws in China and leads us back to the earlier argument that intellectual property laws are a transplant to Chinese law and not 'indigenous' to the legal evolution in China.[152] This can be emphasized by the fact that no other attempts of building an own indigenous copyright system in China can be found in the records.[153] The Great Qing Copyright Law granted a general protection for a copyright work for the life of the author plus thirty years.[154] The use of the work contrary to the fair dealing clause as stipulated by the law was subject to fines.[155]

However, the law was only effective for one year before the Qing Dynasty was brought down[156] and the provisional government enacted a different Copyright Law in 1911; thus, the Great Qing Copyright Law was never actually enforced.[157] This clearly shows that the system of forcing laws onto another nation from the outside is not very helpful because the disregard of the Chinese culture will not lead to an acceptance in the country and hence, improvement.[158] The perception of a society needs to change

149 As a comparison: The first copyright statute in England was promulgated 200 years earlier. WIPO, *Introduction to Intellectual Property: Theory and Practice* (London: Kluwer Law International 1997), 24.
150 Nie, *The Enforcement of Intellectual Property Rights in China* (2006), 179.
151 Yufeng and Ng, "Understanding the Great Qing Copright Law" *J. Copyright Soc'y U.S.A.* 56 (2008-2009), 772.
152 Li, "The Sky is High and the Emperor is Far Way" *Bol Mex Derecho Comp* 36, 108 (2003), 954; also see Ocko, "Copying, Culture, and Control" *Yale J.L.& Human.* 8, 2 - Article 10 (1996), 560.
153 Qu, *Copyright in China* (2002), 2,3.
154 Ibid., 21.
155 Ibid.
156 Kong, *WTO, Internationalization and the Intellectual Property Rights Regime in China* (2005), 6.
157 Yufeng and Ng, "Understanding the Great Qing Copright Law" *J. Copyright Soc'y U.S.A.* 56 (2008-2009), 772; see also Nie, *The Enforcement of Intellectual Property Rights in China* (2006), 179.
158 Alford, *To Steal a Book Is an Elegant Offense: Intellectual Property Law in Chinese Civilization* (1995), 2.

over time so that concepts that are not indigenous in the culture can grow and be understood and adapted by the people.

3. The Reign of the Kuomintang

After the Qing dynasty was finally overruled in the first decade of the 20th century, China was facing many struggles with warlords. During that time the Kuomintang (KMT 國民黨) and the Communists were cooperating in order to fight the aggressors and reunite China as a whole.[159] However, the KMT was not comfortable with the Communists as a partner and instructed several violent coups until it solely gained power in 1928.[160] The KMT pursued the transformation of the government and the independence of China with the result of abolishing extraterritoriality within China as a main goal.[161] During its reign, the KMT also tried to create effective laws of which one is the Copyright Law of 1928.[162]

This law granted protection for authors of literary, artistic and technical works including but not limited to books, essays, stories, music, drama, paintings, copybooks, photographs, engravings and models.[163] The works as well as the assignment of a right needed to be registered with the Ministry of the Interior of the National Government.[164] Further, Article 22 provided that registration was rejected by the Ministry of the Interior if the work was contrary to KMT principles or if it or rather its content was prohibited by other laws.[165] In Article 14 of the Regulation for the Enforcement of the Copyright Law it was stipulated that protection might be granted to foreigners for a period of 10 years if it was useful to the Chinese and the respective foreigner's country gives a mutual protection to Chinese

[159] Qu, *Copyright in China* (2002), 25.
[160] Ibid.
[161] Werner Levi, *Modern China's Foreign Policy*, Minnesota Archive Editions (St. Paul, USA: University of Minnesota Press, 1953), 190.
[162] *The Copyright Law - trans. N.F. Allman* (1928), *The Chinese Law Review* (1929-1931) 4 (2) 1-5.
[163] Ibid., Article 1.
[164] Ibid., Article 2 and Article 15.
[165] Ibid., Article 22.

works.[166] If infringement occurred, the owner of the copyright could bring legal action against the infringer according to Article 23.[167] The sanctions for the infringement of the copyright were stipulated in the fourth chapter as being monetary fines with the amount varying based on the kind of violation.[168]

This law was seen as a major step towards the recognition of intellectual property rights in China but the KMT controlled the registration very rigorously; this basically led to almost no change in the legal practice thereof.[169] At that time the Chinese citizens were not aware of these laws and no legal structure existed that could have executed such laws.[170]

4. The Era of Mao Zedong – Approach to Law and Development of Copyright

Mao Zedong, the leader of the communist party in China gained power when the People's Republic of China was created in 1949 and with his rise to power all laws that existed at that time were abolished.[171] The Chinese Communist Party (CCP) had three phases of changing China from feudalism to capitalism and then from socialism to their favourable communism.[172] The CCP adopted the theories of Marxism when establishing their own ideology.[173] According to the Marxist understanding, rights are not necessary in a state where everyone is equal and no social problems

[166] *Detailed Regulations for the Enforcement of the Copyright Law* (1928), *The Chinese Law Review* (1929-1931) 4 (2) 6-7.
[167] *The Copyright Law - trans. N.F. Allman* (1928), *The Chinese Law Review* (1929-1931) 4 (2) 1-5 Article 23.
[168] Ibid., Article 33 to Article 39.
[169] Qu, *Copyright in China* (2002), 27.
[170] Ibid.
[171] Kong, *WTO, Internationalization and the Intellectual Property Rights Regime in China* (2005), 16; Wang, "Law-making functions of the Chinese courts" *Front. Law China* 1, 4 (2006), 527-528; Sidel, "Copyright, Trademark and Patent Law in the People's Republic of China" *Tex. Int'l L.J.* 21 (1985-1986), 261. - Sidel is referring to Shen Ren'Gan and Zhong Yingke "Banquanfa Qiantan" (A Discussion of Copyright Law) (1982) at 100-04.
[172] Qu, *Copyright in China* (2002), 28.
[173] Stephen C. Angle, *Human Rights and Chinese Thought - A Cross-Cultural Inquiry* (Cambridge, UK: Cambridge University Press, 2002), 200.

exist such as in complete communism.[174] However, the concepts of Marxism and socialism were amended to suit the Chinese standards; this can be called the Maoist communism.[175] The theories of Confucianism and capitalism were held to be contrary to the Communist thinking because Mao saw Confucianism as an old doctrine of feudalism and capitalism as a way to only protect the strong people whereas communism was supposed to protect the working class.[176] The Maoist theories focussed on the collective ownership that basically meant state ownership rather than securing individual rights.[177] After the abolishment of all the existing laws and the legal system created by the KMT[178], there was no alternative legislation at that time – the CCP had not enacted laws or directives for the protection of the author or a copyright in the liberated areas yet.[179] Some policy statements of the CCP included the right for freedom of expression and publication but none of these statements were expressed in the legislation and therefore had no effect.[180] During that time, copyright was recognized partially in China because the State Administration for Publication which was under the auspices of the Ministry of Culture published the *"Resolutions on the Improvement and Development of Publishing Work"* at the First National Publishing Conference in 1950 that ordered the recognition of authors and prohibited others to reproduce, copy or distort the work without the author's permission.[181] The resolutions contained a clause that granted the creators of works a 'basic remuneration' according to the quantity that was printed and gave the right to the creators to prevent others from altering

[174] Ibid., 201-202.
[175] Nie, *The Enforcement of Intellectual Property Rights in China* (2006), 93.
[176] Ibid., 92.
[177] Natalie P. Stoianoff, "The Influence of the WTO over China's Intellectual Property Regime" *Syd. Law Rev.* 34 (2013), 68.
[178] Kong, *WTO, Internationalization and the Intellectual Property Rights Regime in China* (2005), 16.
[179] Sidel, "The Legal Protection of Copyright in the PRC" *Colum.-VLA Art&L.* 9 (1984-1985), 478-479. - Sidel is referring to Shen Ren'Gan and Zhong Yingke "Banquanfa Qiantan" (A Discussion of Copyright Law) (1982) at 100-04.
[180] Ibid., 479.
[181] The Resolutions are discussed by Sidel using his own translations at Sidel, "Copyright, Trademark and Patent Law in the People's Republic of China" *Tex. Int'l L.J.* 21 (1985-1986), 261.

the work.[182] Shortly after promulgation of the resolutions, the massive infringement of the book "The International Situation and the Korean War" by the Dalian Bookstore showed the weakness of the current copyright enforcement and emphasized the need for a stronger protection.[183] After experiencing many problems with the resolutions of 1950, the State Administrative Council promulgated the *"Provisional Regulations on Management of Book and Periodical Publishing, Printing and Distribution"* in 1952, which provided copyright protection and stated fines for the infringement of the author's copyright.[184] During that time, the conception of copyright improved in China although an extensive law had not existed yet.[185] In 1956, the Chinese Ministry of Culture tried to establish a new copyright regulation that was supposed to protect foreign authors in particular; however, this document remained internal and has never been published.[186]

In 1958, the regime introduced the *Tentative Provision for Payment for Published Works in Literature and Social Science*, which secured that authors were remunerated but did not constitute any other right an author might have.[187] During the Cultural Revolution, it was shown that the Maoist did not even recognize the copyright rationales that consisted of Marxist or Leninist theories.[188] Also, the remaining provisions and remuneration rules that were established during the era of Mao Zedong were not accepted

182 Qu, *Copyright in China* (2002), 35; Sidel, "Copyright, Trademark and Patent Law in the People's Republic of China" *Tex. Int'l L.J.* 21 (1985-1986), 261-262.
183 Sidel, "Copyright, Trademark and Patent Law in the People's Republic of China" *Tex. Int'l L.J.* 21 (1985-1986), 261-262. - Sidel is referring to Shen Ren'Gan and Zhong Yingke "Banquanfa Qiantan" (A Discussion of Copyright Law) (1982) at 106-08.
184 *Provisional Regulations on the Management of Book and Periodical Publishing, Printing and Distribution Sectors* (1952 - promulgated 16 August 1952), State Administrative Council (provided by China Copyright and Media - Rogier Creemers).
185 Qu, *Copyright in China* (2002), 36.
186 Ibid.
187 Kong, *WTO, Internationalization and the Intellectual Property Rights Regime in China* (2005), 16.
188 Stoianoff, "The Influence of the WTO over China" *Syd. Law Rev.* 34 (2013), 69.

anymore once the Cultural Revolution had started in 1966.[189] Authors, creators and scientists had so many restrictions laid upon them by the government that the free creation of the mind was diminished.[190] A common saying during the Cultural Revolution, which demonstrates the negligence of intellectual property rights, was:

> *"Is it necessary for a steel worker to put his name on a steel ingot that he produces in the course of his duty? If not, why should a member of the intelligentsia enjoy the privilege of putting his name on what he produces?"*[191]

This saying clearly shows that the Chinese population did not see the need to protect intellectual property at all and explains why it was and still is very complicated to establish an intellectual property protection in China. One of Mao's ideologies was "*subordinating the needs of the part to the needs of the whole*"[192] which led to more motivation than the fact of receiving a small remuneration for the work[193].

The Chinese citizens worked hard to strengthen the community as a whole rather than gaining personal benefits out of it. The CCP was of the opinion that integrity would bring them far and aimed at the support of everyone. The Chinese citizens were first fascinated by the solidarity and support they achieved but the attempt to maintain integrity led to many manipulations and corruption as well as nepotism which resulted in the alienation of supporters of the CCP regime.[194] Summarizing, it can be said that the copyright conception and protection in China did not improve at all during

[189] Nie, *The Enforcement of Intellectual Property Rights in China* (2006), 180.
[190] Ibid., 181.
[191] Alford, *To Steal a Book Is an Elegant Offense: Intellectual Property Law in Chinese Civilization* (1995), 56.
[192] Chapter 24 'Correcting Mistaken Ideas' - The Role of the Chinese Communist Party in the National War (October 1938), Selected Works, Vol. II., p.201 at David Quentin and Brian Baggins, "Quotations from Mao Tse Tung - 1927-1964 - Peking Foreign Language Press - Mao Tse Tung Internet Archive (marxist.org) 2000", 1966 (https://www.marxists.org/reference/archive/mao/works/red-book/ch24.htm, accessed: 6 March 2021).
[193] Qu, *Copyright in China* (2002), 31.
[194] Ibid., 33.

the time of Mao Zedong and the Cultural Revolution but rather had taken a step backwards.[195]

5. Copyright after the Cultural Revolution – Open Door Policy

After the Cultural Revolution, the new Chinese regime in power wanted to improve the standing of China in the world and the 'Four Modernizations Policy' was established that strived to increase China's agricultural sector, the industry and the science and technology sector to international standards.[196] The reform of the foreign policy, also called 'open door policy' can be traced back to Deng Xiaoping who was the reformist leader of China after the Cultural Revolution and had the main aim of improving the economic development of the People's Republic of China.[197] This foreign policy was also held up by Deng's successor Jiang Zemin after he gained power in 1989.[198] The CCP wanted to reconstruct the whole economy and although intellectual property rights were contrary to socialist understanding[199], they were thought to be essential for the 'four modernizations program' to be fulfilled.[200] Intellectual property protection was supposed to bring foreign investment, encourage foreign trade, improve the market as a whole and hence, the CCP recognized that those were necessary in order to establish a strong Socialist country.[201]

Also, the CCP understood that foreign investors feared to invest in China unless their intellectual property rights were secured in some way.[202] The first engagement concerning the protection of intellectual property rights

---

[195] Ibid., 39.
[196] Nie, *The Enforcement of Intellectual Property Rights in China* (2006), 181.
[197] Yang, "The Development of Intellectual Property in China" *World Pat. Inf.* 25, 2 (2003), 136.
[198] Ibid.
[199] Peter K. Yu, "Piracy, Prejudice, and Perspectives: An Attempt to Use Shakespeare to Reconfigure the U.S.-China Intellectual Property Debate" *B.U. Int'l L.J.* 19, 1 (2001), 21.
[200] Nie, *The Enforcement of Intellectual Property Rights in China* (2006), 181.
[201] Ibid.
[202] Qu, *Copyright in China* (2002), 39.

can be found in the Sino-US Trade Agreements in 1979.[203] In 1985, an institution was founded that had the objective of drafting a copyright law for the People's Republic of China, named the National Copyright Office.[204] In the same year, Interim Regulations for copyright were promulgated that can be seen as the first real legal document acknowledging the construct of copyright in China.[205] The concept of copyright also received recognition in the General Principles of Civil Law, which took effect in 1987. It stipulated in Article 94:

> *"Citizens and legal persons shall enjoy rights of authorship (copyrights) and shall be entitled to sign their names as authors, issue and publish their works and obtain remuneration in accordance with the law."*[206]

However, the definition was very general and it was likely that it could have resulted in many interpretational problems in front of the courts. Although the Chinese government was very eager on establishing a sound copyright protection during that time, there were still many parts that had to be improved over time.

In 1990, the first real Copyright Law of the People's Republic of China was enacted and it can be said that it is one of the most important laws that shaped the modern protection of intellectual property rights in China.[207] During that era, the government introduced the 'Four Modernizations Plan' to become a market-driven economy and one of the four goals was to improve science and technology; the adoption of the intellectual property laws during that time clearly shows that China understood the need of intellectual property protection to achieve an improvement in these fields.[208]

---

[203] Pitman B. Potter and Michel Oksenberg, "A patchwork of IPR protections" *CBR* 26, 1 (1999), 8. – Further international agreements will be discussed in detail in the following section.
[204] Kong, *WTO, Internationalization and the Intellectual Property Rights Regime in China* (2005), 17.
[205] Qu, *Copyright in China* (2002), 44.
[206] Article 94 *General Principles of the Civil Law of the People's Republic of China* (1986) (provided by WIPO).
[207] Kong, *WTO, Internationalization and the Intellectual Property Rights Regime in China* (2005), 17.
[208] Ibid.

Moreover, the Chinese government published the *Implementing Regulations of Copyright Law*[209] and the Regulations on the Protection of Computer Software[210] in 1991. In 1994, additional regulations were adopted that stipulated penalties for commercial copyright piracy.[211] The content of the Copyright Law of 1990 including its amendments and regulations are discussed in greater detail in the following chapter.

6. International Relations and International Law

Since the concept of intellectual property rights was very new to the People's Republic of China, it was necessary to get assistance from the Western powers that had more experience in the field of intellectual property law. Cooperating with the United States of America and the other Western powers such as Germany was very important for the international acceptance of the Chinese intellectual property legislation and its worldwide recognition.

The harmonization of intellectual property law has been approached for many years. Concerning copyright law, it has succeeded in some parts when looking at the international agreements that have been signed by many states. The most important agreements regarding copyrights are

- the Berne Convention for the Protection of Literary and Artistic Works (Berne Convention),
- the Rome Convention for the Protection of Performers, Producers of Phonograms and Broadcasting Organizations
  (Rome Convention),

[209] *Regulations for the Implemenation of the Copyright Law of the People's Republic of China* (1991 - 24 May 1991, promulgated 30 May 1991, effective 1 June 1991), National Copyright Administration of the People's Republic of China (provided by WIPO). – The Regulations were amended in 2013
[210] *Regulations for the Protection of Computer Software* (1991 - promulgated 4 June 1991, effective 1 October 1991), State Council of the People's Republic of China (provided by AsianLII). – The Regulations were amended in 2013.
[211] *Decision of the Standing Committee of the National People's Congress on Punishment of the Crimes of Infringing Copyright* (1994 - promulgated and effective 5 July 1994, invalidated 1 October 1997), Standing Committee of the National People's Congress (provided by AsianLII).

- the Agreement on Trade-Related Aspects of Intellectual Property Law (TRIPS) and
- the contracts of the World Intellectual Property Office (WIPO) such as the World Copyright Treaty (WCT), the World Performances and Phonograms Treaty (WPPT) and the Beijing Treaty on Audiovisual Performances (Beijing Treaty).

All these international agreements have shaped the Copyright Law of the People's Republic of China as it is today. Additionally, Article 142 of the General Principles of Civil Law of 1986[212] stipulated that the Chinese legislation is also applicable to foreigners that engage in economic activity in China which showed that China had understood the need to protect foreigners in order to increase the rate of foreign investments.

The following gives an overview of China's international relations and the international agreements it has acceded to which had an influence on the copyright legislation.

a) U.S.-Chinese Relations prior to China's Accession to the WTO

The United States of America had pressured China to create a copyright law since 1979 because the government was of the opinion that a strong protection of copyrights given to U.S. citizens and corporations in China would assist the U.S. firms to enter the Chinese market.[213] The agreements between the U.S. and China have shaped the development of Chinese intellectual property laws tremendously and have led to the accession of China to international organizations and agreements. The major agreements between China and the United States with regard to intellectual

---

212 *"The Application of law in civil relations with foreigners shall be determined by the provisions in this chapter. If any international treaty concluded or acceded to by the People's Republic of China contains provisions differing from those in the civil laws of the People's Republic of China, the provisions of the international treaty shall apply, unless the provisions are ones on which the People's Republic of China has announced reservations. International practice may be applied on matters for which neither the law of the People's Republic of China nor any other treaty concluded or acceded to by the People's Republic of China has any provisions."*, see Article 142 *General Principles of the Civil Law PRC (1986).*

213 June Cohan Lazar, "Protecting Ideas and Ideals: Copyright Law in the People's Republic of China" *Law & Pol'y Int'l Bus.* 27 (1995-1996), 1185.

property right protection, including copyright protection are discussed in the following section.

aa) The Memorandum of Understanding of 1992[214]

Real negotiations concerning intellectual property rights started in 1991 when the U.S. Trade Representative Office initiated a Special 301 investigation[215] of China's intellectual property legislation and enforcement.[216] This was the result of numerous complaints by U.S. companies that were unsatisfied with the Chinese attempt to balance the newly established laws with the Communist ideology in China.[217] Also, the Trade Representative made it clear that trade sanctions would have happened if the enforcement of the intellectual property law would not be improved.[218] It was very important for both countries to find a solution because the United States were major investors for China and China had been exporting many goods to the United States.[219]

In 1992, the Memorandum of Understanding (MoU 1992) between China and the U.S. was signed as a result of the negotiations between those two

---

[214] Hereinafter 'MoU 1992'.

[215] In 1988, the U.S. Congress passed the *Omnibus Foreign Trade and Competitiveness Act of the United States of America* (1988), 19 U.S.C. ch. 17 §§2901 et seq., Pub.L. No. 100-418, 102 Stat. 1107. This led to an amendment of section 182 of the *Trade Act of 1974 of the United States of America* (1974), 19 U.S.C. ch. 12 §§2101 et seq. The United States Trade Representative is ordered to analyse the protection of intellectual property rights and the possibility of American firms that rely on their intellectual property rights to access the markets of other countries. The countries that fail to fulfil certain requirements can be investigated for possible trade sanctions under the Special 301 provisions of the Trade Act, 19 U.S.C. § 2411.

[216] Butterton, "Pirates, Dragons and U.S. Intellectual Property Rights in China" *Arizona L.R.* 38 (1996), 1085.

[217] Lazar, "Protecting Ideas and Ideals: CR Law of PRC" *Law & Pol'y Int'l Bus.* 27 (1995-1996), 1188.

[218] Ibid.

[219] Yang, "The Development of Intellectual Property in China" *World Pat. Inf.* 25, 2 (2003), 138.

countries.[220] This MoU 1992 was a necessary step for the negotiations between the two countries and prevented an approaching trade war.[221] By signing the MoU in 1992 China was obligated to join certain international agreements concerning intellectual property rights. Regarding copyright, the MoU 1992 stipulated in Article 3 (1), that China had to accede to the Berne Convention for the Protection of Literary and Artistic Works[222] with the aim of ratifying the Convention and taking it into effect by 1 June 1993. According to Article 3 (2) MoU 1992, China was also obligated to join the Convention for the Protection of Producers of Phonograms Against Unauthorized Duplication of their Phonograms.[223] Following the accession to these international conventions, the State Council of the People's Republic of China published the *Provisions on the Implementation of International Copyright Treaties*[224] to deal with possible conflicts between Chinese legislation and international treaties. Article 19 of these Provisions stipulates that

> *"Where pre-existing administrative regulations relating to copyright may conflict with these Rules, these Rules shall apply. Where these Rules may conflict with international copyright treaties, the international copyright treaties shall apply."*[225]

This MoU 1992 was one of the first steps for the Chinese copyright law to reach international standards.

---

[220] *Memorandum of Understanding Between the Government of the United States of America and the Government of the People's Republic of China on the Protection of Intellectual Property* (1992), 34 I.L.M. 676, 34 I.L.M. 676 (1995), 1995 WL 374160 (I.L.M.).

[221] Yang, "The Development of Intellectual Property in China" *World Pat. Inf.* 25, 2 (2003), 138; Lazar, "Protecting Ideas and Ideals: CR Law of PRC" *Law & Pol'y Int'l Bus.* 27 (1995-1996), 1188.

[222] *Berne Convention* (1979), TRT/BERNE/001.

[223] Hereinafter 'Geneva Convention'.

[224] *Provisions on the Implementation of the International Copyright Treaties* (1992 - promulgated 25 September 1992, effective 30 September 1992), State Council of the People's Republic of China (provided by WIPO).

[225] Article 19 ibid.

However, although the Chinese copyright law looked good on paper, the major concern for the U.S. after promulgation of the law in 1990 was the lack of effective enforcement.[226] Following many complaints by American companies that were dissatisfied with the enforcement of their rights in China, the U.S. Trade Representative put China on the list of Priority Foreign Countries in 1994.[227] China's reaction to this treatment by the Americans was disappointment and anger because they were working hard at fulfilling the requirements of the MoU 1992.[228] The actions of the United States with the Special 301 investigations and the watch lists have been seen as very bad for the world trade by many industrialized and developing countries because such unilateral actions by the U.S. are not helpful for balancing the needs of all parties involved in comparison to the conclusion of multilateral agreements.[229]

bb) The Memorandum of Understanding of 1995[230]

In 1995, the Memorandum of Understanding between the United States of America and the People's Republic of China (MoU 1995) was signed after an eleventh-hour accord between the Chinese and the U.S. officials on 26 February 1995.[231] This agreement prevented a trade war that was very likely to happen due to China's dissatisfaction with the American move to

[226] Lazar, "Protecting Ideas and Ideals: CR Law of PRC" *Law & Pol'y Int'l Bus.* 27 (1995-1996), 1189.
[227] Kim Newby, "The Effectiveness of Special 301 in Creating Long Term Copyright Protection for U.S. Companies Overseas" *Syracuse J. Int'l L. & Com.* 21 (1995), 43; Geoffrey Crothall, "Beijing slams 'irrational' US policy over piracy" *South China Morning Post (Section: Business News), Beijing, at 4* (1 July 1994).
[228] *The Foreign Ministry spokesmen Shen Guofang said: "We express our profound regret at this move which will harm the Sino-US economic and trade relationship"* and *"China has done a lot of work to ensure the observance of the law and prosecution of those who violate the law..."* Geoffrey Crothall Crothall, "Beijing slams 'irrational' US policy over piracy".
[229] Newby, "Special 301 and Copyright Protection Overseas" *Syracuse J. Int'l L. & Com.* 21 (1995), 52.
[230] Hereinafter 'MoU 1995'.
[231] Jeffrey W. Berkman, "Intellectual Property Rights in the P.R.C.: Impediments to Protection and the Need fo the Rule of Law" *Pacific Basin L.J.* 15, 1 (1996), 6.

put China on the Priority Watch List in 1994 and the threatened trade sanctions of more than US$1 billion on several Chinese products; as a countermeasure, China threatened the United States with several trade sanctions on American goods.[232] The MoU 1992 had not dealt with the enforcement issue of the intellectual property laws, which proved to be the failure of the MoU 1992; U.S.T.R. Mickey Kantor put far more emphasis on this issue in the negotiations for the MoU 1995 that created a dual enforcement system consisting of judicial and administrative measures for right holders.[233]

The agreement consisted of two parts being a letter from the PRC Minister of Foreign Trade and Economic Cooperation, Wu Yi, to the U.S. Trade Representative Micky Kantor concerning the implementation of measures in China and an annex to the letter, called the Action Plan, for effective protection and enforcement of intellectual rights.[234]

The letter gives a summary of the Action Plan, as well as some promises concerning the handling of intellectual property rights in China.[235] A very important declaration is that China started to acknowledge the importance of intellectual property rights for the development of their economy.[236] Another great achievement of the MoU 1995 was that China was bound to *"publish all laws, rules, regulations, administrative guidance, or other official documents concerning any limitation on, regulation, or permission*

[232] Elaine Kurtenbach, "U.S., China Seek Trade Solution, New Business - Piracy, Auto, Energy Issues at Stake", 17 February 1995 (http://community.seattletimes.nwsource.com/archive/?date=19950217&slug=2105560, accessed: 6 March 2021); also Newby, "Special 301 and Copyright Protection Overseas" *Syracuse J. Int'l L. & Com.* 21 (1995), 44; see also Connie Neigel, "Piracy in Russia and China: A Different U.S. Reaction" *Law & Contemp. Probs.* 63, 4 (2000), 194.

[233] *China-United States: Agreement Regarding Intellectual Property Rights* (1995), 34 I.L.M. 881, 34 I.L.M. 881 (1995), 1995 WL 528321 (I.L.M.), 882; see also Berkman, "Intellectual Property Rights in the PRC" *Pacific Basin L.J.* 15, 1 (1996), 7.

[234] *MoU U.S.-China IP Enforcement 1995* (1995), 34 I.L.M. 881, 34 I.L.M. 881 (1995), 1995 WL 528321 (I.L.M.).

[235] Berkman, "Intellectual Property Rights in the PRC" *Pacific Basin L.J.* 15, 1 (1996), 8.

[236] *MoU U.S.-China IP Enforcement 1995* (1995), 34 I.L.M. 881, 34 I.L.M. 881 (1995), 1995 WL 528321 (I.L.M.) 883.

required to engage in all activities identified above".[237] This obligation can be seen as a huge step towards a more transparent legal system, which helped the Western countries to understand the Chinese intellectual property laws. On the contrary, the United States were obligated to assist China in the improvement of the enforcement system, for example by training Chinese customs officials or equipping them with technical devices that assisted in securing enforcement.[238]

The Action Plan consists of two parts in which the first part (1) deals with the enforcement system of intellectual property rights and the second part (2) exemplifies the promises made in the letter concerning the training of personnel, the dissemination of information and the improvement of the recognition of intellectual property rights in China.[239]

Before the MoU was achieved, China's reaction to negotiations with the U.S.T.R. was very positive; the Foreign Ministry's spokesman Shen Guofang stated that the termination as well as the prevention of infringement and piracy was a sincere intention of the People's Republic of China.[240] Both the United States and the PRC would gain a lot from the new MoU 1995 because intellectual property right holders in China, Chinese and foreigners, would achieve greater rights and the trade between both countries was likely to increase.[241] However, the U.S. government was not entirely happy with the outcome of the MoU 1995 because the enforcement of intellectual property rights still was not guaranteed by the agreement and many problems developed in due course.[242]

cc) The 1996 Accord

China failed to achieve the goals set out in the MoU 1995, which led to a significant development in the piracy sector as many copied products such

---

[237] Ibid., 884.
[238] Ibid., 885.
[239] Ibid., 887 ff; Berkman, "Intellectual Property Rights in the PRC" *Pacific Basin L.J.* 15, 1 (1996), 9.
[240] Frank V. Prohaska, "The 1995 Agreement regarding Intellectual Property Rights between China and the United States: Promises for International Law or Continuing Problems with Chinese Piracy" *Tulsa J. Comp. & Int'l L.* 4, 1 (1996), 177.
[241] Ibid., 178.
[242] Ibid., 181.

as videocassettes, computer software and compact disks were exported after the MoU had been agreed on.[243] The Clinton Administration sent a report to Congress about the failure of the Chinese to keep up to the agreement and noted that it was thinking of introducing sanctions on Chinese products in the amount of US$2 billion this time.[244] The report also said: *"piracy remains rampant, and economic damage to U.S. industries continues to rise"*.[245] The new U.S. Trade Representative made a statement in front of the subcommittee on Trade of the U.S. House Ways and Means Committee about the Chinese-American relationship that, although China has worked in terms of the agreement and achieved some success, it has not put on the key areas including the shutdown of piracy plants which resulted in damages for the American and the international industries, especially in the computer software and music industries.[246] In order to prevent trade sanctions, she demanded that China (1) must interfere in factories producing pirated products, (2) improve enforcement in the problematic areas (i.e. Guangdong Province), (3) intensify the control mechanism at the Chinese borders (especially cargo shipments) and (4) allow U.S. companies to access the Chinese computer software, sound recording and motion picture markets.[247] All four demands were part of the MoU 1995 and the fulfilment of these could be seen as necessary to sustain the U.S.-Chinese trade relationship. Shortly before the threatened sanctions were due, the Chinese authorities shutdown some of the major companies producing pirated goods.[248] Nevertheless, the U.S.T.R. was still not satisfied with the Chinese actions and informed the Chinese ambassador that a trade

---

243 Richard W. Stevenson, "U.S. Cites China for Failing to Curb Piracy in Trade" *The New York Times, Washington* (1 May 1996).

244 Ibid.

245 Ibid.

246 Charlene Barsherfsky (U.S. Trade Representative) "U.S.-China Relationship - Statement in front of the Subcommittee on Trade of the House Ways and Means Committee" U.S. Department of State Dispatch Vol 7 Iss 25 (17 June 1996), Document No. 9609133739, 324-325.

247 Ibid.

248 David E. Sanger, "Chinese Pirate Factories Have Roots Abroad, U.S. Study Says" *The New York Times, Washington* (3 June 1996); David E. Sanger, "Signs Emerge Of China Deal On Sanctions" *The New York Times, Washington* (13 June 1996).

war could not be avoided if the actions remained so ineffective.[249] Again, China and the U.S. avoided a trade war at the last minute when they reached an agreement on 17 June 1996 (The 1996 Accord).[250] In this agreement, the Chinese government agreed to deal more efficiently with the producers of pirated products as well as their retailers; also, in contrast to the MoU 1995, the Chinese government agreed to use police officers instead of administrative offices to pursue their aims, because the former have more authority.[251] During the weeks before the accord was reached, already 15 compact disk factories had been closed which showed that the Chinese government took it more seriously this time.[252] However, it needs to be noted that the accord was not an agreement replacing the MoU 1995 but more a regulation of how to enforce it.[253]

dd) Summary

These agreements between China and the United States show how important the relationship between the two countries is and how dependent they are on each other concerning economic trade. The Memorandums of Understanding of 1992 and 1995 and the 1996 Accord were major steps towards an intellectual property system in China and can be seen as very important phases of intellectual property development.

b) Berne Convention for the Protection of Literary and Artistic Works[254]

The Berne Convention dates back to 1886 when ten states agreed upon an international contract concerning literary and artistic works.[255] Nowadays,

249 Paul Blustein, "Hopes Raised For Ending China Copyright Dispute" *The Washington Post, Washington, D.C., at D10 (Volume 119, Issue 191)* (13 June 1996); Sanger, "Signs Emerge Of China Deal On Sanctions".
250 Seth Faison, "U.S. and China Agree on Pact To Fight Piracy" *The New York Times at A1* (18 June 1996).
251 Ibid.
252 Ibid.
253 Mrs. Charlene Barshefsky (U.S.T.R.) pointed that out as stated in Seth Faison; ibid.
254 Hereinafter 'Berne Convention'.
255 Article 3 (1) *Berne Convention* (1979), TRT/BERNE/001.

the Berne Convention has been signed by 178 states.[256] China became a signatory to the convention in 1992 comparing it to Germany that was a signatory of the Berne Convention in 1886 with ratification in 1887 and the United States of America that only acceded to the Convention in 1988.[257] China had to accede to the Berne Convention in terms of the MoU 1992.[258] In fact, acceding to the Berne Convention was China's first action after the MoU 1992 had been concluded.[259] According to Article 36 (1) Berne Convention, *'any country party to this Convention undertakes to adopt, in accordance with its constitution, the measures necessary to ensure the application of this Convention'*.[260] Concerning the implementation, China chose to adopt the process of self-execution because Chinese officials thought that the differences between the Chinese domestic law and the Berne Convention would be dealt with automatically.[261]

One of the major principles of the Berne Convention is that all authors enjoy the same rights in each member state – apart from the country of origin – as the national authors.[262] The laws applicable to the work in the country of origin are the national laws.[263] The country of origin is understood to be the country of first publication or if the work is unpublished the home country of the author.[264] In general, the Convention sets minimum standards to implement copyrights laws. Two important standards of the Berne Convention are the minimum duration of fifty years after the author's death and the guidelines to the basic limitations.[265] Article 2 of the

---

256 WIPO, "WIPO-Administered Treaties - Contracting Parties > Berne Convention" (http://www.wipo.int/treaties/en/ShowResults.jsp?treaty_id=15, accessed: 6 March 2021).
257 Ibid.
258 *MoU U.S. - China IP Protection 1992* (1992), 34 I.L.M. 676, 34 I.L.M. 676 (1995), 1995 WL 374160 (I.L.M.).
259 Stephanie L. Sgambati, "China's Accession to the Berne Convention: Bandaging the Wounds of Intellectual Property Piracy in China" *Fordham Intell. Prop. Media & Ent. L.J.* 3, 1 (1992), 162.
260 Article 36 (1) *Berne Convention* (1979), TRT/BERNE/001.
261 Sgambati, "China's Accession to the Berne Convention" *Fordham Intell. Prop. Media & Ent. L.J.* 3, 1 (1992), 166,168.
262 Article 5 *Berne Convention* (1979), TRT/BERNE/001.
263 Article 5 III ibid.
264 Article 5 IV ibid.
265 Art 7, Art 2bis ibid.

Convention defines which rights it ought to protect and contains a catalogue of all sorts of different material forms that is extended continuously.

c) Universal Copyright Convention

The Universal Copyright Convention (UCC) was created by the United Nations Educational, Scientific and Cultural Organization (UNESCO) and agreed upon in 1952 as an alternative international copyright convention to the Berne Convention.[266] The motivation for this agreement came from the developing countries, the United States of America and Latin America that did not want to join the Berne Convention for several reasons.[267] The developing countries were of the opinion that the Berne Convention only benefited the strong western countries, because they were not able to meet the high demands stipulated by the Berne Convention.[268] The United States as well as most Latin American countries had already acceded to a different multilateral agreement, the Buenos Aires Convention, which did not require them to disclaim certain formalities as the Berne Convention did.[269]

China became a signatory of the UCC in 1992.[270] It can be said that the Universal Copyright Convention acted as a model law for the Chinese copyright law.[271] Also, it can be argued that the UCC aimed at bringing together the Berne Convention and the Pan American Treaty.[272]

Similar to the Berne Convention, minimum standards for the protection of copyright are set out by the Universal Copyright Convention but the UCC's conditions are not as strict as the conditions laid out in the Berne

[266] UN Educational, Scientific and Cultural Organization (UNESCO) *Universal Copyright Convention* (1952), U.N.T.S. No. 13444, vol. 943, pp. 178-325.
[267] Jørgen Blomqvist, *Primer on International Copyright and Related Rights* (Cheltenham, UK and Northhampton, USA: Edward Elgar Publishing, 2014), 9.
[268] Ibid.
[269] Joseph S. Dubin, "The Universal Copyright Convention" *Cal. L. Rev.* 42, 1 (1954), 98.
[270] WIPO, "Other IP Treaties - IP-related Multilateral Treaties < Contracting Parties/Signatories < Universal Copyright Convention 1952" (http://www.wipo.int/wipolex/en/other_treaties/parties.jsp?treaty_id=208&group_id=22, accessed: 6 March 2021).
[271] Yang, "The Development of Intellectual Property in China" *World Pat. Inf.* 25, 2 (2003), 138-139.
[272] Blomqvist, *Primer on International Copyright and Related Rights* (2014), 9.

Convention.[273] The UCC looked promising for countries that had very different copyright systems and laws and were not able to adapt to the requirements of the Berne Convention yet.[274] The UCC stipulated that both published and unpublished works gained national treatment and that an author's work gets protection in its home state if the author has published it in another member state subject to certain requirements.[275]

d) Access to WTO and TRIPS

The General Agreement on Tariffs and Trade (GATT)[276] was established in 1948 with China being one of the founding members; however, the Taiwanese government that was representing China at that time ordered the withdrawal from GATT in 1950.[277] During the 1990's, China was actively prevented from entering the WTO by the United States of America because of all the intellectual property disputes occurring between the United States and China.[278] In 1999, China eventually agreed to the requirements of the United States and started amending its laws according to the agreements of the WTO.[279]

In 2001, China became a member state of the World Trade Organization and by that time, its laws had to comply with all agreements that are part of the WTO.[280] The most important agreement concerning intellectual property rights is the TRIPS agreement, which is not an individual contract by the WTO but part of the WTO-Convention which was an extension of the GATT discussed and concluded in the Uruguay Round in 1994. China

---

[273] Matthew A. Murphy, "Copyright" in *Intellectual Property Law of China*, ed. Michael J. Moser (Huntington, NY, U.S.A.: Juris Publishing Inc., 2011), 269.
[274] Ibid.
[275] The work needs to include the symbol ©, the author's name and the year of first publication; see Article II and III UN Educational, Scientific and Cultural Organization (UNESCO) *UCC* (1952), U.N.T.S. No. 13444, vol. 943, pp. 178-325.
[276] *General Agreement on Tariffs and Trade* (1947), 55 U.N.T.S. 194.
[277] Nie, *The Enforcement of Intellectual Property Rights in China* (2006), 153.
[278] Stoianoff, "The Influence of the WTO over China" *Syd. Law Rev.* 34 (2013), 72.
[279] Patricia Blazey and YiJun Tian, *Intellectual Property Law in China*, ed. Patricia Blazey and Kay-Wah Chan, trans., The Chinese Commercial Legal System (Sydney, Australia: Thomson Lawbook Co., 2008), 326.
[280] WTO "Accession of the People's Republic of China" Protocol WT/L/432.

was not part of the weaker countries that were granted a so-called 'transition period' and hence, it had to comply with all the minimum standards set down in TRIPS by 2001. Germany was one of the founding members when the WTO was created on 1 January 1995 and all the agreements that were concluded up until then came into force on the same day. Concerning intellectual property rights in general, Article 3 TRIPS sets out that all members of the WTO have to be dealt with equal in each Member State and must not be discriminated. Copyright is dealt with in Articles 9-13 of the TRIPS Agreement whereas Article 14 TRIPS concerns the ancillary copyright of performers, producers of phonograms and broadcast organizations. Article 9 TRIPS stipulates that the members have to comply with the minimum standards set out in the Berne Convention and Article 10 TRIPS includes computer programs and compilation of data as being protected by copyright. TRIPS also specifies the enforcement of intellectual property rights by ordering the members to decide upon remedies based on the facts of a particular case and the evidence that was shown by the parties.[281]

e) Rome Convention for the Protection of Performers, Producers of Phonograms and Broadcasting Organizations[282]

The Rome Convention was adopted at Rome on 26 October 1961 and was the first international treaty protecting the intellectual property rights of performers. China as well as the United States are not signatories of the Rome Convention, whereas Germany signed it in 1966 (with it coming to force in 1966).[283] However, many of the principles of Rome are also incorporated in TRIPS.[284]

[281] Article 41 *TRIPS Agreement* (1994), 1869 UNTS 299; 33 ILM 1197 (Annex 1C of the Marrakesh Agreement establishing the World Trade Organization, signed in Marrakesh, Morocco on 15 April 1994, 33 I.L.M. 1125).
[282] Hereinafter 'Rome Convention'.
[283] WIPO, "WIPO-Administered Treaties - Contracting Parties > Rome Convention" (http://www.wipo.int/treaties/en/ShowResults.jsp?treaty_id=17, accessed: 6 March 2021).
[284] For more detail look at WIPO, "Implications of the TRIPS Agreement on Treaties Administered by WIPO", 2012 - WIPO Publication No. 464 (E) (http://www.wipo.int/edocs/pubdocs/en/intproperty/464/wipo_pub_464.pdf, accessed: 6 March 2021).

f) WIPO Contracts (WCT and WPPT)

WIPO is an international organization for the protection of intellectual property rights around the world that the People's Republic of China joined in 1980.[285] Even though TRIPS was introduced by the WTO in 1995, WIPO still saw the need for further treaties and introduced the WIPO Copyright Treaty (WCT)[286] and the WIPO Performances and Phonograms Treaty (WPPT)[287] in 1996. The WIPO treaties were more attractive to developing countries because such could choose from a variety of treaties and also make reservations on certain points of the agreements – an option that is not given to members of the WTO.[288] First, focus is laid upon the development and the necessity of the additional copyright contracts and secondly, the content is discussed.

aa) Process

During the discussion on TRIPS at the end of the Uruguay round it became obvious that TRIPS will not satisfy all needs to harmonize the copyright law especially concerning the fast developing field of communication technology.[289] First, it was considered to adapt the Berne Convention and create an ancillary copyright but an amendment of a treaty with so many signatories did not seem practicable as it required an unanimous decision; similar problems occurred concerning the Rome Convention.[290] Also, the

285 WIPO, "China - Legal Information" (http://www.wipo.int/members/en/details.jsp?country_id=38, accessed: 6 March 2021).

286 *WIPO Copyright Treaty* (1996), S. Treaty Doc. No. 105-17 (1997); 36 ILM 65 (1997) (provided by WIPO).

287 *WIPO Performances and Phonograms Treaty* (1996), S. Treaty Doc. No. 105-17, 36 ILM 76 (1997) (provided by WIPO).

288 Sisule F. Musungu and Graham Dutfield, "Multilateral agreements and a TRIPS-plus world: The World Intellectual Property Organization (WIPO)" *TRIPS Issues Papers (Quaker United Nations Office, Geneva)*, 3 (2003), 10.

289 Mihály Ficsor, "The WIPO "Internet Treaties" The United States as the Driver: The United States as the Main Source of Obstruction - As seen by an Anti-Revolutionary Central European" *J. Marschall Rev. Intell. Prop. L.* 6, 17 (2006), 19.

290 Musungu and Dutfield, "Multilateral agreements and a TRIPS-plus world: The World Intellectual Property Organization (WIPO)" *TRIPS Issues Papers (Quaker United Nations Office, Geneva)*, 3 (2003), 15.

inclusion into the TRIPS negotiations was not possible anymore; to dissolve this problem WIPO set up two expert's committee with the goal of finding a solution to new problems regarding digital technology and the Internet.[291] One committee had the task to deal with the copyright issues, whereas the other committee dealt with the rights of performers and producers of phonograms.[292] The committee's work decreased during the finalization period of TRIPS because the delegations were afraid to disrupt/interfere with the final TRIPS negotiations.[293] After the signing of TRIPS in 1994, the committees intensified their work again to keep up with the 'Digital Agenda' and find solutions for the handling of digital copyright since it was not practical to continue with copyright discussions in the WTO context.[294]

The WCT and the WPPT were the results of a diplomatic conference, which was held on Certain Copyright and Neighbouring Rights in 1996.[295] Both contracts only came into force in 2002 because WIPO had the precondition of at least thirty countries acceding to the agreements before they could come into force.[296] The United States ratified both treaties in 1999 and they came into force in 2002. China accessed the two treaties in 2007 and they came into force in the same year, whereas Germany only accessed in 2009 with the contracts coming into force in 2010.

---

[291] Ficsor, "The WIPO "Internet Treaties"" *J. Marschall Rev. Intell. Prop. L.* 6, 17 (2006), 19.

[292] WIPO, "Basic Proposal for the Substantive Provisions of the Treaty on Certain Questions Concerning the Protection of Literary and Artistic Works to be Considered by the Diplomatic Conference (Document CRNR/DC/4, 30 August 1996) " in *Diplomatic Conference on Certain Copyright and Neighbouring Rights Questions* (Geneva 1996), p. 2 No. 3.

[293] Mihály Ficsor, *The Law of Copyright and the Internet - The 1996 WIPO Treaties, their Interpretation and Implementation* (Oxford: Oxford University Press, 2002), 1.29.

[294] Ibid., 1.34.

[295] Musungu and Dutfield, "Multilateral agreements and a TRIPS-plus world: The World Intellectual Property Organization (WIPO)" *TRIPS Issues Papers (Quaker United Nations Office, Geneva)*, 3 (2003), 15.

[296] Article 20 *WCT* (1996), S. Treaty Doc. No. 105-17 (1997); 36 ILM 65 (1997); Article 29 *WPPT* (1996), S. Treaty Doc. No. 105-17, 36 ILM 76 (1997).

bb) Major Principles of the WCT and WPPT

Both the WCT and the WPPT can be called the “Internet Treaties” since they were adopted to secure the intellectual property rights in the digital age.[297]

In general, the WCT aimed at adapting the protection of copyright works after the internet use as well as the use of personal computers had increased rapidly in the 1990s; it majorly updated the protection given to artistic and literary works by the Berne Convention for the Protection of Literary and Artistic Works to the new digital era.[298] This can also be seen in the preamble of the treaty that states:

> *“Recognizing the need to introduce new international rules and clarify the interpretation of certain existing rules in order to provide adequate solutions to the questions raised by new economic, social, cultural and technological developments.*
>
> *Recognizing the profound impact of the development and convergence of information and communication technologies on the creation and use of literary and artistic works.”*[299]

The term “literary and artistic works” according to the WCT is said to include computer programs, music, movies, books and art.[300]

The WPPT can be explained as the updated version of the 1961 Rome Convention for the Protection of Performers, Producers of Phonograms

---

[297] Jason R. Boyarski et al., "International Developments - WIPO Copyright Treaty Enters into Force" *Intellectual Property & Technology Law Journal* 14, 3 (March 2002), 30.

[298] Ibid.

[299] Paragraphs II and III of the Preamble of the *WCT* (1996), S. Treaty Doc. No. 105-17 (1997); 36 ILM 65 (1997).

[300] Boyarski et al., "International Developments - WIPO Copyright Treaty Enters into Force" *Intellectual Property & Technology Law Journal* 14, 3 (March 2002), 30.

and Broadcasting Organizations.[301] It majorly protects the rights of producers and artists involved in the creation of phonograms and sound recordings.[302]

Similar to the WCT, the WPPT has the aim of recognizing and including the technological development concerning intellectual property protection.[303]

Both treaties try to achieve an international protection from internet piracy by demanding the acceded countries to implement regulations dealing with the infringement of copyright on the internet and providing ways for the authors to control the use of their works and be compensated in cases when an infringement occurs.[304] They make sure that the right of reproduction is also protected in the digital environment, especially by including an "anti-circumvention" provision, which is supposed to stop people from hacking special technological measures that are created to stop unrightful reproduction.[305] The treaties also stipulate that the national law needs to prohibit the unauthorized alteration or deletion of the electronic information that declares the work and its creator or right-holder.[306]

g) WIPO Treaty – The Beijing Treaty on Audiovisual Performances[307]

The Beijing Treaty[308] was the result of long discussions (almost 20 years) on the protection of audiovisual performances and was adopted by the Diplomatic Conference in Beijing from 20 to 26 June 2012. It should act as an

---

[301] Ibid.
[302] Ibid.
[303] The Preamble of the WPPT states in Paragraph III: "*Recognizing the profound impact of the development and convergence of information and communication technologies on the production and use of performances and phonograms*" *WPPT* (1996), S. Treaty Doc. No. 105-17, 36 ILM 76 (1997).
[304] Boyarski et al., "International Developments - WIPO Copyright Treaty Enters into Force" *Intellectual Property & Technology Law Journal* 14, 3 (March 2002), 30.
[305] Ibid.
[306] Ibid.
[307] Hereinafter 'Beijing Treaty'
[308] *Beijing Treaty on Audiovisual Performances (WIPO)* (2012), TRT/BEIJING/001 (provided by WIPO).

addition and "round-off" of the WPPT.[309] It is the first international intellectual property treaty that was established in China.[310] The harmonization was not as successful as expected after the promulgation of the WPPT and TRIPS, so that the need for another international agreement arose.[311] The main problem of the pre-existing treaties is that they treat the rights to phonograms differently to the rights to audiovisual works, especially concerning the requirement of obtaining permission; also, moral rights are not fully recognized in the previous treaties.[312] The Beijing Treaty stipulates the economic rights of performers of audiovisual performances (fixed and non-fixed) as well as moral rights and rules on the transfer of rights.[313] Furthermore it includes the "three-step" test to decide upon limitations and exceptions and sets out a minimum term of protection of fifty years.[314] The treaty entered into force on 28 April 2020, three months after thirty members have put in place their ratification process.[315] According to Article 30 of the Beijing Treaty, the Director General of WIPO is the depositary of that treaty.

h) Memorandum of Understanding between NCAC and WIPO

In December 2015, the NCAC and WIPO concluded a Memorandum of Understanding on Further Strengthening Bilateral Cooperation between

309 Look at WIPO, "Main Provisions and Benefits of the Beijing Treaty in Audiovisual Performances (2012)", 2016 (http://www.wipo.int/edocs/pubdocs/en/wipo_pub_beijing_flyer.pdf, accessed: 6 March 2021).

310 Qiang Liu and Liang Huang, "On the Beijing Treaty on Audiovisual Performances and the Upgrading of China's Copyright Law" *Journal of Shaoyang University - Social Science Edition* 3, 4 (2014), 19.

311 Ibid. – The Rome Convention was even less up to date.

312 Ibid.

313 See *Beijing Treaty* (2012), TRT/BEIJING/001; Liu and Huang, "On the Beijing Treaty on Audivisual Performances and the Upgrading of China's Copyright Law (English Title)" *Journal of Shaoyang University - Social Science Edition* 3, 4 (2014), 19.

314 Look at WIPO, "Main Provisions and Benefits of the Beijing Treaty in Audiovisual Performances (2012)", 2016 (http://www.wipo.int/edocs/pubdocs/en/wipo_pub_beijing_flyer.pdf, accessed: 6 March 2021).

315 Article 26 *Beijing Treaty* (2012), TRT/BEIJING/001.

the NCAC and WIPO. The MoU has the main objective of enhancing the collaboration of the two organizations.[316]

7. Summary

This historical overview exemplifies that the history of Chinese intellectual property law is not long. This can be explained by looking at the theories of Confucianism and the Communists that focussed on the concept of communal rights rather than individual rights. The People's Republic of China has come from a country with no acceptance of intellectual property rights to a country with much intellectual property legislation in quite a short period (1979 up until now). The law is constantly changing in order to adjust to the international standards.

[316] AFD China Intellectual Property Law Office, "China NAC and WIPO sign MOU to Cooperate in All Respects of Copyright", 24 December 2015 (https://www.lexology.com/library/detail.aspx?g=ca968235-ea70-4743-a2f8-d34752faf7a1, accessed: 6 March 2021).

8. Overview and Accessions

The following table gives an overview of the accessions of China, Germany and the United States to the abovementioned organizations and treaties:

Organization or Agreement	**People's Republic of China**	**Germany**	**United States of America**
WIPO	1980	1970	1970
Berne Convention	1992	1887	1988
UCC	1992	1955	1954
WTO	2001	1995	1995
TRIPS	2001	1995	1995
WCT	2007	2009	1999
WPPT	2007	2009	1999
Beijing Treaty	2014 (ratification)	-	-

Accessions of China, Germany and the U.S. to International Organizations and Agreements

CHAPTER 3 – THE STATUS QUO OF THE CHINESE COPYRIGHT LAW

In order to understand the whole development process of the Chinese Copyright Law it is necessary to look at the current law and its associated regulations, the copyright authorities and the enforcement strategies.

I. The Copyright Law of 1990

The first part gives an overview of the first real copyright legislation in China and demonstrates its development throughout the years up until now.

1. Promulgation and Amendments

As discussed above, the first Copyright Law of China was promulgated in 1990 and took effect on 1 June 1991.[317] Following that, the State Council also issued the *Implementing Regulations*[318] for the Chinese Copyright and the *Regulations for the Protection of Computer Software*[319] in 1991. In 1994, the first law stipulating criminal sanctions for the infringement of copyright took effect after a decree of the Standing Committee of the National People's Congress, but these regulations were invalidated in 1997.[320]

---

317 *Copyright Law of the People's Republic of China* (1990) (provided by WIPO).

318 *Regulations for the Implemenation of the Copyright Law of the People's Republic of China* (1991 - 24 May 1991, promulgated 30 May 1991, effective 1 June 1991), National Copyright Administration of the People's Republic of China.

319 *Regulations for the Protection of Computer Software* (1991 - promulgated 4 June 1991, effective 1 October 1991), State Council of the People's Republic of China.

320 *Decision of the Standing Committee of the National People's Congress on Punishment of the Crimes of Infringing Copyright* (1994 - promulgated and effective 5 July 1994, invalidated 1 October 1997), Standing Committee of the National People's Congress.

a) Reform 2001

In 2001, the copyright law was amended for the purpose of decreasing the deficits regarding the compliance with the TRIPS agreement.[321] In 1998, a first draft was submitted to the Standing Committee of the National People's Congress that did not include any provisions concerning the network environment, because the internet did not play a big role in China in 1998 and network protection was not included in TRIPS either.[322] However, the internet hit the Chinese society at the end of the 20th century which led to the rise of internet piracy.[323] For that reason, the draft in 2000 included the "right to transmit on information networks"[324]; this inclusion shows that China wanted to modernize its law as far as possible and adapt to state-of-the-art technologies.

The extent of the amendment in 2001 was quite considerable because local elements as well as international demands were recognized, four paragraphs were added and fifty-three of the existing paragraphs were changed substantially. In particular, articles that were incompatible with TRIPS, the market economy and the development of information technology were amended.[325] Major changes took place in the area of subject matter and the right to protection was broadened.[326] Concerning the network environment, the protection of works of authors, producers and performers was strengthened by the addition of civil liabilities and administrative penalties in cases in which a technical measure protecting the work was altered or destroyed or electronic right management information was removed or changed intentionally.[327] However, it can be called a failure that China did

[321] Theodor Enders, "Das neue Urheberrecht der Volksrepublik China" *HFR*, 1/2007 (2007), 2 at paragraph 5.
[322] Xiaoqing Feng, "The Protection of Copyright in Network Environment: A Review of Recent Reform of the Chinese Copyright Law" *Information and Communications Technology Law* 11, 2 (2002), 161.
[323] Ibid.
[324] Ibid.
[325] Xiaoqing Feng and Frank Xianfeng Huang, "International Standards and Local Elements: New Developments of Copyright Law in China" *J. Copyright Soc'y U.S.A.* 49 (2001-2002), 921.
[326] Feng, "The Protection of Copyright in Network Environment" *Information and Communications Technology Law* 11, 2 (2002), 161.
[327] Look at Article 47 (6) and (7) *Copyright Law of the People's Republic of China* (1990/2001 version) (provided by WIPO); Feng, "The Protection of

not manage to include any provisions on limitations to the right to transmit on information networks because the stipulation of certain limitations is one of the basic principles in Chinese Copyright Law for establishing a balance between the public interest of the society and commercial interest of the copyright holders.[328]

In summary, it can be argued that the 2001 amendment of the Chinese Copyright Law has been a great achievement in fulfilling the 'international obligation under the TRIPS Agreement'.[329] However, it cannot be said that the law was fully TRIPS-compliant by 2001.[330]

Another aspect worth noticing is that by amending the law to suit international demands, China has – in some parts accepted – that its ideologies and hence its economy had to be amended in order to play a role in the world; it can be concluded that this transformation occurred because of the advancement of technology and the 'liberalization of thoughts' (解放 思想 Jiěfàng sīxiǎng).[331]

b) WTO-Panel Report in 2009

On 26 January 2009, the WTO Dispute Settlement Body (DSB) published a panel report[332] about "China – Measures Affecting the Protection and Enforcement of Intellectual Property Rights". As discussed earlier, the relationship between the United States of America and the People's Republic of China concerning the protection of intellectual property rights has been difficult for a long time and the disputes moved to another level once China

---

Copyright in Network Environment" *Information and Communications Technology Law* 11, 2 (2002), 162.

[328] Feng, "The Protection of Copyright in Network Environment" *Information and Communications Technology Law* 11, 2 (2002), 162.

[329] Feng and Huang, "International Standards and Local Elements" *J. Copyright Soc'y U.S.A.* 49 (2001-2002), 921.

[330] Enders, "Das neue Urheberrecht der Volksrepublik China" *HFR*, 1/2007 (2007), at paragraph 5.

[331] Feng and Huang, "International Standards and Local Elements" *J. Copyright Soc'y U.S.A.* 49 (2001-2002), 921.

[332] WTO "China - Measures Affecting the Protection and Enforcement of Intellectual Property Rights - Report of the Panel" (2009), WT/DS362/R (09-0240).

joined the WTO in 2001.[333] Before China had accessed the WTO, the United States could only use threats of trade sanctions and threats not to support China's accession to the WTO as a form of pressure. With China now being a member, the United States can use the dispute settlement process of the WTO.

After all discussions and bilateral agreements with China, the United States were dissatisfied with the results and sought a consultation with China in 2007 (April/June) according to Articles 1 and 4 of the Understanding in Rules and Procedures Governing the Settlement of Disputes (DSU)[334] and Article 64 TRIPS but the DSB did not lead to a solution and therefore requested the insertion of a panel (August).[335] The United States argued that China's steps concerning

- the thresholds for criminal procedure and penalties,
- the disposal of goods confiscated by customs authorities that infringe intellectual property rights and
- the denial of copyright and related rights protection and enforcement to works that have not been authorized for publication or distribution within China

were infringing the TRIPS agreement.[336] It is not the goal of a WTO dispute to declare a winner and a loser at the end.[337] The outcome of the Panel was that some parts in the legislation – that the United States claimed as not being TRIPS-conform – were affirmed whereas other parts were not to

---

[333] Rostam J. Neuwirth, "Der WTO-Bericht zu China - Measures Affecting the Protection and Enforcement of Intellectual Property Rights: ein Kommentar " *GRUR Int.* 58, 5 (2009), 367.

[334] *Understanding on Rules and Procedures Governing the Settlement of Disputes* (1994), 869 UNTS 401; 33 I.L.M. 1226 (Annex 2 of the Marrakesh Agreement establishing the World Trade Organization, signed in Marrakesh, Morocco on 15 April 1994 , 33 I.L.M. 1125).

[335] Neuwirth, "Der WTO-Bericht zu China: ein Kommentar" *GRUR Int.* 58, 5 (2009), 367.

[336] Especially Article 61 I and II, Article 41 I, Article 59 in conjunction with Article 46 and Article 9 I TRIPS; WTO "China - Measures Affecting the Protection and Enforcement of Intellectual Property Rights - Report of the Panel" (2009), WT/DS362/R (09-0240), 1-3.

[337] Peter K. Yu, "The TRIPS Enforcement Dispute" *Neb. L. Rev.* 89, 4 (2010), 1082.

be seen in breach with TRIPS. This is probably the reason that neither China nor the United States pursued an appeal to the Appellate Body.[338] The Report concluded that Article 4 of the 2001 Chinese Copyright Law was inconsistent with the TRIPS requirements, the custom measures were partly inconsistent with Article 59 TRIPS and that the United States had not established an inconsistency of China's criminal thresholds.[339] However, this report merely acted as an ascertainment by an official WTO organ of deficits in Chinese intellectual property protection and provided a certain signpost for the improvement of Chinese intellectual property legislation.[340] No further consequences resulted from this.

c) Reform in 2010

It can be argued that the WTO report resulted in the amendment of the copyright law in 2010. According to the preamble of the law, the Standing Committee of the Eleventh National People's Congress only amended two articles at the 13th meeting in 2010. First, Article 4 was adjusted to suit the demands from the WTO panel report now saying:

> *"Copyright holders shall not violate the Constitution or laws or jeopardize public interest when exercising their copyright. The State shall supervise and administrate the publication and dissemination of works in accordance with the law".*[341]

This change is significant because before that Article 4 Chinese Copyright Law did not grant a copyright to works that are prohibited by law, which meant that all works that had not been accepted by the administration yet were not being granted any protection.[342] The U.S. was of the opinion that

---

[338] Ibid.

[339] WTO "China - Measures Affecting the Protection and Enforcement of Intellectual Property Rights - Report of the Panel" (2009), WT/DS362/R (09-0240), 8.1, p. 134.

[340] Neuwirth, "Der WTO-Bericht zu China: ein Kommentar" *GRUR Int.* 58, 5 (2009), 374-376.

[341] Article 4 *Copyright Law of the People's Republic of China* (1990/2010 version) (provided by WIPO).

[342] Article 4 of the 2001 Law said: "Works the publication or distribution of which is prohibited by law shall not be protected by law. Copyright owners, in

this infringed the minimum rights set out in the Berne Convention – the WTO panel agreed with that.[343] Secondly, Article 26 was added to the Copyright Law dealing with the requirement of registration when licensing or assigning copyright.[344] This requirement is mandatory according to the *Measures for the Registration of Pledge on Copyright.*[345]

The new PRC Copyright Law was announced on 26 February 2010 and took effect on 1 April 2010.

exercising their copyright, shall not violate the Constitution or laws or prejudice the public interest." *Copyright Law PRC* (1990/2001 version); see also Annie Tsoi, "Principle Impact of Copyright Law Amendments" *China Law & Practice* (May 2010), 1-2.

[343] Tsoi, "Principle Impact of Copyright Law Amendments" *China Law & Practice* (May 2010), 1-2.

[344] Article 4 *Copyright Law PRC* (1990/2010 version).

[345] Article 4 *Measures for the Registration of Pledge on Copyright* (2010 - issued 25 November 2010, effective 1 January 2011), National Copyright Administration of the People's Republic of China (provided by WIPO).

d) Current Copyright Laws and Regulations

The following graphic shows the most important regulations relating to the Chinese Copyright Law:

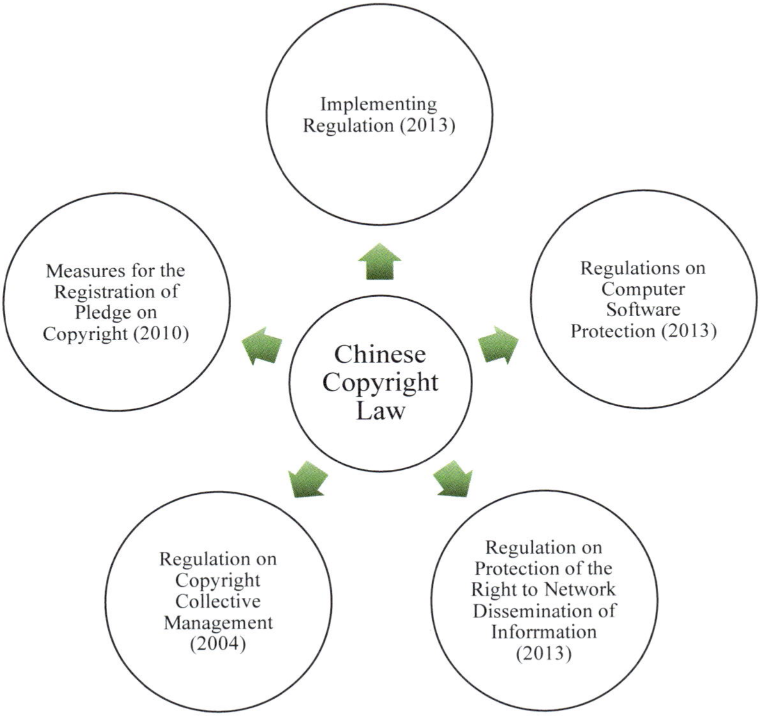

2. Content Overview

This part gives an overview of the currently enacted Chinese Copyright Law of 2010 focussing on the major principles of copyright, being the work term, the author, the exploitation rights and the limitations or fair dealing clauses. By analysing the main principles, one can compare and contrast the system of Chinese copyright to the American and German systems to understand why the Chinese Copyright Law is formulated the way it is and what difficulties it is facing.

a) Work Term

First, the work term including the requirements to qualify as a copyright protected work as well as the different types of copyright are briefly explained. The definition of the work term is of major importance for a creator to determine his/her rights under the respective laws.[346] Secondly, the exceptions to this provision are shown.

Article 1 of the Copyright Law lays out that copyright is given to works of literature, art and science.[347] The Copyright Law does not define the exact requirements a works needs to fulfil in order to qualify as an artistic, literary or scientific copyright protected work. This definition is dealt with in the Implementing Regulations.[348] Article 2 thereof defines works as "intellectual creations" that are original and can be reproduced in a tangible form in the area of literature, art and science.

aa) Intellectual Creation and Originality

"Creation" (作品 zuòpǐn) is stipulated as any kind of intellectual activity that results in works of art, literature or science.[349] However, organizational work for others, ancillary work et cetera are not to be seen as "creative" in terms of the Copyright Law as shown in Article 3 (2) of the Implementing Regulations. However, the Copyright Law does not protect the idea itself but rather the expression of the idea.[350] This is also laid out in the Guide to the Berne Convention that was written by the International Bureau of WIPO in 1978. Article 2 of the Berne Convention is discussed in paragraph 2.3. of the Guide, which states that the patent law is responsible for protecting ideas whereas the copyright law is protecting *"the words, notes, drawings, etc."* in which an idea is embodied.[351] Article 9 (2) TRIPS also

---

[346] Sanqiang Qu, *Intellectual Property Law in China* (Alphen aan den Rijn, Netherlands: Kluwer Law International, 2012), 89.
[347] Article 1 *Copyright Law PRC* (1990/2010 version).
[348] *Regulations for the Implementation of the Copyright Law of the People's Republic of China* (2013 - issued 2 August 2002, effective 15 September 2002, amended 8 January 2011, amended 30 January 2013, effective 1 March 2013), State Council of the People's Republic of China (provided by WIPO).
[349] Article 3 ibid.
[350] Qu, *Intellectual Property Law in China* (2012), 90.
[351] 2.3 *Guide to the Berne Convention for the Protection of Literary and Artistic Works (Paris Act ,1971)* (1978, Geneva), World Intellectual Property Organization (provided by WIPO). – The International Bureau of WIPO - The

stipulates that the expression and not the idea itself shall be protected by copyright.

Chinese scholars support the opinion that the author's personality is the major component when defining whether a work is an intellectual creation.[352] In the courts, this requirement has been interpreted very strictly.[353]

Secondly, "originality" (独创性 dúchuàng xìng) is required for works that are protected by the Copyright Law. "Original" in the copyright meaning should not be understood as being novel or inventive, it rather is understood to be an "original" work of the creator meaning that it is not entirely copied from another work and comprises a form of "intellectual effort, judgment and discrimination" of the creator.[354] The courts have often interpreted the requirement of originality very broadly.[355] The Chinese legislation does not include a regulation on the creativity level that a work needs to fulfil in order to enjoy copyright protection.[356] The only document, in which the originality of a copyright protected work has been dealt with, can be found in Article 15 of the *Interpretations of the Supreme People's Court Concerning Several Issues on Application of Law in Hearing Correctly the Civil Copyright*; these state that works of different authors about the same topic can nevertheless each enjoy protection if they are "*creative and independently completed*".[357] This shows that the major requirement is that the work is not copied from someone else but rather created independently.

Guide is not an authentic interpretation of the Berne Convention but rather an explanation of WIPO concerning the nature, aims and scope of the Convention.

[352] Qu, *Copyright in China* (2002), 91.

[353] Ibid.

[354] Qu, *Intellectual Property Law in China* (2012), 92.

[355] Qu, *Copyright in China* (2002), 90.

[356] Qu, *Intellectual Property Law in China* (2012), 94.

[357] *Interpretation of the Supreme People's Court Concerning Several Issues on Application of Law in Hearing Correctly the Civil Copyright* (2002 - adopted 12 October 2002, effective 15 October 2002), Supreme People's Court of the People's Republic of China (provided by WIPO).

bb) Reproducibility

The last requirement is that it must be capable of *"being reproduced in a tangible form"*. The value of literary, artistic and scientific works originates once the work is out in the public domain and can be disseminated; at this stage, it becomes important for the creator to regulate the dissemination and gain benefits from it.[358] Tangible in the copyright sense does not mean that a completed physical work needs to exist but rather that it can be captured in some kind of form that can be reproduced (copied).[359] One example can be shown when looking at oral works. According to Article 4 (2) of the Implementing Regulations, an expression of oral works means spoken language and names as examples lectures, court debates and improvisational speeches. However, concerning oral works it is very hard to provide proof of their existence in a court case.[360]

cc) Types of Copyright Works

Article 3 of the Chinese Copyright Law lays out a list, which includes but is not limited to the following types of works:

- *"written works,*
- *oral works,*
- *musical, dramatical, qǔyì*[361]*, choreographic and acrobatic works,*
- *works of the fine arts and architecture,*
- *photographic works,*
- *cinematographic works and works created by a process analogous to cinematography,*
- *graphic works such as drawings of engineering designs and product designs, maps and sketches, and model works,*
- *computer software."*[362]

Article 4 of the Implementing Regulations substantiates the works and their respective expressions. In Article 3 (9) Chinese Copyright Law it is stipulated that other works can be protected as well, which emphasizes that

[358] Qu, *Intellectual Property Law in China* (2012), 94.
[359] Enders, "Das neue Urheberrecht der Volksrepublik China" *HFR*, 1/2007 (2007), 11.
[360] Qu, *Intellectual Property Law in China* (2012), 96.
[361] 曲艺 = Chinese folklore
[362] Article 3 *Copyright Law PRC* (1990/2010 version).

the list is not closed. However, these works must have some kind of provision in either laws or administrative regulations.

Article 6 of the Chinese Copyright Law stipulates that the qǔyì works (= folklore) will be dealt with in a separate regulation by the State Council. Qǔyì works includes cross talk (相声 xiàngsheng), clapper talk (快书 kuài shū), special Chinese drumming (大鼓 dàgǔ) and storytelling (评书 píngshū) and is mainly presented by spoken performance.[363] However, such regulations by the State Council have not been formulated yet, so that the qǔyì works are also protected by the current copyright regulations.

Databases are not named in Article 3 Chinese Copyright Law. They are specifically dealt with in Article 14 Chinese Copyright Law. According to that, a copyright can exist in a compilation with a certain degree of originality[364] as long as it does not discriminate any form of copyright in the pre-existing works that are piled together. The protection of databases is one of the requirements of TRIPS that is laid down in Article 10 (2) TRIPS. Article 14 Chinese Copyright Law provides the corresponding provision to this.

Copyright protection is given to computer software according to Article 3 (8) Chinese Copyright Law – the State Council has promulgated a special regulation regarding the protection thereof.[365] The protection of computer software is dealt with in a separate section.[366]

---

[363] Article 4 (5) *Regulations for the Implementation of the Copyright Law of the People's Republic of China* (2013 - issued 2 August 2002, effective 15 September 2002, amended 8 January 2011, amended 30 January 2013, effective 1 March 2013), State Council of the People's Republic of China.

[364] Here, originality can be found in the way a compilation is arranged and in the way the pre-existing works are selected by the creator (compiler); for more information look at Qu, *Intellectual Property Law in China* (2012), 100.

[365] *Regulations on Computer Software Protection* (2013 - issued 20 December 2001, effective 1 January 2002, amended 8 January 2011, amended 30 January 2013, effective 1 March 2013), State Council of the People's Republic of China (provided by WIPO).

[366] See *Chapter 3 I. 3* of this dissertation.

dd) Exceptions to Copyright Protection

The Chinese Copyright Law includes some exceptions to copyright protection that are discussed in the following.

(1) Article 5 Works

Works that are generally excluded from copyright protection are dealt with in Article 5 Chinese Copyright Law that states that protection shall not be given to the following:

- *"Laws and regulations, resolutions, decisions and orders of State organs, other documents of a legislative, administrative or judicial nature and their official translations,*
- *News on current affairs and*
- *Calendars, numerical tables and forms of general use, and formulas."*[367]

The first category is excluded from copyright protection because public (state) documents are the expression of public actions and hence, should not receive protection because they are not created by an individual and further to that are formulated in order to reach the wide mass of people in a short time.[368]

The second category includes all sorts of information about current events by radio, television, internet, newspapers, magazines and the like because such reports are meant to provide the people with facts and information on current happenings; also, the nature of news is not suitable for copyright protection because they are mainly a retelling of events without a creative and subjective part of an individual.[369]

The third category includes all kind of works that are used widely and therefore belong to the public domain rather than to individual people.[370]

[367] Article 5 *Copyright Law PRC* (1990/2010 version).
[368] Qu, *Intellectual Property Law in China* (2012), 102.
[369] Ibid., 103.
[370] Ibid.

(2) Illegal Works

Up until the amendment of the Copyright Law in 2010, China did not grant protection to works of which the publication or distribution were prohibited by law.[371] This article was part of the WTO dispute that took place between the United States and China from 2007 until 2009[372], when the DSB published the Panel report. The Panel came to the conclusion, that Article 4 of the 2001 Chinese Copyright Law was inconsistent with the obligations stipulated in Article 5 (1) Berne Convention (like Article 9.1. TRIPS) and Article 41.1. TRIPS.[373] Following this report, China amended Article 4 of the Chinese Copyright Law, which now does not deprive authors of illegal works of the protection but sets out that the exploitation of rights shall be done without violating the Constitution, laws or jeopardize public interests.[374]

The Panel Report tries to set out the criteria for prohibited works after China's submissions to the Panel and names the following categories[375] as prohibited:

> [Content/works that]
>
> *"(1) are against the fundamental principles established in the Constitution;*
>
> *(2) jeopardize the unification, sovereignty and territorial integrity of the State;*

---

[371] Article 4 *Copyright Law PRC* (1990/2001 version).

[372] For more detailed information on the WTO dispute, see *Chapter 3 I. 1. b)* of this dissertation.

[373] WTO "China - Measures Affecting the Protection and Enforcement of Intellectual Property Rights - Report of the Panel" (2009), WT/DS362/R (09-0240), 134.

[374] *Copyright Law PRC* (1990/2010 version).

[375] The criteria are mainly taken from the content review regulations and the Panel states examples such as Article 26 of the Regulations on the Administration of Publications or Article 25 of the Regulations on the Administration of Films.

(3) divulge State secrets, jeopardize security of the State, or impair the prestige and interests of the State;

(4) incite hatred and discrimination among ethnic groups, harm their unity, or violate their customs and habits;

(5) propagate cults and superstition;

(6) disrupt public order and undermine social stability;

(7) propagate obscenity, gambling, violence, or abet to commit crimes;

(8) insult or slander others, or infringe upon legitimate rights and interests of others;

(9) jeopardize social ethics or fine national cultural traditions;

(10) other contents banned by laws, administrative regulations and provisions of the state."[376]

In summary, a copyright arises in all works that fulfil the copyright requirements set out above, but the exercise of such right is restricted when the work is violating the Constitution, laws or the public interest.

b) Copyright Subject

This section deals with the establishment of the copyright subject. In order to depict the rightful subject, a distinction needs to be made between general works and special works.

[376] WTO "China - Measures Affecting the Protection and Enforcement of Intellectual Property Rights - Report of the Panel" (2009), WT/DS362/R (09-0240), 7.79, p. 22.

aa) The Authorship in General Works

First, the standard form of authorship in general works is shown.

(1) Primary Authors

The so-called copyright subject is generally the author of a work. The authorship of copyright protected works is dealt with in section two of Chapter II of the Chinese Copyright Law (2010). It can be said that China has not used the pure 'principle of creativity' as it is incorporated, for example in the German Copyright Law[377], because Article 11 of the Chinese Copyright Law, a priori, sets out that the copyright, in general, belongs to its author but is subject to certain exceptions.[378] The author is defined to be the citizen that is responsible for the creation of the work.[379] As explained in the section on the definition of the work term, a *"creation (...) means intellectual activities in which (...) works are directly created"*[380]. Article 3 (2) of the Implementing Regulations stipulates that mere assistance, organization or the like is not understood to be a creation.

However, the citizen is not the only subject that is eligible for copyright ownership. Article 11 (3) Copyright Law stipulates that a legal entity or other organization can be the author of a work if the work is created *"under the auspices and according to the intention"* of such and the legal entity or other organization is responsible for the work. In that case, a transfer of the rights is not necessary because the legal entity or organization automatically becomes the author.[381]

---

[377] „Urheber ist der Schöpfer des Werkes" (English: The author is the creator of the work); § 7 *Urheberrechtsgesetz Deutschland (German Copyright Act)* (1965).

[378] See Adolf Dietz, "Das chinesische Urheberrecht: Copyright oder droit d'auteur?" in *Urheberrecht im Informationszeitalter - Festschrift für Wilhelm Nordemann zum 70. Geburtstag am 8. Januar 2004*, ed. Ulrich Loewenheim (München: Verlag C.H. Beck, 2004), 531-532.

[379] Article 11 Paragraphs 1-2 *Copyright Law PRC* (1990/2010 version).

[380] Article 3 (1) *Regulations for the Implementation of the Copyright Law of the People's Republic of China* (2013 - issued 2 August 2002, effective 15 September 2002, amended 8 January 2011, amended 30 January 2013, effective 1 March 2013), State Council of the People's Republic of China.

[381] See Enders, "Das neue Urheberrecht der Volksrepublik China" *HFR*, 1/2007 (2007), 5, recital 12.

(2) Derived Authorship

According to Article 19 Chinese Copyright Law, the rights of a natural person[382] shall be transferred according to the Law of Succession after the death of the author as long as the term of protection has not run out. The rights of the legal entity or other organization shall be transferred to the succeeding entity or in absence of a successor are transferred to the State.

bb) The Authorship in Special Works

The Chinese Copyright law has stipulated various provisions on different kinds of works that do not fall under the normal case. In the following, the rules concerning the authorship in special works are explained.

(1) Transformations of Other Author's Works

Article 12 Chinese Copyright Law sets out the rules regarding transformations of existing works including adaptation, translation, annotation or arrangement. The copyright in the transformed work shall vest in the transformer without prejudice to the copyright in the pre-existing work. Also, the transformer needs to obtain permission and pay remuneration if necessary.[383]

(2) Joint Authorship

Article 13 Chinese Copyright Law lays out that a jointly created work (two or more authors) and its rights collectively belong to the co-authors. Furthermore, Article 13 (2) Chinese Copyright Law stipulates that if a joint work is separable into parts each author can exploit his/her rights as long as it does not interfere with the rights in the combined work as a whole. Hence, the joint works are a combination of separate copyright protected works of the co-authors and the copyright in the complete work.[384] This results in an "oeuvre of the whole" with a uniform term of protection.[385]

In order for copyright protection to arise in a joint work, the concurrent will of the co-authors must be present including the objective of the

---

[382] Meaning the rights stipulated in Article 10 (5) to (17) Chinese Copyright Law.

[383] See Qu, *Intellectual Property Law in China* (2012), 109.

[384] Theodor Enders and Alexandra Steiner, "Urheberrechtsreform und Urheberrechtsdurchsetzung" *ZChinR* 17, 2 (2010), 100.

[385] Ibid.

work.[386] Further, the activities of all co-authors need to show that they actually have worked together in the creation of the work, meaning that they acknowledge each other's work and participated in the creation in a substantial and direct way.[387]

In the case where a joint work is inseparable, Article 9 of the Implementing Regulations sets out that the copyright must be collectively exploited by the co-authors *"under a unanimous agreement"* but in the absence thereof any co-author may not hinder the other in the exploitation of the right unless it is justified or concerns the transfer of rights; the monetary gains however, always need to be shared reasonably among all co-authors.[388] In the case of the death of a co-author with no successor, the other co-authors will obtain the economic rights of the deceased.[389]

(3) Compilations

A compilation is a work of assortment of pre-existing works, parts thereof, data or other materials that does not constitute a work in the meaning of the Copyright Law but due to the selection or arrangement of its contents gains the status of originality.[390] Databases fall under that description.[391] According to Article 14 Chinese Copyright Law, the copyright of such work is vested in the person who compiled/arranged the compilation and can exploit such as long as it does not hinder the rights in pre-existing works.

(4) Cinematographic Works

Article 15 Chinese Copyright Law specifies that cinematographic works belong to the producer while the other participating persons (director, cameraman, scriptwriter et cetera) have the right of authorship in the individual

---

[386] Qu, *Intellectual Property Law in China* (2012), 110; also see Wei, *Der Urheberrechtsschutz in China mit Hinweisen auf das Deutsche Recht* (1994), 50-51.

[387] Qu, *Intellectual Property Law in China* (2012), 110.

[388] Article 9 *Regulations for the Implementation of the Copyright Law of the People's Republic of China* (2013 - issued 2 August 2002, effective 15 September 2002, amended 8 January 2011, amended 30 January 2013, effective 1 March 2013), State Council of the People's Republic of China.

[389] Qu, *Intellectual Property Law in China* (2012), 110.

[390] Article 14 *Copyright Law PRC* (1990/2010 version).

[391] Look at *Chapter 3 I. 2. a) dd).*

parts, shall receive remuneration for the use thereof and if such parts are separable works these authors can exercise their copyright independently.

(5) Works Created in the Course of Employment

Article 16 of the Chinese Copyright Law deals with the shift of copyright exploitation from the employee to the employer if the work is *"created in the course of employment"*; such work exists when it is created *"in the fulfilment of tasks*[392] *assigned to him (the citizen) by a legal entity or other organization"*. Article 16 sentence 2 sets out that the actual author, namely the citizen, is the owner of the copyright but he/she has to grant his/her employer a usage right of the copyright meaning that the employer is allowed to exploit the work over a period of two years in which the author is not allowed to grant an identical exploitation right to a third person without permission. After the expiration of that period, the author is allowed to grant third parties a right to exploitation but the gains have to be split between the author and the entity in consonance with the contract concluded between them.[393]

The rights that are stipulated in the first half of the article are subject to limitations that are laid out in the second paragraph of Article 16. This will result in the author being limited to the right to have his/her name mentioned and in some cases, receive remuneration.[394] The complete copyright of a work created in the course of employment will only be vested fully in the author if the work is not one of the following:

- Works that are mainly created with the material and technical resources[395] of the employer and hence, the employer has the responsibility (i.e. drawings of engineering designs, maps, computer software);

[392] "Tasks" is defined in Article 11 (1) of the Implementing Regulations as *"the duties the citizen shall fulfil in the legal person or organization by which he is employed"; Regulations for the Implementation of the Copyright Law of the People's Republic of China (2013 - issued 2 August 2002, effective 15 September 2002, amended 8 January 2011, amended 30 January 2013, effective 1 March 2013), State Council of the People's Republic of China.*
[393] Article 12 ibid.
[394] See Dietz, "Das chinesische Urheberrecht: Copyright oder droit d'auteur?" (2004), 532.
[395] Material is defined as the "*funds, equipment or materials purposely provided to the author (...) for the creation of a work*", see Article 11 (2) *Regulations for*

- Works created in the course of employment where the copyright lies with the entity in accordance with laws, regulations or contracts.[396]

From the above limitations, a rough rule of thumb can be established saying that the copyright in works that take in a lot of investment and resources of the entity or organization will usually be vested in the entity or organization whereas works that do not create many costs and focus more on the creativity and talent of the creator will primarily be with the actual creator.[397]

Another interesting aspect here is that the exception made in Article 11 paragraph 1 Chinese Copyright Law that *"except where otherwise provided for in "this" law, the copyright shall belong to its author"*[398] is in a sense expanded to include other laws and regulations and contracts as possible exceptions of the general principle.[399]

(6) Commissioned Work

Many other jurisdictions have not stipulated any rules regarding commissioned works (= works that are created by order of another).[400] A separate provision concerning commissioned works exists in the Chinese Copyright Law. They are dealt with in Article 17 Chinese Copyright Law, which gives the parties the freedom of contract in deciding the owner of the copyright. The creator can even transfer the whole copyright to the commissioning party, meaning that both the economic and the moral rights are shifted to the commissioning party.[401] The second sentence of Article 17 provides for a statutory presumption that the creator will be the copyright

the Implementation of the Copyright Law of the People's Republic of China (2013 - issued 2 August 2002, effective 15 September 2002, amended 8 January 2011, amended 30 January 2013, effective 1 March 2013), State Council of the People's Republic of China.

[396] Article 16 paragraph 2 *Copyright Law PRC* (1990/2010 version).

[397] Wei, *Der Urheberrechtsschutz in China mit Hinweisen auf das Deutsche Recht* (1994), 56-57.

[398] Article 11 paragraph 1 *Copyright Law PRC* (1990/2010 version).

[399] Dietz, "Das chinesische Urheberrecht: Copyright oder droit d'auteur?" (2004), 532.

[400] Qu, *Intellectual Property Law in China* (2012), 114.

[401] Ibid.; also see Wei, *Der Urheberrechtsschutz in China mit Hinweisen auf das Deutsche Recht* (1994), 62.

owner if there is no agreement or contract. This is very different to the German Copyright Law because the copyright itself cannot be transferred in these cases; the commissioning party can only obtain the usage rights (exploitation rights) by contract with the creator.[402]

(7) Special Rule Regarding the Works of Unidentified Authorship

Sometimes works exists where it is impossible to figure out who the author of the work is (i.e. author has not signed his/her name). Nevertheless, these works are also protected under the Copyright Law although it is very complicated to calculate the protection period because there is no author's age that can be used as a reference.[403] However, in order to stimulate circulation of the work, Article 13 Implementing Regulations stipulates that the copyright *"shall be exercised by the owner of the original copy of work"*[404] with the exception of the right of authorship as long as an identification has not been successful.[405]

(8) Special Rule Regarding the Physical Transfer of an Original Work

This special rule has been established to deal with works of fine arts and the like because of the value originals have on the respective markets.[406] Article 18 Chinese Copyright Law sets out that the transfer of ownership in an original does not include the transfer of the copyright of the work.[407] Hence, the rights in that work need to be separated into property and intellectual property rights. Nevertheless, Article 18 also grants the "right to exhibit" to the owner of the original work of fine arts.

---

402 Enders and Steiner, "Urheberrechtsreform und Urheberrechtsdurchsetzung" *ZChinR* 17, 2 (2010), 101.

403 See Qu, *Intellectual Property Law in China* (2012), 114.

404 Article 13 *Regulations for the Implementation of the Copyright Law of the People's Republic of China* (2013 - issued 2 August 2002, effective 15 September 2002, amended 8 January 2011, amended 30 January 2013, effective 1 March 2013), State Council of the People's Republic of China.

405 See Qu, *Intellectual Property Law in China* (2012), 114.

406 Also see ibid.

407 Article 13 *Regulations for the Implementation of the Copyright Law of the People's Republic of China* (2013 - issued 2 August 2002, effective 15 September 2002, amended 8 January 2011, amended 30 January 2013, effective 1 March 2013), State Council of the People's Republic of China.

c) Content and Exercise of Copyright

The copyright in a work rises to existence without the requirement of registration.[408] According to Article 6 Implementing Regulations, the copyright in a work is effective starting with the date of the completion. This is derived from the Berne Convention which stipulates that a copyright in a work shall exist *"whether published or not"*[409] and the enjoyment *"shall not be subject to any formality"*[410]. Hence, Article 2 Chinese Copyright Law states:

> *"Chinese citizens, legal entities or other organizations shall, in accordance with this Law, enjoy the copyright in their works, whether published or not."*[411]

This specification stands in contrast to patent and trademark law where an application with examination and approval is obligatory for the establishment of a right.[412]

Nowadays copyright protected works can nevertheless be registered, but the registration does not constitute the right but helps to enforce it because a registration can be used as evidence in court (preliminary proof).[413] The following shows how the registration of copyright works has increased during the last years:[414]

---

408 China as a signatory to the Berne Convention has to guarantee copyright protection without a prior registration of the work, because Article 5 (2) of the Berne Convention stipulates that the emergence of copyright shall not be dependent on any form of formalities.
409 Article 3 (1) (a) *Berne Convention* (1979), TRT/BERNE/001.
410 Article 5 (2) ibid.
411 Article 2 *Copyright Law PRC* (1990/2010 version).
412 Also see Qu, *Intellectual Property Law in China* (2012), 117.
413 Also see Jinping Shi, "Copyright registration in China", 20 December 2015 (http://www.ccpit-patent.com.cn/node/2759, accessed: 6 March 2021).
414 NCAC "Report on the National Copyright Registration in 2014" (3 March 2015); NCAC "Report on the National Copyright Registration in 2015" (4 February 2016); NCAC "Report on the National Copyright Registration in 2016" (3 Feburary 2017); NCAC "Announcement of the General Office of the National Copyright Administration on the National Copyright Registration in 2017" (13 February 2018); NCAC "Report on the National Copyright

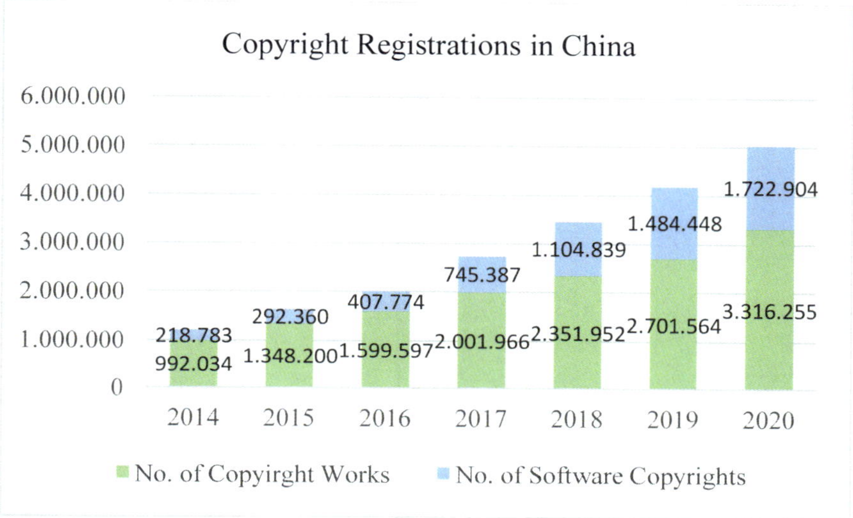

The diagram shows that the registration of new copyright works has increased steadily from 2014 onwards. In particular, in relation to the registration of software copyrights there has been a remarkable increase of around 787% from 2014 to 2020.

This once again shows that China is growing fast and focus is placed on technologies. A greater number of copyright registrations further shows that the Chinese people/ companies understand the need and importance of intellectual property protection.

Furthermore, Article 2 paragraphs 2 and 3 Chinese Copyright Law set out that a foreigner or stateless person enjoys a copyright in China if the author's country of origin or of habitual residence has an agreement with China or is member to the same international treaties as China or if the

Registration in 2018" (1 March 2019); NCAC "Announcement of the National Copyright Administration on the National Copyright Registration in 2019" (25 March 2020); NCAC "Announcement of the National Copyright Administration on the National Copyright Registration in 2020" (16 March 2021).

work in question is first published in the territory of China. Article 6 Implementing Regulations specifies that a copyright shall be acquired on the date of creation.[415]

In 1995, the NCAC introduced the possibility to register copyright works on a voluntary basis and receive a certificate that does not act as an acquisition certificate but rather as a proof of the copyright[416], especially in disputes where the time of creation is important to decide which work has been created first.[417]

Article 10 of the Chinese Copyright Law stipulates that copyright includes both personal and property rights, which is discussed in greater detail in the following.

aa) Personal (Moral) Rights

The Chinese Copyright Law contains four personal rights, namely the

- the right of publication,
- the right of authorship,
- the right of revision and
- the right of integrity.[418]

The importance of the protection of personal rights of the author is emphasized when looking at Article 29, which stipulates that no one (i.e. producer, publisher, performer et cetera) may violate the author's personal rights[419] when exploiting the work.[420]

---

[415] Article 6 *Regulations for the Implementation of the Copyright Law of the People's Republic of China* (2013 - issued 2 August 2002, effective 15 September 2002, amended 8 January 2011, amended 30 January 2013, effective 1 March 2013), State Council of the People's Republic of China.
[416] Also see Shi, "Copyright registration in China", 20 December 2015 (http://www.ccpit-patent.com.cn/node/2759, accessed: 6 March 2021).
[417] Qu, *Intellectual Property Law in China* (2012), 121.
[418] Article 10 (1)-(4) and Article 20 *Copyright Law PRC* (1990/2010 version).
[419] Meaning the right of publication, the right of authorship and the right of integrity (Article 10 (2)-(4) Chinese Copyright Law).
[420] Also see Xin Li, *Urheberrecht in Deutschland und der Volksrepublik China - ein Rechtsvergleich* (Hamburg: Verlag Dr. Kovač, 2015), 82.

Personal rights are not transferrable.[421] The four rights are explained in greater detail in the following.

(1) The Publication Right

The right to publish a work is understood to be the decision of making it available to the general public. The Chinese Copyright Law does not differentiate between the basic right to publish the work and the right to explain and communicate the content of the respective work.[422] This right can only be executed once, because once the creator decides to publish the work it is in the public sphere and a further distribution after the first publication will not be understood as a "second" publication.[423] The classification of the publication right into one of the two groups of rights is debated among experts as some say that it strictly belongs to the personal rights whereas others argue that the publication right has a "dual nature".[424] The latter is more convincing because it argues that in order to make use of the work (or better: exploit the work) the creator makes the simultaneous decision of making the work available to the public by for example exhibiting it or distributing it.[425] However, as explained above, the right to publication is solely granted to the author as he/she can decide the time and place of publication disregarding economic elements of the right.[426] This is a feature that the publication right shares with the other "real" personal rights in Article 10 Chinese Copyright Law.[427]

There is an exception when another person than the creator can exercise the right of publication. According to Article 17 Implementing Regulations, the successor or legatee of an author can exercise the publication right within a period of 50 years after the authors death unless a publication

[421] *Argumentum e contratio* of the third paragraph of Article 10 *Copyright Law PRC* (1990/2010 version).
[422] Li, *Urheberrecht in Deutschland und der Volksrepublik China - ein Rechtsvergleich* (2015), 83.
[423] See Qu, *Intellectual Property Law in China* (2012), 122.
[424] Ibid.
[425] Ibid., 122-123.
[426] Ibid., 123.
[427] Wei, *Der Urheberrechtsschutz in China mit Hinweisen auf das Deutsche Recht* (1994), 64.

is against the author's will.[428] Where a legatee or successor is absent, the owner of the original work has the right of publication.[429] When it comes to works where the author cannot be identified, Article 13 Implementing Regulations sets out that apart from the authorship right all rights, including the right to publication, shall be vested in the owner of the original work.[430]

Although the right of publication partially belongs to the personal rights, it passes on from the creator to the author in cases of cinematographic works, works created in the course of employment and commissioned works.[431]

However, it should also be noted that the right to publish a work could be limited by other person's private rights as the involved persons need to give their consent to publication.[432]

(2) The Authorship Right

The right of authorship is the right of the creator to be acknowledged as the author when the work is used or distributed to the public. It covers the right to put the author's own name onto the work (true name, alias, anonymous et cetera) as well as to prevent others from claiming authorship in this respective work.[433] The decision of an author not to sign his/her name to the work does not constitute a waiver of the right of authorship because the author could change his/her mind and sign his/her name at a later stage.[434]

(3) The Revision Right

The revision right can be explained as a right of the author to prevent others from altering it including actions such as adding, deleting and modifying

---

[428] Article 17 *Regulations for the Implementation of the Copyright Law of the People's Republic of China* (2013 - issued 2 August 2002, effective 15 September 2002, amended 8 January 2011, amended 30 January 2013, effective 1 March 2013), State Council of the People's Republic of China.
[429] Article 17 ibid.
[430] Article 13 ibid.
[431] Articles 15, 16 and 17 *Copyright Law PRC* (1990/2010 version).
[432] Qu, *Intellectual Property Law in China* (2012), 123.
[433] Ibid.
[434] Ibid., 124.

parts of the work.[435] Equally to the authorship right, the revision right allows the author to alter the work as much as he/she wants to and at the same time prevent others from changing it against his/her will; the revision right protects the concept of the author of the work who has made the decision to create the work as it is – an alteration could damage the author's honour and reputation.[436] Article 34 paragraph 1 Chinese Copyright Law grants a special revision right to book publishers as long as the author has given permission (i.e. either single permission or general permission in the contract).[437] The second paragraph of Article 34 Chinese Copyright Law grants an alteration right to newspaper and periodical publishers concerning *"editorial modifications and abridgments in the language"* and a consent of the author is only needed for changes to the content of the work.[438]

(4) The Integrity Right

The final personal copyright is the integrity right that protects the author's work from mutilation and distortion. This right is derived from Article 6 (1) of the Berne Convention and has the aim of protecting the "honour or reputation" of the author. This right is closely linked to the revision right because, although consent might be given by the author to alter a work, the person modifying it has to respect the integrity of the work and must not falsify or defame it in any way.[439]

bb) Economic Rights

The economic rights include the usage rights that are understood to be actual rights to use the work as well as to exploit the work. In total, there are twelve economic rights that consist of the following:

- right of reproduction,
- rights of distribution,
- right of rental,
- right of exhibition,

[435] Ibid.
[436] Ibid.
[437] Article 34 *Copyright Law PRC* (1990/2010 version); see Li, *Urheberrecht in Deutschland und der Volksrepublik China - ein Rechtsvergleich* (2015), 84.
[438] Article 34 *Copyright Law PRC* (1990/2010 version); see Li, *Urheberrecht in Deutschland und der Volksrepublik China - ein Rechtsvergleich* (2015), 84.
[439] Also see Qu, *Intellectual Property Law in China* (2012), 125.

- right of performance,
- right of presentation,
- right of broadcasting,
- right of communication,
- right of cinematography,
- right of adaptation,
- right of translation,
- right of compilation[440]

The various rights are now discussed in greater detail.

(1) The Reproduction Right

The reproduction right is the right to produce one or multiple copies of a work by several methods such as *"printing, photocopying, lithographing, making a sound recording or video recording, duplicating a recording, or duplicating a photographic work, or by other means"*[441]. The reproduction right is one of the elemental rights of copyright and is also laid down in Article 9 of the Berne Convention that defines the right to reproduce a work *"in any manner or form"*.[442]

(2) The Distribution Right

The distribution right is the right of the copyright owner to decide if he/she makes the work or copies of the work available to the public by either selling or donating it.[443] Once a work or its copies are distributed to the public, the author loses his/her power to intervene so that the acquirer can sell or donate the work again.[444] The right is exhausted after it has been executed for the first time.

(3) The Rental Right

The rental right is only applicable to cinematographic works or works created by a process analogous to cinematography and to computer software (if main object of rental). The owner of the copyright can exercise it by

[440] Article 10 (5)-(16) *Copyright Law PRC* (1990/2010 version).
[441] Article 10 (5) ibid.
[442] See also Qu, *Intellectual Property Law in China* (2012), 127.
[443] Article 10 (6) *Copyright Law PRC* (1990/2010 version).
[444] Qu, *Intellectual Property Law in China* (2012), 129.

giving an authorization to third persons to use a work for a specific time period (commercial rental).[445]

(4) The Exhibition Right

The exhibition right is the right to display the work of fine art or a photographic work and/or its copies in the public.[446] Different to the other economic rights, here, the owner of the original work has the right to exhibit his/her work.[447]

Also, interesting to note here is the fact that if the author decides to display (at that moment) unpublished work he/she exercises both the publication right as well as the exhibition right at the same time.[448]

(5) The Performance Right

The performance right is the right to perform or communicate the performance of a work to the public in any form.[449] Performance includes both the live performance of a work as well as the performance of the work by technical means.[450] However, the Chinese Copyright Law does not specify the explicit ways of performance so that it is open to interpretation.

(6) The Presentation Right

The presentation right is the right to show a work[451] by projector or a similar technological instrument.[452] This right is a newer right in the Chinese Copyright Law and shows that China wants to improve the rights of copyright holders.[453]

---

[445] Article 10 (7) *Copyright Law PRC* (1990/2010 version).
[446] Article 10 (8) ibid.
[447] Qu, *Intellectual Property Law in China* (2012), 130.
[448] Ibid.
[449] Article 10 (9) *Copyright Law PRC* (1990/2010 version).
[450] This can be derived from the WCT that stipulates a right to communicate a work to the public; Article 8 *WCT* (1996), S. Treaty Doc. No. 105-17 (1997); 36 ILM 65 (1997).
[451] Including fine art, photography, cinematography, works analogous to cinematography and other works.
[452] Article 10 (10) *Copyright Law PRC* (1990/2010 version).
[453] Qu, *Intellectual Property Law in China* (2012), 131.

(7) The Broadcasting Right

The broadcasting right is the right to broadcast or disseminate the work in different ways.[454] It includes the wireless broadcast of the work as well as the communication via loudspeaker or any other analogous instrument that transmits signs, sound or images.

(8) The Communication Right

The communication right refers to the right of the author to make a work accessible at a place and time decided by the public through the information network either by wire or wireless means.[455] In comparison to the previously discussed broadcasting right, the communication right was introduced to include the making available of the work independent from broadcasting organizations through the information network where the user/listener can decide exactly to what time and where he/she will make use of the work.[456]

(9) The Cinematography Right

The cinematography right is the right to fix an adaptation of a work by cinematography or an analogous process.[457] Cinematography can also be explained as the process of filming or turning works into motion picture by the use of technology.[458] The production of a film involves several rights of different copyright owners (i.e. adaptation rights that arise by changing an original to a script, production rights, distribution rights et cetera) who have to get the consent of the author of the primary (original) work.[459]

(10) The Adaptation Right

The adaptation right refers to the right to change/adapt/alter an original work into a new work that also fulfils the originality requirement.[460] As an example a person who wants to change a novel into a play has to get the

[454] Article 10 (11) *Copyright Law PRC* (1990/2010 version).
[455] Article 10 (12) ibid.
[456] Qu, *Intellectual Property Law in China* (2012), 132.
[457] Article 10 (13) *Copyright Law PRC* (1990/2010 version).
[458] Qu, *Intellectual Property Law in China* (2012), 132.
[459] Ibid., 132-133.
[460] Article 10 (14) *Copyright Law PRC* (1990/2010 version).

authorization of the author of the novel and has to create a new original work from it.

(11) The Translation Right

The translation right is the right to change the original language of a work into another language.[461] The translator of an original work has to respect the primary author by translating the work very accurately and not changing the meaning thereof which requires a good understanding of the content.[462]

(12) The Compilation Right

The compilation right refers to the right to make a compilation of pre-existing works or parts thereof or to arrange them and create a new work.[463] In contrast to an adaptation of the work, the original works or parts of it are not altered but only put together in an arrangement fulfilling the originality requirements laid out above.[464] Interesting to note is, that if someone arranges works into a new work without having the consent of the owners of the originals, he/she would interfere with the reproduction right and not the compilation right.[465]

(13) Other Rights

The list is not exclusive and leaves room for other rights enjoyed by copyright owners in Article 10 (17) Chinese Copyright Law. This leaves room for the rights that are laid down in international agreements or bilateral agreements as well as possible rights resulting from the advancement of technology.

In view of the fast-developing technology and the globalization which lead to increasing bilateral and multilateral discussions it is positive that China has opted for an open list so that the judiciary has the possibility to adapt to "newer" developments. Despite this "flexibility" China should amend the legislation or issue regulations in regular intervals so that the law remains comprehensible.

---

461 Article 10 (15) ibid.
462 Qu, *Intellectual Property Law in China* (2012), 133.
463 Article 10 (16) *Copyright Law PRC* (1990/2010 version).
464 Qu, *Intellectual Property Law in China* (2012), 133.
465 Ibid.

d) Term of Protection

Copyright is an intellectual property right that grants the owner a monopoly over a certain period of time. The scope of this monopoly is defined by each country's legislation.[466] As a reference point either the author's age or the time of publication can be used. Many countries have used the author's age plus a certain period.[467] China makes use of both concepts depending on the type of work in question. Section 3 of the Chinese Copyright Law begins with the protection term of copyrights. Here, it has to be distinguished between the moral rights and the economic rights.

aa) Protection of Moral Rights

According to Article 20, there is no limitation in the protection period concerning moral rights, meaning that the term of protection concerning the rights of authorship and revision as well as the protection of integrity of the work are granted eternally. After the author's death, the protection of the right should be carried out by his/her successor, the agency or in absence thereof by the copyright administration.[468]

bb) Protection of Economic Rights

Article 21 stipulates that the economic rights (Article 10 (5) until (17) Chinese Copyright Law) are protected as long as the author's life plus another fifty years after the author's death.[469] Concerning works of joint authorship, the period will be calculated from the time of death of the last author of the work.

cc) Protection of Works Created for a Legal Entity

A different term of protection has to be applied in the cases where a legal entity or other organization enjoys the copyright – may it be because the work has been created in the course of employment[470] or the legal entity or organization holds the copyright from the beginning. Here, the term is fifty

[466] Also see ibid., 137.
[467] This can be explained by looking at Article 7 (1) of the Berne Convention, which sets out the general concept to use the author's age. Also see ibid.
[468] Ibid., 138.
[469] The fifty years expire on 31 December of the fiftieth year after the author's death.
[470] The right of authorship does not fall within that protection period because Article 20 is applied to that.

years counted from the first publication of the work[471] with the limitation that no protection will be granted if the publication of the work has not occurred within fifty years after completion. A problem can be seen when looking at the legal certainty of this regulation.[472] As explained above the ownership of works created in the course of employment as well as commissioned works can be decided upon by contracts between the parties. Third parties do not necessarily know of the contractual terms and hence, will not know when the protection term expires.[473]

dd) Photographic and Cinematographic Works

Exactly the same approach has been chosen for the protection of the right of publication of cinematographic and photographic work (Article 21 paragraph 3 Chinese Copyright Law) because such works are protected for fifty years starting from publication and are no longer protected if not published within the first fifty years after completion.[474]

ee) Protection of Works of Unknown Authorship

The same term of protection (fifty years counted from publication) is granted to works of unknown authorship unless the author can be identified at some point[475]; then, the general term of Article 21 paragraph 1 will be applied again. However, the legislation is incomplete here, because it remains unclear, whether such work receives protection if it is not published within the fifty years after completion of the creation.[476] Also it is unclear if a work of a so far unknown author will be protected if the author is only identified after the fifty years counted from the publication have lapsed.

---

[471] The fifty years expire on 31 December of the fiftieth year after publication.

[472] Dietz, "Das chinesische Urheberrecht: Copyright oder droit d'auteur?" (2004), 532-533.

[473] Ibid.

[474] Also see Wei, *Der Urheberrechtsschutz in China mit Hinweisen auf das Deutsche Recht* (1994), 91.

[475] Article 18 *Regulations for the Implementation of the Copyright Law of the People's Republic of China* (2013 - issued 2 August 2002, effective 15 September 2002, amended 8 January 2011, amended 30 January 2013, effective 1 March 2013), State Council of the People's Republic of China.

[476] Wei, *Der Urheberrechtsschutz in China mit Hinweisen auf das Deutsche Recht* (1994), 92.

In contrast to that, the German copyright legislation does not separate economic and moral rights when it comes to the term of protection. According to Article 64 German Copyright Act (Urheberrechtsgesetz), the term of protection of all rights to a work is the life of the author plus another seventy years.[477]

e) The Exercise of Copyright

The author of a work can decide whether he/she wants to exercise the rights himself/herself or allow others to exercise the copyright. The copyright owner can either authorize others to exercise certain rights and receive remuneration for it[478] or transfer the rights partially or wholly to others and receive a specific fee for the transfer[479]. Of course, a donation of the rights is also possible. By an *argumentum e contrario* it can be said that the personal rights cannot be transferred because Article 10 paragraph 2 and 3 Chinese Copyright Law only name the rights stipulated in Article 10 paragraph 1 (5)-(17). The different ways of exercising the copyright are discussed in greater detail in the following.

aa) Permission to Use

Article 10 paragraph 2 Chinese Copyright Law grants the right to the copyright owner to authorise others to exercise the copyright, in other words to permit someone else to make use of the rights in a work. This process is called licensing and can be executed in several ways. The owner can either grant an exclusive right to one particular person or give various licenses to various persons. Article 24 Chinese Copyright Law sets out that a person who wants to exploit the copyright of someone else must conclude a copyright licensing contract with the owner that has to contain the following:

- category of the right to be exploited,
- the nature of the license (exclusive or non-exclusive),
- territory covered by the license and duration of the license,
- remuneration rate and payment conditions,
- liability if contract is breached,
- other matter that seem to be necessary to the parties.[480]

[477] *UrhG (Germany)* (1965).
[478] Article 10 paragraph 2 *Copyright Law PRC* (1990/2010 version).
[479] Article 10 paragraph 3 ibid.
[480] Article 24 ibid.

Article 23 Implementing Regulations stipulates that a licensing contract concerning an exclusive license needs to be in written form with the exceptions of works that are to be published in a newspaper or periodical.[481] The licensee may not exploit any right that is not specifically licensed by the contract.[482]

The contents of the exclusive exploitation right shall be concluded by the contract.[483] The Implementing Regulations also deal with the situation when an agreement concerning an exclusive license is absent or unclear. According to Article 24 of the Implementing Regulations, the licensee shall have the right to prevent others, including the copyright owner himself/herself, from exercising the copyright in question.

Sublicensing of a copyright is only allowed if the copyright owner consents in writing to the grant of a sublicense to a third party; this can be part of the licensing contract or a later granted permission.[484]

bb) Transferring Copyrights

Article 10 paragraph 3 Chinese Copyright Law gives the possibility to the author to transfer the copyright in a work in part or in whole to another person and in return receive remuneration for it. Article 25 Chinese Copyright Law sets out that the transfer of copyright requires a written contract that needs to contain the following:

- title of the work,
- category of the right transferred and territory covered by the transfer,
- transfer fee rate,
- payment conditions,
- liability if contract is breached,

---

481 *Regulations for the Implementation of the Copyright Law of the People's Republic of China* (2013 - issued 2 August 2002, effective 15 September 2002, amended 8 January 2011, amended 30 January 2013, effective 1 March 2013), State Council of the People's Republic of China.

482 Article 27 *Copyright Law PRC* (1990/2010 version).

483 Article 24 *Regulations for the Implementation of the Copyright Law of the People's Republic of China* (2013 - issued 2 August 2002, effective 15 September 2002, amended 8 January 2011, amended 30 January 2013, effective 1 March 2013), State Council of the People's Republic of China.

484 Article 24 ibid.

- other matters that seem to be necessary to the parties.[485]

Article 25 Implementing Regulations stipulates that the copyright transfer contract needs to be registered with the administrative departments.

The transferee may not exploit any right that is not specifically transferred by the contract.[486]

cc) Remuneration

Remuneration is dealt with in Article 28 Chinese Copyright Law. This article lays down the contractual autonomy of the parties because they can freely decide upon the remuneration that needs to be paid in return for the exploitation of the work or they can make use of the rates fixed by the administrative department. Article 28 also sets out that such fixed rights shall be used in absence of a specific regulation in the contract.

dd) Special Copyright Contracts

Besides the general rules regarding the assignment and licensing of copyrights there are some special contracts that are discussed in greater detail. The Chinese Copyright Law has devoted a separate section to deal with publication, performance, sound recording, video recording and broadcasting (Article 30 to Article 46 Chinese Copyright Law).

(1) Publishing Contract

Books, newspapers and magazines are the three different forms of publishing. The publishing contracts can be split into two different kinds of contracts – the book publishing contract and the newspaper and magazine (periodicals) publishing contract.[487]

Article 30 Chinese Copyright Law sets out that a book publisher who wants to publish a book needs to agree with the copyright owner on a contract and pay remuneration. A publishing contract is an exclusive contract and the copyright owner is prohibited to deliver the book to another publisher

---

485 Article 25 *Copyright Law PRC* (1990/2010 version).
486 Article 27 ibid.
487 Wei, *Der Urheberrechtsschutz in China mit Hinweisen auf das Deutsche Recht* (1994), 104.

to be published.[488] Article 32 Chinese Copyright Law stipulates the rules and fulfilment of a publishing contract:

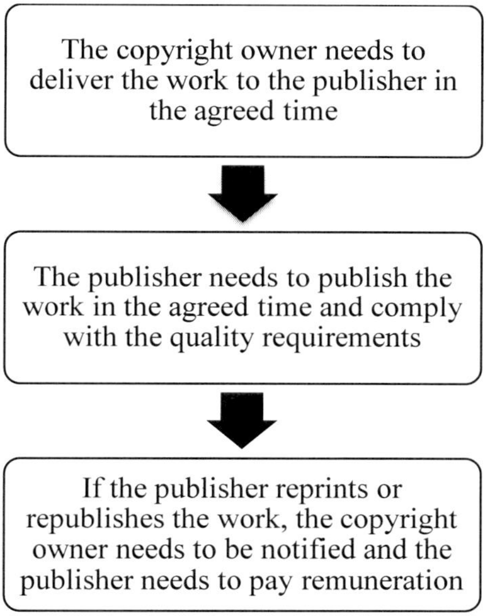

If the publisher is not able to publish the book in the contractually agreed time he/she has to bear civil liabilities.[489] If the first edition of the book is sold out and the publisher denies the reprint or republication, the copyright owner has the possibility to end the contract.[490] The copyright owner of the book can authorize the book publisher to alter the work in form of revisions or abridgements.[491] The Implementing Regulations contain a further provision regarding the content of an exclusive book publishing contract if the contract does not include arrangements concerning the specific content of the contract; in such cases the publisher has "*the exclusive right to publish the book in the same language and in the form of original or revised version*".[492]

[488] Article 31 *Copyright Law PRC* (1990/2010 version).
[489] Article 32 paragraph 2 ibid.
[490] Article 32 paragraph 3 ibid.
[491] Article 34 paragraph 1 ibid.
[492] Article 28 *Regulations for the Implementation of the Copyright Law of the People's Republic of China* (2013 - issued 2 August 2002, effective 15

Concerning newspapers and periodicals the time frame of submission is much shorter and fixed by law, unless agreed otherwise in a contract.[493] Here, the copyright owner is not allowed to submit the work to another publisher for a certain period of time if he/she has not received any notification by the publisher – if a newspaper is involved the time period must not be longer than fifteen days whereas a magazine publisher has thirty days counted from the submission of the work. The second paragraph of Article 33 opens up the possibility for other newspaper and periodical publishers to reprint a work in return for the payment of remuneration to the copyright owner unless the copyright owner has opposed to such reprint.[494] In comparison to the book publisher, a newspaper or periodical publisher does not need the authors consent if he/she wants to make editorial modifications and abridgements in the language of the work.[495] However, an alteration of the content of the work can only be made with the consent of the author.[496]

Concerning works that are created by adaptation, translation et cetera, Article 35 Chinese Copyright Law stipulates that the publisher needs the consent of both the creator of the new work as well as the creator of the pre-existing work that the new work is based on.

(2) Performance Contract

The performance contract is the contract between a performer, either a single person or a group, with the copyright owner regarding the performance of such work. Article 37 Chinese Copyright Law sets out that the performer needs to acquire the consent of the copyright owner and – in return of the exploitation of the work in form of a performance – pay a specified remuneration to the owner.[497] Equivalent to the book publisher, a performer needs to obtain the consent of both the owner of the pre-existing work and

---

September 2002, amended 8 January 2011, amended 30 January 2013, effective 1 March 2013), State Council of the People's Republic of China.

[493] Article 33 *Copyright Law PRC* (1990/2010 version).

[494] According to Article 30 of the *Regulations for the Implementation of the Copyright Law of the People's Republic of China* (2013 - issued 2 August 2002, effective 15 September 2002, amended 8 January 2011, amended 30 January 2013, effective 1 March 2013), State Council of the People's Republic of China.

[495] Article 34 paragraph 2 *Copyright Law PRC* (1990/2010 version).

[496] Article 34 paragraph 2 ibid.

[497] The same procedure is to be carried out by the organizer of a performance.

the owner of the newly created work in cases of the adaptation, translation and the like.[498]

(3) Sound and Video Recording Contract

The sound and video contracts are similar to the performance contracts. According to Article 40 paragraph 1 Chinese Copyright Law, a producer of sound and video recordings needs to have the consent of the copyright owner and has to pay remuneration to such when exploiting the work. Concerning works created by ways of adaptation, translation and the like, again, both the permission of the owner of the pre-existing work and the newly created work is needed.[499] Similar to Article 33 paragraph 2 Chinese Copyright Law[500] a producer of sound recordings can – for the purpose of creating a sound recording – use a musical work that has been legally recorded before without the consent of the copyright owner as long as remuneration is paid unless he/she has objected to such reuse.[501] Such objection needs to be declared at the time the work is legally recorded.[502]

Further, Article 41 Chinese Copyright Law stipulates that the performer and the producer of a sound recording need to conclude a contract including the remuneration for the performer when a sound recording of a performance is being made. Article 42 Chinese Copyright Law deals with the cases in which the producer has allowed a third party to reproduce, distribute or make the sound recording available to the public through information network and stipulates that such third party has to pay remuneration to the copyright owner and the producer.

(4) Broadcasting Contract

The fourth section is dedicated to the broadcasters. Here, it needs to be distinguished between unpublished and published works. Article 43 paragraph 1 Chinese Copyright Law sets out that a radio or television station

---

[498] Article 37 paragraph 2 *Copyright Law PRC* (1990/2010 version).
[499] Article 40 paragraph 2 ibid.
[500] Another publisher is allowed to reprint or excerpt the work published by another publisher unless the copyright owner has objected to such methods.
[501] Article 40 paragraph 3 *Copyright Law PRC* (1990/2010 version).
[502] Article 31 *Regulations for the Implementation of the Copyright Law of the People's Republic of China* (2013 - issued 2 August 2002, effective 15 September 2002, amended 8 January 2011, amended 30 January 2013, effective 1 March 2013), State Council of the People's Republic of China.

needs the permission of the copyright owner when broadcasting an unpublished work of another person and pay remuneration to such. Whereas paragraph 2 of Article 43 stipulates that a published work can be broadcasted without the permission as long as remuneration is paid.

In cases where the broadcaster wants to broadcast a cinematographic work, a work created by a process analogous to cinematography or a video recording he/she has to get the consent of the producer and additionally the consent of the copyright owner in cases of video recordings and pay remuneration to the respective persons.[503]

(5) Collective Copyright Management

Another possibility for copyright owners to have their rights exercised is the way of collective copyright management.

The first Copyright Law of 1990 did not contain a regulation regarding the collective copyright management – it was first introduced in the *Implementing Regulations of 1991* in Article 54 which allowed the exercise of copyright by collective management.[504] The first revision of the Chinese Copyright Law in 2001 included a new paragraph on collective copyright management and ordered that regulations concerning their establishments, rights, obligations, et cetera shall be formulated separately by the State Council.[505] Such regulations were promulgated in 2004 and came into effect on 1 March 2005 and were slightly amended in 2013.[506]

In the current law, Article 8 Chinese Copyright Law grants the possibility to copyright owners of copyright exercise by collective copyright management. Once the copyright owner has decided to have his/her rights exercised in that way, the collective copyright organization can act in its own name for the owner and is also given the right to be a party in legal or

[503] Article 46 *Copyright Law PRC* (1990/2010 version).

[504] *Regulations for the Implemenation of the Copyright Law of the People's Republic of China* (1991 - 24 May 1991, promulgated 30 May 1991, effective 1 June 1991), National Copyright Administration of the People's Republic of China; Wei, *Der Urheberrechtsschutz in China mit Hinweisen auf das Deutsche Recht* (1994), 108.

[505] Article 8 *Copyright Law PRC* (1990/2001 version).

[506] *Regulations on Copyright Collective Administration* (2004 - adopted 22 December 2004, effective 1 March 2005, amended 4 December 2013), State Council of the People's Republic of China (provided by WIPO).

arbitration proceedings concerning the respective copyright. Article 8 paragraph 2 Chinese Copyright Law sets out that collective copyright organizations are non-profit organizations.

Article 2 Regulations on Copyright Collective Management stipulates the activities of the organizations when exercising copyright owner's rights as the following:

- conclusion of licensing contracts with users,
- collecting fees from such,
- distribution of licensing fees to owners,
- participation in litigation or arbitration proceedings.[507]

In total, there are five collecting organizations in China:

- the Music Copyright Society of China (MCSC),
- the China Written Works Copyright Society (CWWCS),
- the Images Copyright Society of China (ICSC),
- the China Audio-Video Copyright Association (CAVCA) and
- the China Film Copyright Association (CFCA).[508]

The MCSC was the first collective copyright organization in China and was founded in 1992.[509] These organizations need to be founded by Chinese citizens and have to be officially registered.[510] Article 7 (2) Regulations on Copyright Collective Management sets out that the organizations

---

[507] Article 2 ibid.

[508] See Lijing Li, *Die kollektive Urheberrechtswahrnehmung durch Verwertungsgesellschaften in der Bundesrepublik Deutschland und in der Volksrepublik China*, Band 97, Studienreihe zum Gewerblichen Rechtsschutz und zum Urheberrecht (Hamburg: Verlag Dr. Kovač, 2012), 58-59.

[509] Music Copyright Society of China, "General Introduction" (http://www.mcsc.com.cn/en/situation.html, accessed: 3 March 2021); Wei, *Der Urheberrechtsschutz in China mit Hinweisen auf das Deutsche Recht* (1994), 109.

[510] See Li, *Die kollektive Urheberrechtswahrnehmung durch Verwertungsgesellschaften in der Bundesrepublik Deutschland und in der Volksrepublik China* (2012), 78; for more details regarding the definition and formation of a collective administration organization, look at ibid., 76-79, 176-180.

in each area have a monopoly position[511] because no business scope of an organization must interfere with an already existing organization.[512]

Article 19 Regulations on Copyright Collective Management sets out that in order to authorize a copyright collective organization, the copyright holder needs to conclude a written contract about the administration of the rights by the respective organization – by that authorization and the fulfilment of all necessary steps, the copyright owner will become a member of the respective organization.[513] Furthermore, Article 19 Regulations stipulates that a copyright collective administration might not refuse a contract with a copyright owner once all requirements of such association are fulfilled.[514]

Article 20 Regulations on Copyright Collective Management prohibits the copyright owner to exercise or authorize others to exercise the rights that are part of the contract with the collective copyright association.[515]

Article 23 Regulations on Copyright Collective Management orders the association to conclude written licensing contracts with the licensees that have a maximum duration of two years[516] and the association must not conclude exclusive licensing contracts with anyone.[517]

f) Copyright Related Rights (Neighbouring Rights)

The Chinese Copyright Law also recognizes copyright related rights in Articles 30 to 46. Related rights are granted to the distributors of copyright works. These include the rights of the following:

---

[511] It must be noted that there are still some organizations that were founded before the monopoly position was legally consolidated in the Regulations; such organizations still handle copyrights of copyright owners so that in some areas more than one organization is operating in the same business scope; ibid., 93-94.
[512] Ibid., 90-91.
[513] Article 19 *Regulations on Copyright Collective Administration* (2004 - adopted 22 December 2004, effective 1 March 2005, amended 4 December 2013), State Council of the People's Republic of China.
[514] Article 19 ibid.
[515] Article 20 ibid.
[516] A renewal is possible.
[517] Article 23 *Regulations on Copyright Collective Administration* (2004 - adopted 22 December 2004, effective 1 March 2005, amended 4 December 2013), State Council of the People's Republic of China.

- publishers (Articles 30 to 36),
- performers (Articles 37 to 39),
- producers of sound and video recordings (Articles 40 to 42),
- broadcasters (Articles 43 to 46).

The Implementing Regulations stipulate that

> *"The term "rights and interests related to copyright" as referred to in the Copyright Law and these Regulations means the rights enjoyed by publishers in the typographical designs of their books or periodicals, the rights enjoyed by performers in their performances, the rights enjoyed by producers of sound and video recordings in their sound and video recordings, and the rights enjoyed by radio and television stations in their broadcasting programmes".*[518]

Furthermore, the Implementing Regulations set out that the owners of copyright related rights must not prejudice the rights of the copyright owners of the works they exploit when publishing, performing, recording and broadcasting.[519]

The structure of the Chinese Copyright Law is not very systematic in this section because these articles, as explained in the previous part[520], contain the rules on the exercise of copyright and the contracts of publishers, broadcasters et cetera with copyright owners. This "mix-up" of related rights and the exercise of rights shows the lack of understanding of copyright when the law was made in 1990.[521]

---

[518] Article 26 *Regulations for the Implementation of the Copyright Law of the People's Republic of China* (2013 - issued 2 August 2002, effective 15 September 2002, amended 8 January 2011, amended 30 January 2013, effective 1 March 2013), State Council of the People's Republic of China.
[519] Article 27 ibid.
[520] See *Chapter 3 I. 2. e) dd)* of this dissertation on the exercise of copyright and special copyright contracts.
[521] Wei, *Der Urheberrechtsschutz in China mit Hinweisen auf das Deutsche Recht* (1994), 112.

aa) The Rights of a Publisher

Article 36 Chinese Copyright Law grants the right to the typographical design (layout design) of a published book or periodical to the publisher (出版者 chūbǎnzhě) and gives him/her both the right to authorize a third person to use/exploit it and the right to prevent others from making unauthorized use of it. Typographical design is the choice of publishing material such as fonts, style, order of words and size.[522] The publisher's right has a limited time of duration, namely ten years, counting from the first publication where the typographical design is used.[523]

Furthermore, Article 31 Chinese Copyright Law stipulates that once a publishing contract is signed the publisher has an exclusive right and thereby receives protection by law so that others cannot publish the work under their accounts. This right is not a so-called neighbouring right that arises naturally but more a right established by the contract with the copyright owner. This is due to the fact that the right to a typographical design has some form of creativity and therefore needs to be treated similar to copyrights whereas the exclusive publishing right is just an economical right given by the contract.[524]

bb) The Rights of a Performer

According to Article 5 (6) Implementing Regulations, a performer (表演者 biǎoyǎnzhě) is *"an actor, or a performing group or any other person who performs literary or artistic works"*[525].

The performer has the right to claim performership and to protect the image of his/her performance from distortion.[526] These rights are similar to the authorship as well as the integrity right of copyright owners. The right to

[522] Qu, *Intellectual Property Law in China* (2012), 149.
[523] Article 36 paragraph 2 *Copyright Law PRC* (1990/2010 version).
[524] Qu, *Intellectual Property Law in China* (2012), 150.
[525] Article 5 (6) *Regulations for the Implementation of the Copyright Law of the People's Republic of China* (2013 - issued 2 August 2002, effective 15 September 2002, amended 8 January 2011, amended 30 January 2013, effective 1 March 2013), State Council of the People's Republic of China.
[526] Article 38 (1) and (2) *Copyright Law PRC* (1990/2010 version).

prevent others from the distortion of the performance is aiming at protecting the performer's reputation and prestige.[527] Both the performership right and the right to protect the performance from distortion are personal rights and therefore, are granted to the performer perpetually.[528]

Article 38 (3) to (6) Chinese Copyright Law grant the right to the performer to allow others live broadcasting, making of sound and video recordings, reproduction and distribution and making the work available to the public through information network; however, Article 38 paragraph 2 clarifies that third persons can only exploit such rights once they have the consent of the copyright owner and pay remuneration to such. These economical performer's rights are granted for fifty years.[529]

cc) The Rights of a Producer of Sound or Video Recordings

According to Article 5 (4) and (5) Implementing Regulations, a producer (制作者 zhìzuò zhě) of a sound/video recording is the person who first makes the sound/video recording.[530]

Article 42 Chinese Copyright Law grants the right to the producers of sound or video recordings to authorize others to reproduce, distribute or rent the sound or video recording or to make it available to the public through information network; in return, the producer receives remuneration from the third person.[531] The producer's right is granted for fifty years.[532] However, such authorization to third persons is only possible if the third person also has the permission of the copyright owner of the original work and pays remuneration to such.[533]

---

[527] Qu, *Intellectual Property Law in China* (2012), 153.
[528] Article 39 paragraph 1 *Copyright Law PRC* (1990/2010 version); see also Qu, *Intellectual Property Law in China* (2012), 154.
[529] Article 39 paragraph 2 *Copyright Law PRC* (1990/2010 version). - Expiring on 31 December of the fiftieth year after the performance takes place.
[530] Article 5 (4) and (5) *Regulations for the Implementation of the Copyright Law of the People's Republic of China* (2013 - issued 2 August 2002, effective 15 September 2002, amended 8 January 2011, amended 30 January 2013, effective 1 March 2013), State Council of the People's Republic of China.
[531] Article 42 paragraph 1 *Copyright Law PRC* (1990/2010 version).
[532] Article 42 paragraph 1 sentence 2 ibid. - Expiring on 31 December of the fiftieth year after the first completion of the recording.
[533] Article 42 paragraph 2 ibid.

dd) The Rights of a Broadcaster

Article 45 Chinese Copyright Law grants two rights to radio and television stations (广播电台 guǎngbò diàntái and 电视台 diànshìtái; short "broadcasters"). Without the permission of the broadcasters, third persons cannot broadcast their programs and also cannot make sound or video recordings of their programs or reproduce such recordings. These two broadcaster's rights are granted for fifty years.[534]

g) Limitations

Article 13 TRIPS stipulates that

> *"Members shall confine limitation or exceptions to exclusive rights to certain special cases which do not conflict with a normal exploitation of the work and do not unreasonably prejudice the legitimate interests of the right holder."*[535]

This obligation under TRIPS is reflected in Article 22 and 23 Chinese Copyright Law that deal with the limitations on rights: rights are limited by two ways – fair use and statutory license. Ways of limitations on rights should be implemented by the legislators for the aim of a harmonious interplay of the economic rights of the right holder and the needs of the general public, meaning the promotion of culture, information and education.[536]

The different limitations to Chinese Copyright Law are discussed in more detail in the following.

aa) Fair Use

Article 22 Chinese Copyright Law sets out the rules for using a copyright protected work without the permission of the respective owner and without paying remuneration to such as long as the person using the works cites

---

[534] Article 45 paragraph 2 ibid. - Expiring on 31 December of the fiftieth year after the first broadcasting of a program.

[535] Article 13 *TRIPS Agreement* (1994), 1869 UNTS 299; 33 ILM 1197 (Annex 1C of the Marrakesh Agreement establishing the World Trade Organization, signed in Marrakesh, Morocco on 15 April 1994, 33 I.L.M. 1125).

[536] Also see Qu, *Intellectual Property Law in China* (2012), 162.

the name and the title of the work and does not prejudice it.[537] Fair use can be defined as the *"reasonable and limited use of a copyrighted work"*[538]. The affirmation of a fair use situation can act as a defence when the right holder is claiming that another person has infringed the work.[539] In total, there are twelve different scenarios stipulated in the legislation in which the fair use exception applies:

(1) Personal Study, Research or Appreciation

Another person can use the right holders work for personal study, research or appreciation. Such personal use constitutes fair use because the personal rights of the user; however, the use must not be of a commercial nature.[540] The fair use exception will not apply if any commercial activity is involved. The use of an unpublished work does not fall under this exception.[541]

(2) Quotation in Own Work

Another usage that falls under the limitations of copyright is the inclusion of quotations in the user's own work. According to Article 22 (2) Chinese Copyright Law, this includes cases of *"introducing or commenting a certain work, or explaining a certain point"*[542]. The user has to make sure to name the author and title of the work to provide readers with a sufficient and accurate source of the quoted content. According to Article 22 (2), the quotation has to be "appropriate". "Appropriate" means that the used quotation must be in context of one of the abovementioned cases, must not be the substantial part of the work and the rights of the copyright owner should not to be infringed in any way.[543] The use of an unpublished work does not fall under this exception.[544]

---

[537] Article 21 *Regulations for the Implementation of the Copyright Law of the People's Republic of China* (2013 - issued 2 August 2002, effective 15 September 2002, amended 8 January 2011, amended 30 January 2013, effective 1 March 2013), State Council of the People's Republic of China.
[538] Qu, *Intellectual Property Law in China* (2012), 162.
[539] Also see ibid., 162-163.
[540] Also see ibid., 163.
[541] Article 22 (1) *Copyright Law PRC* (1990/2010 version).
[542] Article 22 (2) ibid.
[543] See Qu, *Intellectual Property Law in China* (2012), 164.
[544] Article 22 (2) *Copyright Law PRC* (1990/2010 version).

(3) Use in the News

The use of another's work in a report of current events in a newspaper, a periodical, in a radio or television show and in other forms of media constitutes the third fair use exception to copyright as long as the representation or quotation is unavoidable for the report, the author's name and work's title are named properly and the further rights of the copyright owner are not prejudiced in any way.[545] The use of an unpublished work does not fall under this exception.[546]

(4) Publication or Broadcasting of an Article on Political, Economic or Religious Topics

According to Article 22 (4) Chinese Copyright Law, publishers and broadcasters can republish or rebroadcast content that has been published or broadcasted by another publisher or broadcaster as long as current political, economic or religious topics are concerned. However, this exception is not valid if the author of the work has opposed the republication or rebroadcasting of the work.[547]

(5) Publication or Broadcasting of a Speech at a Public Gathering

Another limitation to copyright is the publication or broadcasting of a public speech by newspaper and periodical publishers or radio and television stations.[548] However, this is only possible if the holder of the speech has not opposed the publication or broadcasting of the speech. A public gathering is an assembly of people where everyone can freely go to and listen and the orator wants to spread his/her content to the wide public.[549]

(6) Translation or Reproduction for Teaching and Research Purposes

According to Article 22 (6) Chinese Copyright Law, teachers and scientific researchers can reproduce small quantities or translate published works for the purpose of teaching or scientific research as a long as the translation or reproduction has not been published for dissemination. However, the users

545 Article 22 (3) ibid.; also see Qu, *Intellectual Property Law in China* (2012), 164.
546 Article 22 (3) *Copyright Law PRC* (1990/2010 version).
547 Article 22 (4) ibid.
548 Article 22 (5) ibid.
549 See Qu, *Intellectual Property Law in China* (2012), 164.

also must clearly indicate the source (author's name and title of work) and must not interfere with other legal rights of the author.[550]

(7) Use in the Fulfilment of Official Duties

Article 22 (7) Chinese Copyright Law concerns State organs and allows them to use another's published work for the fulfilment of official duties. However, the source needs to be clearly stated and no other rights of the author must be infringed. State organs include legislators, law enforcers and judicial and military authorities that have to make use of such works for the purpose of official duties such as law enactment, policies or national management.[551]

(8) Reproduction for Use in Library for Display or Preservation

A public institution such as a library, an archive, a memorial hall or an art gallery are allowed to reproduce a publish work of their collection without the copyright owner's permission to show or preserve the work.[552] As Article 22 (8) Chinese Copyright Law does not specifically name "published" works as the other paragraphs do, this limitation can be interpreted to include both published and unpublished works.

(9) Free Performance to the Public

Another limitation to copyright is the possibility of performing a published work in the public sphere without charging the spectators for the live performance as well as without paying the performers for such performance (e.g. flash mobs).[553] However, similar to the other limitation situations, the author's name and tile of the work need to be indicated.

(10) Display in an Outdoor Public Place

According to Article 22 (10) Chinese Copyright Law, spectators of art that has been put up for display in an outdoor public place are allowed to copy, draw, photograph or video record the works without permission.

[550] Also see ibid., 164-165.
[551] Ibid., 165.
[552] Article 22 (8) *Copyright Law PRC* (1990/2010 version).
[553] Article 22 (9) ibid.

(11) Translation from Han Language to Minority Chinese

The translation of a published work that has been created in the Han language into a minority Chinese language can be done without permissions if such translation has the purpose to publish or distribute the translated work in the country side.[554] The limitation can only be applied to works of Chinese citizens, legal entities or other organizations.[555] This limitation has been established for the purpose of encouraging the scientific and cultural development of ethnic minorities as well as their respective languages.[556] Also, the name of the author and the work title need to be indicated. It can be argued that this limitation deprives the author of the right to provide the translations on his/her own.

(12) Transliteration into Braille

The last case where a limitation to copyright is given is the transliteration of public works into braille.[557]

(13) Fair Use and Information Communication Technology

The Chinese Copyright Law does not include provisions on the fair use regarding the digital environment. Article 10 WCT deals with the possibility of introducing exceptions to copyright in special cases (similar to the abovementioned Article 13 TRIPS).[558] Unfortunately, none of these provisions include exceptions in the digital environment. However, Member States of the WCT have made Agreed Statements concerning the WCT at the Diplomatic Conference in 1996. The Agreed Statement on Article 10 WCT reads

> *"It is understood that the provisions of Article 10 permit Contracting Parties to carry forward and appropriately extend into the digital environment limitations and exceptions in their national laws which have been considered acceptable under the Berne Convention. Similarly, these*

[554] Article 22 (11) ibid.
[555] Article 22 (11) ibid.
[556] Qu, *Intellectual Property Law in China* (2012), 166.
[557] Article 22 (12) *Copyright Law PRC* (1990/2010 version).
[558] *WCT* (1996), S. Treaty Doc. No. 105-17 (1997); 36 ILM 65 (1997).

> *provisions should be understood to permit Contracting Parties to devise new exceptions and limitations that are appropriate in the digital network environment.*"[559]

China has implemented such limitations and exceptions by the *Regulations on the Protection of Right of Dissemination via Information Network*[560]. Article 6 of the Regulations stipulates that a work can be made available through information network without the permission of the copyright owner and without the payment of any kind of remuneration in the following circumstances:

- use in one's own work (by quotation),
- use in the news for the purpose of reporting current events,
- use by teachers or scientific researchers (small quantity of copies),
- use in the fulfilment of official duties,
- translation into Chinese minority language,
- making the work perceptible for blind persons,
- use in article published over information network regarding political or economic topics,
- making available of a public speech.[561]

Article 7 of the Regulations sets out that a library, archive, memorial hall, museum, or art gallery may show a digital work, which is legally published, or a digital reproduction of a work in its collection for the purpose of display or preservation.[562]

Here, it can be seen that China has included most of the exceptions of the Chinese Copyright Law in its Regulations on the Protection of Right of

---

[559] "Concerning Article 10" *Agreed Statements concerning the WIPO Copyright Treaty* (1996 - adopted by the Diplomatic Conference on 20 December 1996), WIPO (provided by WIPO).
[560] *Regulations on the Protection of Right of Dissemination via Information Network* (2013 - issued 18 May 2006, effective 1 July 2006, amended 16 January 2013, issued 30 January 2013, effective March 2013), The State Council of the People's Republic of China (provided by HFGIP).
[561] Article 6 ibid.
[562] Article 7 ibid.

Dissemination via Information Network. However, private use is not included in the Regulations. This is due to the fact that it is very difficult for an individual to limit the use in the internet for one person only and therefore the number of persons who benefit from the dissemination via information network is too large and would be harmful to the author's copyright.[563]

bb) Statutory Licensing

A statutory license can be defined as a license that arises automatically as long as the author has not opposed to such. It means that a work can be used without the owner's permission as long as the right remuneration is paid.[564]

(1) For the Creation of a Textbook

According to Article 23 Chinese Copyright Law, third persons can make use of "*passages from a work, a short written work, musical work, a single work of the fine arts or photographic work which has been published*" for the compilation of a textbook used in the compulsory education[565] and for the national education plan.[566] No permission is required for such purposes but remuneration needs to be paid accordingly and the textbook needs to name the source, namely the author and the title of the work. Additionally, the work must not be prejudiced by the use in a textbook.[567]

Although this statutory license arises automatically, an author can object to such use in advance.[568]

Article 23 paragraph 2 Chinese Copyright Law sets out that this statutory license for the compilation of textbooks is also applied to the rights of publishers, performers, producers of sound and video recordings as well as radio and television stations.

[563] Qu, *Intellectual Property Law in China* (2012), 167.
[564] Wei, *Der Urheberrechtsschutz in China mit Hinweisen auf das Deutsche Recht* (1994), 83.
[565] In China: 9 years.
[566] Article 23 paragraph 1 *Copyright Law PRC* (1990/2010 version).
[567] Article 23 paragraph 1 last sentence ibid.
[568] Article 23 paragraph 1 ibid.

Further, obligations are stipulated in the Implementing Regulations of the Copyright Law.[569] Article 22 of the Implementing Regulations sets out that the administrative department for copyright of the State Council, namely the NCAC, has to fix and issue specific remuneration rates in cooperation with the department for pricing of the State Council and Article 32 of the Implementing Regulations further specifies that such remuneration needs to be paid within two months from the use of the work.

Furthermore, the Regulation on the Protection of the Right to Network Dissemination of Information stipulates that the rules set out in Article 23 Chinese Copyright Law are also valid in the information network meaning that excerpts of works and the like can be used for the production of courseware that is spread through the information network and made available to registered students of distance education institutions.[570] All the other requirements such as the payment of the remuneration apply here is as well.

(2) For the Reprint or the Use of an Excerpt by Newspapers or Periodicals

The second statutory license in the Chinese Copyright Law can be found in Chapter 4 that deals with the rights related to copyright. Article 33 paragraph 2 Chinese Copyright Law grants another newspaper or periodical publisher to reprint a work that has previously been published by another publisher, use an abstract thereof or use it as reference material. No permission by the copyright owner is required for the described acts but remuneration needs to be paid.

Similar to the "textbook license" the license arises automatically unless the copyright owner declares opposition to the reprinting or excerpting.[571] Fur-

[569] *Regulations for the Implementation of the Copyright Law of the People's Republic of China* (2013 - issued 2 August 2002, effective 15 September 2002, amended 8 January 2011, amended 30 January 2013, effective 1 March 2013), State Council of the People's Republic of China.
[570] Article 8 *Regulations on the Protection of Right of Dissemination via Information Network* (2013 - issued 18 May 2006, effective 1 July 2006, amended 16 January 2013, issued 30 January 2013, effective March 2013), The State Council of the People's Republic of China.
[571] Article 33 paragraph 2 *Copyright Law PRC* (1990/2010 version).

thermore, Article 30 Implementing Regulations stipulates that the opposing copyright owner needs to attach such declaration to the work to its first publication in a newspaper or periodical.[572]

As abovementioned, the remuneration needs to be fixed by the NCAC and needs to be paid within a period of two months from exploitation of the work.[573]

However, the Regulation on the Protection of the Right to Network Dissemination of Information does not stipulate any rules for these circumstances.

(3) For Phonogram Producers

The third statutory license is incorporated in Article 30 paragraph 3 Chinese Copyright Law and allows producers of sound recordings to use a musical work (of which a lawful sound recording exists) for the production of a sound recording. Such exploitation of a musical work does not require the permission of the copyright owner but remuneration needs to be paid in form of fixed rates and within the two-months-deadline.[574] This statutory license was introduced in the Chinese Copyright Law to prevent a monopolistic position of the phonogram producer who has acquired a permission to use the musical work first and to promote fair competition on the market.[575]

However, the copyright owner can prohibit the exploitation with a declaration that needs to be made at the time of the legal recording of the work.[576]

---

[572] Article 30 *Regulations for the Implementation of the Copyright Law of the People's Republic of China* (2013 - issued 2 August 2002, effective 15 September 2002, amended 8 January 2011, amended 30 January 2013, effective 1 March 2013), State Council of the People's Republic of China.
[573] Article 22 and Article 32 ibid.
[574] Article 22 and Article 32 ibid.
[575] Qu, *Intellectual Property Law in China* (2012), 171.
[576] Article 31 *Regulations for the Implementation of the Copyright Law of the People's Republic of China* (2013 - issued 2 August 2002, effective 15 September 2002, amended 8 January 2011, amended 30 January 2013, effective 1 March 2013), State Council of the People's Republic of China.

(4) For Broadcasting Organizations

The last statutory licenses in the Chinese Copyright Law are stipulated for broadcasting organizations and have the aim of promoting the dissemination of information to the general public by restricting the scope of the broadcasting right of copyright owners.[577]

Article 43 paragraph 2 Chinese Copyright Law sets out that a radio or television station can broadcast a published work of another without the permission from the copyright owner as long as remuneration is paid.[578]

Article 44 Chinese Copyright Law allows broadcasting organizations to broadcast a previously published sound recording as long as remuneration is paid and the broadcasting is not contrary to a bilateral agreement of the parties.[579]

In these circumstances, it is not possible for the copyright owner to declare opposition in advance.

cc) The Three-Step Test

The three-step test is a principle laid out in the international agreements. It allows Member States to grant certain exceptions to copyright subject to three conditions:

- First, the limitations cannot be too broad and hence, need to relate to special cases;
- Secondly, the limitation must not lead to an impediment of the normal exploitation rights of the respective copyright owner;
- Thirdly, the use of the work without prior consent must not unreasonably prejudice the legitimate interests of the copyright owner.[580]

---

[577] Qu, *Intellectual Property Law in China* (2012), 172.
[578] Article 33 paragraph 2 *Copyright Law PRC* (1990/2010 version).
[579] Article 33 paragraph 2 ibid.
[580] Look at Article 13 TRIPS: *"Members shall confine limitations or exceptions to exclusive rights to certain special cases which do not conflict with a normal exploitation of the work and do not unreasonably prejudice the legitimate interests of the right holder.";* Article 9 (2) Berne Convention: *"It shall be a matter for legislation in the countries of the Union to permit the reproduction of such works in certain special cases, provided that such reproduction does not conflict*

Article 21 Implementing Regulations reads

> *"The exploitation of a published work which may be exploited without permission from the copyright owner in accordance with the relevant provisions of the Copyright Law shall not impair the normal exploitation of the work concerned, nor unreasonably prejudice the legitimate interests of the copyright owner."*[581]

The three-step test was incorporated into the Chinese Copyright System before China's access to the WTO.

h) Infringing Actions

The different forms of infringement are depicted in the following.

aa) Primary Infringement

The infringing actions of a copyright protected work are stipulated in Article 47 Copyright Law and include but are not limited to[582]

- the publication of a work without the permission of the owner,

---

with a normal exploitation of the work and does not unreasonably prejudice the legitimate interests of the author."; Article 10 (1) WCT: *"Contracting Parties may, in their national legislation, provide for limitations of or exceptions to the rights granted to authors of literary and artistic works under this Treaty in certain special cases that do not conflict with a normal exploitation of the work and do not unreasonably prejudice the legitimate interest of the author."*; Article 16 (2) WPPT: *"Contracting Parties shall confine any limitations of or exceptions to rights provided for in this Treaty to certain special cases which do not conflict with a normal exploitation of the performance or phonogram and do not unreasonably prejudice the legitimate interests of the performer or of the producer of the phonogram."*

[581] *Regulations for the Implementation of the Copyright Law of the People's Republic of China* (2013 - issued 2 August 2002, effective 15 September 2002, amended 8 January 2011, amended 30 January 2013, effective 1 March 2013), State Council of the People's Republic of China.

[582] Section 11 of Article 47 clarifies that the list is not complete and other actions can also lead to the infringement of copyright and the rights related to the copyright.

- the publication of a co-work by one of the joint authors without the permission of the others,
- being named in a work another person has created to gain fame, although no participation has taken place,
- the distortion or mutilation of another's work,
- plagiarism of another's work,
- the exploitation of a work for exhibition, film-making or the like without the permission,
- the exploitation without the payment of the remuneration,
- renting a cinematographic work or the like without permission,
- the exploitation of the typographical design of a published book or periodical without the permission,
- the broadcast, communication to the public or recording without permission of the performer.[583]

bb) Secondary Infringement

Secondary infringement is dealt with in Article 48 of the Copyright Law and includes

- the reproduction, distribution, performance, presentation, broadcast or compilation of a work or making it available to the public without permission,
- the publication of a book without having a publication right,
- the reproduction or distribution of a sound recording or video recording of a performance or offering such on the information network without the performer's permission,
- the reproduction or distribution of a sound recording or video recording or offering such on the information network without the performer's permission,
- the rebroadcast or reproduction of a radio or television program without permission,
- intentionally overcoming technological barriers that have been installed to protect a work,
- the removal or alteration of the electronic rights management information that is attached to the work with intent,

[583] Article 47 *Copyright Law PRC* (1990/2010 version).

- the production or sale of a pirated work.[584]

cc) Criminally Relevant Infringement

A regulation on a possible criminal liability concerning copyright infringement could not be found in the primary Copyright Law of 1990.[585] This was part of the copyright disputes of China with the rest of the world and is one condition of TRIPS. In Article 61 TRIPS it is laid out that the national law must set out criminal liability in cases of willful commercial copyright infringement. Sanctions should include imprisonment and/or monetary fines.[586]

The possibility of criminal proceedings is given by Article 48 Chinese Copyright Law where a procedure is provided for cases that constitute a crime in terms of the Criminal Law. The Criminal Law of the People's Republic of China[587] deals with intellectual property crimes in Articles 213 to 220. Copyright crimes in particular are dealt with in Article 217 and 218 of the Criminal Law. According to Article 217 Chinese Criminal Law, the following acts are defined to be an infringement:

- unauthorized copying and distribution or broadcasting through information networks of works (including written, musical, fine art, audiovisual works, computer software and other works);
- publication of books in which another holds the exclusive right of publication;
- unauthorized duplication and distribution or dissemination of audiovisual works through the information network;
- unauthorized duplication and distribution or dissemination of audio and video recordings of performances through the information network;

[584] Article 48 ibid.
[585] The 1990 Chinese Copyright Law only provided for acts of infringement in Article 47 that only led to civil liabilities for the infringer and in some cases, administrative penalties; Article 47 *Copyright Law PRC* (1990).
[586] Article 61 *TRIPS Agreement* (1994), 1869 UNTS 299; 33 ILM 1197 (Annex 1C of the Marrakesh Agreement establishing the World Trade Organization, signed in Marrakesh, Morocco on 15 April 1994, 33 I.L.M. 1125).
[587] *Criminal Law of the People's Republic of China* (1979/1997 version) (provided by WIPO); *Criminal Law of the People's Republic of China (Amendment XI)* (2021) (provided by npc.goc.cn).

- production and sale of artistic works with fake signatures of others; and
- unauthorized deliberate avoidance or destruction of technical measures taken by the copyright owner.

The Criminal Law has only recently been amended in December 2020 and took effect on 1 March 2021.[588] In this recent amendment, the dissemination of works through the information network, the unauthorized use of audio and video recording of performances and the circumvention/destruction of technical measures have been added to the list of criminally relevant activities. It is very positive to note that China is improving the criminal scope of copyright infringement taking into consideration the technological advancement.

i) Liability

The following section shows how an infringer can be held liable. China opens up three ways for the liability of infringers, namely civil liability, administrative liability and criminal liability.

aa) Civil Liability

According to Article 47 Chinese Copyright Law, anyone committing one of the abovementioned infringement actions has to bear liabilities that include

- the cease of the infringing actions, namely stopping distribution of an infringing work or destruction of infringing reproductions;[589]
- the elimination of possible bad effects by, for example, publically showing a counterstatement to eliminate possible damages to the right holder's reputation;[590]
- the apology to the infringed person by placing an apology in the news;[591]

[588] *Criminal Law PRC (Amendment XI)* (2021).
[589] Wei, *Der Urheberrechtsschutz in China mit Hinweisen auf das Deutsche Recht* (1994), 131-132.
[590] Ibid., 132.
[591] Ibid.

- the payment of compensation for damages that includes both material and immaterial damage.[592]

According to Article 49 Chinese Copyright Law, the infringer has to compensate the infringed person for actual losses suffered and in cases where such loss is unknown, pay compensation to the amount of the illegal gains; sentence 2 of Article 49 further stipulates that such compensation has to include the reasonable expenses the right owner had to take on in order to stop the infringing actions by and convict the infringer. If none of these can be used as the calculation basis, the court has the possibility to decide on the amount of compensation with a maximum of 500,000 Yuan.[593] It can be said that the courts will assume the existence of fault unless the infringer opposes; therefore, the infringed person only needs to prove the infringement of his/her rights.[594]

bb) Administrative Liability

Article 48 Chinese Copyright Law is a combination of civil liabilities as well as administrative sanctions. The abovementioned civil liabilities also apply in the infringement situations listed in Article 48. Cases in which the public interest is harmed open up the possibility for administrative sanctions. The administrative department may issue an order to the infringer

- to cease the infringement;
- for confiscation of the illegal gains;
- for confiscation or destruction of the infringing copies; and
- for payment of a fine.[595]

In serious cases, the administrative department may additionally issue an order

- for confiscation of the material, devices and instruments that have been used for the infringing actions.[596]

---

[592] Ibid., 132-133.

[593] For a more detailed summary of damages and the calculation thereof, look at Yong Wan, "Copyright Damages in China" *J. Copyright Soc'y U.S.A.* 61 (2013-2014).

[594] Ibid., 527.

[595] Article 48 *Copyright Law PRC* (1990/2010 version).

[596] Article 48 ibid.

(1) Administrative Fine

The calculation of the fine named in Article 48 Chinese Copyright Law is not further defined in the law but the Implementing Regulations include an Article on such. According to Article 36 Implementing Regulations, there are two different scenarios on how to calculate the fine.

If the illegal business income is above 50,000 Yuan, the fine can be from one time but less than five times the volume of the illegal business.

If the illegal business income is below 50,000 Yuan or no income is generated, a fine of not more than 250,000 Yuan can be chosen by the administrative department taking the seriousness of the case into account.

(2) China's Recent Measures for Improvement

Here, it can be seen that China has already improved the administrative procedure as it changed Article 36 of the previous *Regulations for the Implementation* (2002) from the maximum of three times the amount of the illegally gained sum to five times the amount. This shows that China itself found the fines too low and needed to improve the system in order for it to lead to a more deterrent effect on the infringers to prevent future infringement from happening. Also, the maximum fine, if the illegal business turnover cannot be calculated, has been increased to 250,000 Yuan instead of 100,000 Yuan in the 2002 Regulations, again setting a sign for stronger enforcement.

cc) Criminal Liability

Article 217 Chinese Criminal Law stipulates that someone who commits copyright infringement to acquire profits and *"the amount of unlawful gains is larger"* or *"there are other serious circumstances"* can receive

- a sentence of up to three years,

and/or

- can be fined.[597]

[597] In the recent amendment of the Criminal Law the possibility of criminal detention has been deleted so that the possible penalties are now only imprisonment and/or monetary fine.

In particularly serious cases a sentence can be between three and ten years[598] and a fine.

Article 218 Chinese Criminal Law sets out a sentence of up to five years[599] and/or a fine for the seller if the seller knows that the distributed goods are infringing copyright and a *"huge amount of unlawful gains"* is generated.

Article 220 Chinese Criminal Law stipulates that a unit can also be sentenced to a fine if a crime of Articles 217 and 218 has been committed; the person directly in charge in the unit shall be punished accordingly.

dd) Interim Relief

The Chinese Copyright Law of 1990 did not include any regulations on possible interim measures and measures of securing evidence in a copyright infringement case. Such measures were only introduced to the Chinese Copyright Law of 2001 for China to enter the WTO because Article 50 TRIPS stipulates that such measures need to be implemented in the laws of the Member States. Article 50 1 (a) and (b) TRIPS set out that the judicial authorities in the Member States shall be able to order provisional measures to prevent infringement from occurring to preserve evidence. Furthermore, the judicial authorities can decide such measures without having heard the other party in cases where irreparable harm is likely to be caused.[600] Such TRIPS provisions have been incorporated into the national law by Articles 50 and 51 Chinese Copyright Law, which is discussed in the following.

(1) Interim Measures

The Chinese legislation provides right holders with the possibility to seek an interim relief. Article 50 Chinese Copyright Law stipulates that an injunction can be filed when the claimant can prove an existing or imminent infringement of a copyright that could likely result in irreparable harm. The

598 In the recent amendment of the Criminal Law the range of punishment was increased from a maximum of seven years to ten years.
599 In the recent amendment of the Criminal Law the range of punishment was increased from a maximum of three years to five years.
600 Article 50 2 *TRIPS Agreement* (1994), 1869 UNTS 299; 33 ILM 1197 (Annex 1C of the Marrakesh Agreement establishing the World Trade Organization, signed in Marrakesh, Morocco on 15 April 1994, 33 I.L.M. 1125).

court can order the discontinuation of the production/dissemination of pirated/unauthorized goods and protect the property.

Article 50 paragraph 2 Chinese Copyright Law stipulates that the regulations in Articles 93 to 96 and Article 99 of the Chinese Civil Procedure Law are applicable to the interim measures provided for in the Copyright Law.[601] The law stipulates that the court has forty-eight hours to decide upon a party's petition to preservation and if such petition is successful it needs to be immediately implemented.[602] Furthermore, the preservation measure will lose its effect if the petitioner does not file a lawsuit within thirty days after the court's decision.[603]

(2) Securing Evidence

According to Art 51 Chinese Copyright Law, a right holder can also apply for an injunction if it is likely that evidence will be rendered or disappear during the proceedings; the court has forty-eight hours to decide upon the petition and the preservation measures have to be executed within fifteen days from the decision.[604]

3. The Protection of Computer Software

The protection of computer software is currently not regulated within the Copyright Law. In the following, it is discussed how China protects this important and vastly growing area.

Article 10 TRIPS sets out that computer programs have to be protected as literary works under the Berne Convention. The current *Regulations on*

[601] The Chinese Civil Procedure Law has been revised again in 2012/2013 and 2017 and the Articles have changed in the reformed legislation. The former Articles 93-96 and 99 in former Chapter 8 are now Articles 101-105 and 108 in Chapter 9 of the revised Civil Procedure Law.
[602] Article 101 paragraph 2 *Civil Procedure Law of the People's Republic of China* (1991/2017 version) (provided by cicc.court.gov.cn).
[603] Article 101 paragraph 3 ibid. The 30-day time limit has been increased from 15 days to 30 days in the 2012 amendment.
[604] Article 51 paragraph 2 and 5 *Copyright Law PRC* (1990/2010 version).

Computer Software Protection was promulgated in 2001[605] and amended in 2013. It contains special regulations for the protection of computer software in contrast to the "normal" copyright works.

a) Computer Program

Article 2 of the Regulations sets out that computer software is supposed to be understood as *"computer programs and their relevant documentation"*[606]. Article 4 of the Regulations stipulates that software *"must have been independently developed and fixed on a certain tangible object"*.[607] Software that is created by duplication or partial copying of another software or not solely developed by the developer himself/herself will not get protection.[608] Software copyright protection does not include ideas, process, operating method or mathematical concept.[609] A protection of such would be harmful to the creation of software because ideas, methodology and concepts are crucial for the theory of creation and belong to the public domain.[610]

b) Software Copyright Owner

According to Article 9 of the Regulations, the owner of the software, generally, is the developer of the software. This can be a natural person, a legal person or other organization.[611] Article 10 to 13 of the Regulations stipulate the ownership in cases of co-development, commissioned works, tasks

[605] The Regulation for the Protection of Computer Software issued by the State Council in 1991 were repealed by the 2001 Regulation.
[606] Article 2 *Regulations on Computer Software Protection* (2013 - issued 20 December 2001, effective 1 January 2002, amended 8 January 2011, amended 30 January 2013, effective 1 March 2013), State Council of the People's Republic of China.; Article 3 further defines the terms computer program, documentation, software developer and software copyright owner.
[607] Article 4 ibid.
[608] Qu, *Intellectual Property Law in China* (2012), 212.
[609] Article 6 *Regulations on Computer Software Protection* (2013 - issued 20 December 2001, effective 1 January 2002, amended 8 January 2011, amended 30 January 2013, effective 1 March 2013), State Council of the People's Republic of China.
[610] Qu, *Intellectual Property Law in China* (2012), 212.
[611] See Article 5 *Regulations on Computer Software Protection* (2013 - issued 20 December 2001, effective 1 January 2002, amended 8 January 2011, amended 30

assigned by a State authority and development in the course of employment. These rules are similar to the rules stipulated for "normal" copyright works.

c) Software Copyright Content

The content of rights given to owners of software copyright is similar to the rights given to other copyright works. One interesting difference to note is, that a software copyright owner is not entitled to a right of integrity. The Regulations only set out three personal rights, namely the right of publication, the right of authorship and the right of alteration.

The list of economic rights is not a finalized list but specifically names five economic rights that are given to the software copyright owner:

- right of reproduction,
- right of distribution,
- right of rental,
- right of dissemination via an information network,
- right of translation.

The owner can give an authorization to others for the exercise of such rights and in return receive remuneration for it (Article 8 II of the Regulations). Furthermore, an owner can also transfer the rights, partially or wholly, in return for remuneration. In contrast to the copyright law, the exercise and transfer of rights is not limited to the economic rights so that the personal rights of the software copyright owner can be transferred as well.

d) Term of Protection

The term of protection for software copyright is laid out in Article 14 of the Regulations. Concerning natural persons, the copyright lasts for the life of the natural person plus another fifty years[612], concerning legal persons or organizations the copyright lasts for fifty years ending on 31 December after the first release of the software.[613] If the software is not released it

January 2013, effective 1 March 2013), State Council of the People's Republic of China.

612 ending on 31 December of the fiftieth year after the death, Article 14 paragraph 2 ibid.

613 Article 14 paragraph 2 and 3 ibid.

will lose the protection after fifty years following the date of development.[614]

e) Limitations to Software Copyright

Users of software are granted several rights, which can be seen as limitations to the software owner's copyright. The restrictions to copyright are established for the balance of interests of the different actors, meaning the developers and the users with the aims of promoting a strong software industry in China.[615]

Article 16 of the Regulations gives three rights to users:

- users can install the software on a computer and similar devices as long as the use requirements are complied with;
- users can make backup copies for damage prevention as long as such copies are not given to others;
- users can make necessary modifications so that they can use the software in their environment and can also make improvements to the functionality and performance; such amended software must not be given to others without the owner's authorization.

Article 17 of the Regulations holds an exception for purposes of learning and studying as it stipulates that in certain cases authorization and the payment of remuneration may be dispensable if the designs concepts and principles implied in the software[616] are studied.

The licensing of computer software is dealt with in Articles 18 to 22 of the Regulations.

f) Infringement and Liability

Article 23 of the Regulations sets out the acts of infringement that lead to the civil liability of the infringer. The software of another is infringed if:

- the software is released or registered without authorization of the owner;

---

[614] Article 14 paragraph 3 ibid.

[615] Qu, *Intellectual Property Law in China* (2012), 218.

[616] Also including installation, display, transmission and storage.

- the software is released or registered with a wrong name (name of the infringer) and by doing so the infringer makes use of the developer's fame;
- co-developed software is released or registered without the authorization of all co-developers;
- another name is affixed to the software or the owner's name is altered; in contrast to the abovementioned infringement acts, the software has already been released in this case;[617]
- the software is translated or revised without authorization of the owner.

The list is not exclusive and leaves room for other acts that can result in infringement.[618]

It is very positive that China has opted for this non-exclusive list so that other acts that might become possible due to the technological advancement can also constitute infringement under the current law.

Furthermore, Article 24 of the Regulations sets out the situations where infringement cannot only lead to civil liabilities but also to administrative sanctions and criminal liabilities. These are the following actions:

- the reproduction, fully or partially, of another's software; here, the owner's right of duplication is harmed;
- distribution, rental or dissemination via an information network to the public;
- evasion or demolition of a technical measure for protection of the software with intent;
- deletion or modification of the electronic information on software right management with intent;
- transfer or grant of licenses to others to exploit the owner's copyright without permission.

Administrative liability is arising when the act impairs the public interest; in such cases the administrative authorities can order the infringer to cease

[617] Qu, *Intellectual Property Law in China* (2012), 220.
[618] Article 23 (6) *Regulations on Computer Software Protection* (2013 - issued 20 December 2001, effective 1 January 2002, amended 8 January 2011, amended 30 January 2013, effective 1 March 2013), State Council of the People's Republic of China.

the infringement, confiscate illegal income, confiscate/destroy infringing copies, impose fines, and in severe cases, also confiscate the tools/material used by the infringer or initiate criminal proceedings. Criminal liability shall be investigated on the basis of the Criminal Law.

The last paragraph of Article 24 deals with the fines that can be imposed on the infringer. Positively to note is that the fines for severe infringement acts were significantly increased within the 2013 amendment of the Regulations (from 50,000 Yuan to 200,000 Yuan).

g) Summary

Summarizing, it can be said that the Regulations on Computer Software Protection are exhaustive for the main issues for the protection of computer programs. It is positive to note the China has left open some possibilities to adapt the protection to the advancement of the technology and that the fines have been increased to better deter the infringer. However, open clauses must also be seen critically as they reduce the transparency of the law and thus, make it more difficult for right holders to know their rights and enforce them.

Thus, if new acts of infringement arise, the Regulations should be amended by updating the list of infringing conduct.

4. The Dissemination Right in the Information Network

In the following part, China's legal framework in relation to the protection of infringement over the internet are discussed.

Because of the fast development of digital technology, the concept of copyright needed to adjust drastically in order to still fulfil its purpose of protecting copyright works, especially in the information network. The transmission of work throughout the information network has led to a huge challenge in terms of copyright protection.[619]

As shown earlier, the right to dissemination via the information network belongs to the economic rights that are set out in the Chinese Copyright

[619] Also see Qu, *Intellectual Property Law in China* (2012), 225.

Law. The *Regulations on the Protection of Right of Dissemination via Information Network*[620] contain rules on the liability of different subjects pertaining to infringements in the digital sphere.

The main points stipulated in the Regulations regarding the liability of web service providers and the infringers are discussed in the following.[621]

a) The Rights of the Administration

According to Article 13 of the Regulations, an administrative department can order a web service provider to reveal the information of a suspected infringer including the name, contact information and web address if such provider furnishes services to the suspected infringer.

According to Article 25 of the Regulations, the copyright administrative department can send a warning to the provider or in serious cases confiscate the devices used for Web services, if the provider does not comply with the obligation to reveal the information on an allegedly infringing service receiver.

b) Allegedly Infringing Works on the Information Network

In the following, the process of allegedly infringing work on the information network is discussed depicting what a right holder can do and what the rights and obligations of all persons involved are.

aa) The Rights of the Copyright Owner

If a right owner (of a work, performance, sound or visual recording) discovers an unauthorised use/exploitation of the work either at a web service provider who offers information storage space or at one who offers search

[620] *Regulations on the Protection of Right of Dissemination via Information Network* (2013 - issued 18 May 2006, effective 1 July 2006, amended 16 January 2013, issued 30 January 2013, effective March 2013), The State Council of the People's Republic of China.

[621] Please note that Articles 1 to 12 of the Regulation will not be discussed as they mostly mirror the general stipulations in the copyright Law in relation to the general limitations to the right of dissemination via information network and also concern the applicability of the Regulation.

and link services, he/she can send a written notice to the web service provider.[622] Such notice needs to contain the following information:

- name of the right owner, contact information and address;
- title and web address of the infringing work (or performance, sound or visual recording) that he/she intends to have deleted or the link to be disabled;
- some kind of preliminary evidence that proves an infringement.[623]

The right holder is responsible for the correctness of his/her statement.

bb) The Obligations of the Web Service Providers following the Written Notice

Once a notice has been sent to the web service provider, the responsibility of the provider arises to delete the information (in other words the infringing work, performance, sound or visual recording) or disable the link to such work.[624] Furthermore, the provider needs to forward the notice to the person who has made use of the services of the provider and uploaded the allegedly infringing work.[625] If the written notice cannot be forwarded to the party responsible for uploading the work, such notice needs to be made publically available via information network.[626]

cc) The Rights of the Service Receiver/Infringer

The service receiver is the person who is responsible for the upload of the allegedly infringing work. After having received the notice forwarded by the service provider he/she has the possibility to oppose the deletion/disablement with a written statement if it is believed that the work is not infringing another person's copyright.[627] Such written statements need to contain the following information:

- name, contact information and address of the service receiver;

[622] Article 14 *Regulations on the Protection of Right of Dissemination via Information Network* (2013 - issued 18 May 2006, effective 1 July 2006, amended 16 January 2013, issued 30 January 2013, effective March 2013), The State Council of the People's Republic of China.
[623] Article 14 (1), (2) and (3) ibid.
[624] Article 15 sentence 1 ibid.
[625] Article 15 sentence 1 ibid.
[626] Article 15 sentence 2 ibid.
[627] Article 16 ibid.

- title and web address of the work (or performance, sound or visual recording) that should be restored;
- some kind of preliminary evidence that proves infringement has not taken place.[628]

The service receiver is responsible for the correctness of his/her statement.

dd) The Obligations of the Web Service Providers following the Written Statement

According to Article 17 of the Regulations, the web service provider needs to restore the deleted work or disabled link after such written statement and has the obligation to forward such to the right owner; the right owner must not contact the service provider again with the aim of having the work deleted.

c) Liability

Those who infringe someone else's copyright in a work on the information network will be held liable. Both the web service providers as well as the receiver of web services can be held liable under the following conditions.

aa) Article 18 of the Regulations

Article 18 both gives room for civil penalties and administrative actions. Anyone who infringes the Regulations can be held liable to civil penalty including the termination of the infringement, erasing the impact, apologising to the right holder and paying a compensation for suffered losses. As soon as the public interest is also harmed, the Administrative Department can order the infringer to stop the infringement, confiscate the illegal gains and can impose a fine that will be calculated using the illegally gained revenue, which might be very difficult to determine. Depending on the seriousness of the case, the department can confiscate the equipment and in cases of criminal offenses the department can trigger criminal liability. The following actions will lead to infringement:

- unauthorized making available of content to the public;
- intentionally avoiding or damaging technical measures;
- intentionally deleting or changing any electronic information on management in the published works (or performances, sound or

[628] Article 16 (1), (2) and (3) ibid.

visual recordings) or making available such works knowing that the electronic management information has been deleted or changed without authorization;

- making the content available to help the poor in rural areas with exceeding the specified scope or without paying the announced remuneration or not removing content that a right holder opposed to having it out in the public;
- making available a work without indicating the title and the author's name or without paying the remuneration or without having the technical measures in place that are supposed to prevent others from infringing the right or without preventing reproduction acts that substantially impair the right holder's interest.

bb) Article 19 of the Regulations

Article 19 sets out some further rights of the administrative department and gives them the possibility to the confiscation of illegal gains, devices or components used for the infringing act and in serious cases confiscate the computer and equipment used for providing web services and impose fines and subject them to criminal liability. The following acts will lead to such:

- intentionally producing, importing or supplying others with devices, technical services and the like for the purpose of circumventing technical measures;
- gaining profit by making available content;
- making content available to help the poor in rural areas without previously announcing the title and the author's name and without paying remuneration.

cc) Possible Exemptions of the Web Service Provider regarding Damage Compensation

The responsibility for acts taking place in the information network is very hard to be limited because with the ongoing development of technology it becomes harder and harder to control what content is spread throughout the network. Therefore, the Regulations stipulate some situations under which a web service provider will be exempted from liability for damage compensation.

(1) Article 20 of the Regulations

A web service provider who offers automatic access services according to the instruction of those receiving its services or offers automatic transmission services does not have to pay compensation if the following two criteria are met:

- no selection or alteration of the content is done;
- the works are only available to the designated service receivers.[629]

(2) Article 21 of the Regulations

Furthermore, a provider does not need to pay compensation if he/she only stores content from another provider and automatically makes them available to the service receivers via a technical arrangement for the purposes of the improvement of efficient transmission via the information network. However, exemption does only exist if the following criteria are met:

- no alteration to the content is done;
- no impact is caused to the other provider;
- automatic modification, deletion or screening needs to take place once the other provider has modified, deleted or screened such.

(3) Article 22 of the Regulations

The provider is also exempted from damage compensation in cases where he/she only provides service receivers with storage space for the purpose of supporting the dissemination of content via information network if the following criteria are met:

- information storage needs to be clearly indicated to the service receivers and the name, contact person and web address of the provider needs to be clearly indicated;
- the content must not be altered;
- the provider must not be aware of a possible infringement scenario;
- no economic benefits are gained directly from the stored content;
- the content is immediately deleted after the receipt of a written notice of a right holder.

[629] (access of others is prevented).

(4) Article 23 of the Regulation

The last possible exemption from damage compensation of a web service provider offering search or link services is stipulated in Article 23 of the Regulations. Here, the provider can dispose of his/her liability to pay compensation if he/she disables a link to infringing content after having received a written notice of the right holder unless the provider is or should have been aware of the infringing content beforehand. In the latter, a provider is jointly liable with the infringer.

d) China's Measures against Infringement on the Information Network

China is continuously trying to improve the system. As an answer to the vastly developing technical possibilities that infringers have, the State Council has amended the Regulations on the Protection of Right of Dissemination via Information Network – that were first promulgated in 2006 – in 2013.

The fine stipulated in Articles 18 and 19 was increased from a maximum of 100,000 Yuan to a fine range with no upper limit that is calculated by the illegal business revenue. This can be from 100% up to but less than five times of the amount in cases where the revenue is above 50,000 Yuan. Concerning cases with a non-existent illegal business revenue or a revenue of less than 50,000 Yuan a fine must not be higher than 250,000 Yuan depending on the seriousness of the matter.

This shows that China has seen the need for stricter regulations and hence, better deterrence for possible right infringers.

e) Provisions by the SPC

Furthermore, on 17 December 2012 the SPC introduced the *Provisions of the Supreme People's Court on Certain Issues Related to the Application of Law in the Trial of Civil Cases Involving Disputes over Infringement of the Right of Dissemination through Information Networks* which came into effect on 1 January 2013.[630]

[630] *Provisions of the Supreme People's Court on Certain Issues Related to the Application of Law in the Trial of Civil Cases Involving Disputes over Infringement of the Right of Dissemination through Information Networks* (2012 - issued 17 December 2012, adopted 26 November 2012, effective 1 January

These Provisions provide guidelines to the courts on how to establish whether a web service provider has actual and/or constructive knowledge of the infringing activities and thus, can be held (jointly) liable. They also stipulate, that the courts shall not hold web service providers liable if they are able to prove that no fault is on their side, e.g. if they have adopted technological measures and the occurring infringement was nevertheless difficult to discover.[631] Also, the SPC clarifies that web service providers do not have to actively review their platforms for infringing actions.[632]

Furthermore, the Provisions state in Article 11 that web service providers that obtain economic benefit from the works have a high duty of care which conversely means that there is no automatic liability but that web service providers have the possibility to present counter-evidence to be exempted from liability.

These Provisions by the SPC help to better narrow the infringing conduct of web service providers and complements the Regulation in the case of civil litigation.

f) The Impact of the recently promulgated E-Commerce Law

With the rapid growth of e-commerce, it was necessary for China as the largest e-commerce market to take certain precautions to protect this market. Thus, on 1 January 2019 the E-Commerce Law of the People's Republic of China took effect.[633] Amongst other aims in improving the e-commerce sector, the legislation aims at improving the protection of intellectual property rights in the online environment – in Article 5 it is laid out that e-commerce operators ("operator") shall, inter alia, take part in intellectual property protection. Article 41 E-Commerce Law states

---

2013), Supreme People's Court of The People's Republic of China (provided by HFG Law & Intellectual Property).

[631] Article 8 sentence 3 ibid.

[632] Article 8 sentence 2 ibid.

[633] Article 2 E-Commerce Law stipulates *"[...] "e-commerce" means the business activities of sale of goods or provision of services through the Internet or other information networks. [...] This Law shall not apply to financial products and services, or services of providing news and information, audio and video program, publication and cultural products through information network."*; *E-Commerce Law of the People's Republic of China* (2018) (provided by IP Key).

> *"E-commerce platform operators shall establish their intellectual property rights ("**IPRs**") protection rules, strengthen cooperation with IPR holders and legally protect the IPRs."*[634]

Article 42 stipulates that a right holder has the possibility to notify an e-commerce platform operator ("platform operator") in case of IP infringement providing "prima facie" evidence. The platform operator then has to take necessary measures to stop the infringement such as deletion, blocking et cetera and inform the infringing e-commerce operator, otherwise the platform operator will be held jointly liable. Anyone who sends in wrong notices or notices in bad faith and by that causes loss of operators on the platform will be held liable. According to Article 43, the supposedly infringing operator can then oppose to the alleged infringement also providing "prima facie" evidence. The platform operator has to forward the opposing statement to the right holder who has the possibility to either file a complaint with the competent authority or sue the operator in court within fifteen days. If such action is not taken within the deadline, the platform operator can restore the offers of the operator. Especially in relation to foreign right holders it will be almost impossible to adhere to that deadline because of the several requirements such as notarized documents to file a complaint or lawsuit.

Unfortunately, the E-Commerce Law is not clear on what exactly this "prima facie" evidence provided by the alleged infringer could be. Furthermore, there is no provision regulating the situation where an operator stops the takedown in bad faith.[635] Without stricter measures, it is feared that the operators can "play" with the right holders and unlawfully stop the takedown procedures. This issue has also been addressed by the U.S.T.R. who fears that the new E-Commerce Law might undermine the legal framework for web service providers.[636]

---

[634] Ibid.

[635] For further information on the E-Commerce Law, see SIPS (Joseph Simone), "China's new E-commerce Law", 14 March 2019 (https://www.worldtrademarkreview.com/anti-counterfeiting/chinas-new-e-commerce-law, accessed: 6 March 2021).

[636] The United States Trade Representative "2019 Special 301 Report" (April 2019), 43.

In alignment with the Regulations on the Protection of Right of Dissemination via Information Network, Article 45 lies out that an operator is jointly liable if the infringing conduct of the operator is known or should have been known and fails to take necessary prevention measures. In addition, Article 62 regulates that liability shall also be borne by the operator if they cannot provide the relevant documents to ascertain the facts of the dispute.

It is stipulated in Article 84 E-Commerce Law that – should the platform operator not adhere to the order of the authority to make a rectification within the specified time, a fine between 50,000 and 500,000 Yuan and in severe cases between 500,000 and 2,000,000 Yuan can be imposed. It is positive to note that the ranges of fines are set quite high.

A further positive development for right holders is that the E-Commerce Law regulates that e-commerce operators have to publish their business licenses and in case of e-commerce platforms, users of the platform have to provide its identity, address et cetera to the platform operator.[637] This will make it easier for right holders to identify infringers.

g) Summary

Summarizing, it can be said that the protection of rights in the context of the information network is widely regulated in China's legal framework but that there is still room for improvement to adequately protect the right holders. It is positive to note that the legislators have already increased the fines with the amendment of the Regulation in 2013 and that the fines stipulated in the E-Commerce Law are also relatively high so that they increase the deterrence rate.

With the fast advancement of technology and new types of media constantly arising it is important that the laws, regulations, provisions et cetera are constantly adapted to take the new developments into account.

[637] Articles 15, 27 and 28 *E-Commerce Law PRC* (2018).

II. Classification of the Chinese Copyright System Compared to Other Systems

In order to better understand the structure of the Chinese Copyright system and to place it in context to the different constructs it is necessary to compare the Chinese system to other countries.

The existing copyright law systems can mainly be split up into two different systems – the Anglo-American Copyright system and the European continental Droit d'Auteur system.[638] However, it has to be kept in mind that the copyright law can also differ between countries that follow the same system.[639] For example, although the United States and the United Kingdom follow the Anglo-American system, their copyright laws show some major differences.[640] For this reason and for the purpose of clarity, the analysis in this dissertation will focus on two countries only. The United States of America will represent the Anglo-American system as a common law country, whereas Germany will represent the European Continental system as a coded law country.

1. The Terminology

First, the terminology of the law is looked at. The way a law is named can provide an indication for its character.

The German Copyright Law is named "Urheberrecht", which literally means "Author's law". Here, emphasis is put on the author or the originator of a work and his/her personal creation.[641] It can be argued that the European system, that is used in Germany, aims at giving incentives to creators

[638] Enders and Steiner, "Urheberrechtsreform und Urheberrechtsdurchsetzung" *ZChinR* 17, 2 (2010), 94.
[639] Dietz, "Das chinesische Urheberrecht: Copyright oder droit d'auteur?" (2004), 528.
[640] Especially in the field of moral rights; here, the UK is much closer to the European system. Ibid.
[641] Enders and Steiner, "Urheberrechtsreform und Urheberrechtsdurchsetzung" *ZChinR* 17, 2 (2010), 94.

like artists, writers and researchers and encourages them to make use of their exploitation rights.[642]

The United States call it "The Copyright Act". The term "copyright" emphasizes the verb "to copy" which means "reprinting", "duplicating" or "reproducing"; this clearly shows that the "Copyright Law" focuses on the economic goals of a copyright holder because it protects the unauthorised reproduction of a work.[643]

In comparison, German Copyright focusses on the creator himself/herself as the main protective purpose whereas American Copyright has a more economic nature and focuses on a marketable right as the main protective purpose.

The Chinese Copyright Law is named "zhùzuòquán" (中华人民共和国著作权法 Zhōnghuá Rénmín Gònghéguó <u>Zhùzuòquán</u> Fǎ).

"Zhùzuò" (著作) can be translated as "literary work" and is closer to the wording used in Europe as well. However, in Mandarin the word "bǎnquán" (版权) is also commonly used when talking about the Chinese copyright law. "Ban" stands for "version" or "edition" which relates more to the English term "copyright". In Article 57 of the Chinese Copyright Law it is stipulated that the term "zhùzuò" as it is used in the legislation means "bǎnquán", which is more commonly used in the country when referring to the protection of copyright works.[644]

Hence, it becomes difficult to only use the naming of the copyright law as a factor to categorize Chinese Copyright Law as a continental European Copyright or as an Anglo-American Copyright. For example, the national

---

642 Look at §1 *UrhG* that in some way acts as a preamble to the law by placing the author as the main subject of the law; see also Gunda Dreyer, "Kapitel I, Teil 1, Abschnitt 1 Allgemeines (§1) " in *Urheberrecht: Urheberrechtsgesetz, Urheberrechtswahrnehmungsgesetz, Kunsturhebergesetz - Heidelberger Kommentar*, ed. Gunda Dreyer, Jost Kotthoff, and Astrid Meckel (Heidelberg, Germany: C.F. Müller, 2009), 40-41.

643 Enders and Steiner, "Urheberrechtsreform und Urheberrechtsdurchsetzung" *ZChinR* 17, 2 (2010), 94.

644 See also ibid.

copyright office of China is called "guójiā bǎnquán jú" (国家版权局 – National Copyright Administration) and hence, uses the term "bǎnquán", that can be aligned closer to the American system.[645]

This shows that the wording in China is not as important to the defining character of the copyright system as it might be the case in other countries.[646]

2. General Nature of Chinese Copyright Conception

Regarding the conception of Chinese Copyright Law, it is very difficult to compare it to the Western systems. China has a long history of socialist movements and still sees itself as a socialist state. The "socialist nature" is also reflected in the country's legislation.

China takes a dualistic approach to copyright law meaning that the purpose of the law is both the protection of state interest as well as individual interests.[647] This is reflected in Article 1 Chinese Copyright Law that states that the law aims at protecting the creators and encourages the creation of works that support the socialist culture.[648] Generally, it can be said that Chinese Copyright Law focuses more on the protection of the society compared to Western Countries.[649] The Chinese Copyright Law does not pursue the aim of commercial goals and economic profit but rather protects the authors from the arbitrariness of publishers as well as supports and incentivizes the creation of useful socialist works in China;[650] according to the traditional socialist view a created work belongs to the society and not to the individual author and therefore needs to be useful to the society.[651]

---

[645] Dietz, "Das chinesische Urheberrecht: Copyright oder droit d'auteur?" (2004), 529.
[646] Ibid., 529-530.
[647] Qu, *Copyright in China* (2002), 70.
[648] *Copyright Law PRC* (1990/2010 version).
[649] Qu, *Copyright in China* (2002), 83.
[650] Ibid., 77.
[651] Ibid., 71.

In summary, the conception of copyright in China can be best described as a "traditional socialist copyright".[652] It is difficult to clearly classify it to be similar to the European or the American concepts.

3. The Structure of the Law

A similarity to the European Droit d'auteur system that can be detected in the Chinese Copyright Law is its structure. German Copyright Law consists of five columns, namely

- Column I: The substantive copyright law,
- Column II: Related rights,
- Column III: Contract and licensing law,
- Column IV: Collecting societies and
- Column V: Enforcement of Law.[653]

In contrast to that, the Anglo-American Copyright is missing a systematic approach regarding the related rights, contract and licensing law as well as the rights of collecting societies.[654]

China does not have such a clear structure as the German Copyright Law. In some parts, provisions on different areas (i.e. substantive law and contracting law) are mixed together in certain articles although a separate chapter on licensing and contracting exists.[655] However, the Chinese Copyright Law shows some similarity:

- Chapter 2: Copyright (= substantive copyright law),
- Chapter 3: Copyright Licensing and Transfer Contracts (= general contract and licensing law),

---

[652] Ibid., 70-71.

[653] *UrhG (Germany)* (1965); see also Dietz, "Das chinesische Urheberrecht: Copyright oder droit d'auteur?" (2004), 530.

[654] Dietz, "Das chinesische Urheberrecht: Copyright oder droit d'auteur?" (2004), 530.

[655] i.e. Chapter 4 on related rights of publishers, performers etc. contains regulations regarding the contracts in this field although Chapter 3 deals with these; Chapter 1 on substantive copyright includes in Article 10 paragraph 2 and 3 regulations regarding the licensing and transfer which logically should have been dealt with in Chapter 3; see ibid., 530-531.

- Chapter 4: Publication, Performance, Sound Recording, Video Recording and Broadcasting
  (= related rights and contracts in that area),
- Article 8: Collective copyright administration organizations
  (= collecting societies),
- Chapter 5: Legal Liabilities and Enforcement Measures.

4. The Content of Law – Important Features

In the following some concepts of Chinese Copyright Law are compared to the concepts in Germany and the U.S. to determine further similarities and differences.

a) The Authorship and Protection Term

First, the treatment of ownership/authorship are looked at.

As previously explained, Germany pursues the "principle of creativity" meaning that the person who created the work is deemed to be the author of such.[656]

In the U.S., initial ownership vests with the author of the work but in cases of "works made for hire" the employer is deemed to be the author of the work and owns all rights thereto.[657]

Article 11 Chinese Copyright stipulates that in general, copyright is given to the author of the work but in specific cases provided for by law it can belong to someone different. For example, Article 11 paragraph 3 Chinese Copyright Law stipulates that a legal entity or organization is seen to be the author of a work, if it is created *"under the auspices and according to the intention of a legal entity or other organization, which bears responsibility for the work"*[658].

Regarding works created in the course of employment, Article 16 sentence 2 Chinese Copyright Law specifies that the author enjoys the copyright but grants priority to the employer (legal entity or organization); the employer has the right to exclusively exploit the copyright work for a period of two

[656] § 7 *UrhG (Germany)* (1965). - For further information see Chapter 3 I. 2. b) aa) (1) of this dissertation.
[657] § 201 (a) and (b) *U.S. Copyright Act* (1995), 17 U.S.C. §§ 101 et seq.
[658] Article 13 paragraph 3 *Copyright Law PRC* (1990/2010 version).

years while the copyright itself stays with the author. In contrast to that, Article 16 paragraph 2 Chinese Copyright Law gives the primary copyright, except for the right of authorship, to the employer in cases of drawings of engineering designs and the like (mainly technical products) or in cases where the copyright is assigned by laws, administrative regulations or contracts.[659] A remuneration may be paid to the creator. The second exception in Article 16 paragraph 2 is interesting to note because the primary author cannot only be determined by law and administrative regulations but also by contracts. This provision extends the rules on authorship to situations outside the legislation which the contracting parties can decide upon. Contractual agreements can also define the copyright subject in cases of commissioned works.[660]

Both scenarios show that China has chosen a different route than Germany by departing from the "principle of creativity". The Chinese provisions are in fact much closer to the American Copyright Law as they open up the possibility for legal entities organizations to be seen as the primary author of a work.[661]

Regarding producers of cinematographic works, Article 15 Chinese Copyright Law grants the copyright of a cinematographic work to the producer, whereas involved people such as the scriptwriter, director et cetera have the right of authorship in their works and receive remuneration. This provision can be compared to the German model in §§ 88-89 UrhG as it gives priority to the producer but respects the creators of the individual works by granting them the right of authorship and remuneration.[662]

In general, it can be said that China places emphasis on legal entities, organizations and producers by giving them many rights regarding works that have been created under their auspices or in the course of employment.[663] Thus, an influence of both the Anglo-American system as well as the European system can be seen.[664]

---

659 For further information, see *Chapter 3 I. 2. b)* of this dissertation.
660 Article 17 *Copyright Law PRC* (1990/2010 version).
661 Dietz, "Das chinesische Urheberrecht: Copyright oder droit d'auteur?" (2004), 533.
662 Ibid.
663 Ibid.
664 Ibid.

b) The Personal Copyright Rights

Article 6bis Berne Convention states that the author of a work shall be entitled to certain rights such as the authorship right, the right to prevent modification, distortion or mutilation or any action that would damage his/her honor or reputation.[665]

German Copyright Law recognizes such rights in §§ 12-14 UrhG (= publication right, right to claim authorship, right to integrity). They have an own subsection in the legislation with the title "Personal Copyright Rights" which shows their importance in German Copyright Law. §§ 39 UrhG protects the personal right from modification of a work and sets out that the person who has obtained a usage right must not modify the work unless the parties have agreed otherwise or a denial by the author regarding the title of the work would be unreasonable.

The United States have long refrained from signing the Berne Convention that was established in 1886. As previously mentioned, the U.S. only acceded in 1988. One of the major reason for the refusal to accede was that the concept of moral rights (Article 6bis Berne Convention) was contrary to American Copyright Law[666] up until then.[667] The U.S. promulgated the Berne Convention Implementation Act in 1988 (BCIA)[668] which sets out a "minimalistic approach" of the U.S. in amending their legislation to be compliant with the Berne Convention.[669] The BCIA only repeated the provision in Article 6bis Berne Convention but did not establish any moral

[665] Article 6bis (1) *Berne Convention* (1979), TRT/BERNE/001.

[666] American Copyright follows an utilitarian approach meaning that the incentive of the author or distributor to create a copyright work is the economic (profitable or marketable) right that he/she earns after having created a work; Julie E. Cohen et al., *Copyright in a Global Information Economy*, 4 ed., Aspen Casebook Series (New York, USA: Wolters Kluwer, 2015), 7.

[667] Ibid., 37-38; Samuel Jacobs, "The Effect of the 1886 Berne Convention on the U.S. Copyright System's Treatment of Moral Rights and Copyright Term, and Where That Leaves Us Today" *Mich. Telecomm. & Tech. L. Rev.* 23 (2016), 170, 172.

[668] The BCIA states that with this Act in place, all requirements of Berne are satisfied; see Sec. 2(3) *Berne Convention Implementation Act of the United States of America* (1988), PL 100-568, 102 STAT. 2853.

[669] Cohen et al., *Copyright in a Global Information Economy* (2015), 38.

rights.[670] Two years post accession, the Visual Artists Rights Act (VARA)[671] was established that granted some moral rights to creators of “visual art”. However, such provision is rarely applicable because certain requirements need to be met.[672] Some other legislations name basic moral rights as well but it is clearly visible that the U.S. are not willing to put an emphasis on such and hence, are still not fully complying with the requirements of the Berne Convention.[673]

As previously explained, Chinese Copyright Law has fully implemented personal rights in Article 10 (1)-(4). The importance of personal rights is again emphasized in Article 29 Chinese Copyright Law stipulating that the personal rights may not be infringed by persons (publishers, performers, et cetera) that are legally exploiting the works.[674] Furthermore, Article 20 Chinese Copyright Law sets out that the rights to authorship, revision and integrity are granted endlessly.

This is very close to the handling of personal rights in German Copyright Law[675] and it can be said that China fulfils its obligations required by the Berne Convention.

c) Licensing and Transferring Copyright

The field of licensing and transferring copyrights is very important in characterizing a copyright system.

---

670 Sec. 3(b) *U.S. Berne Convention Implementation Act* (1988), PL 100-568, 102 STAT. 2853; Jacobs, "The Effect of the 1886 Berne Convention on U.S. Copyright System" *Mich. Telecomm. & Tech. L. Rev.* 23 (2016), 174.

671 *Rights of Certain Authors to Attribution and Integrity (Visual Artists Rights Act of the United States of America)* (1990), 17 U.S.C. § 106a.

672 For more details look at: Jacobs, "The Effect of the 1886 Berne Convention on U.S. Copyright System" *Mich. Telecomm. & Tech. L. Rev.* 23 (2016), 175 et seq.

673 Ibid., 169-181, 198-190.

674 Article 10 of the Implementing Regulations also emphasizes that cinematographic changes can only be made if necessary and if such are not distorting or mutilating the work; *Regulations for the Implementation of the Copyright Law of the People's Republic of China* (2013 - issued 2 August 2002, effective 15 September 2002, amended 8 January 2011, amended 30 January 2013, effective 1 March 2013), State Council of the People's Republic of China.

675 Dietz, "Das chinesische Urheberrecht: Copyright oder droit d'auteur?" (2004), 534.

The German Copyright Law is quite clear. §§ 29 UrhG stipulates that copyright in general cannot be transferred but can only be inherited. However, authors can grant usage rights to others according to §§ 29 (2) in connection with §§ 31 UrhG.

The United States have chosen a different path. According to § 201 (d) (1) U.S. Copyright Act, *"The ownership of a copyright may be transferred in whole or in part by any means of conveyance or by operation of law (...)"*[676]. This shows that in the United States a copyright can be transferred as a whole without any exceptions to it.

Chinese Copyright Law is not as clear on the transferal of rights. Article 10 paragraphs 2 and 3 Chinese Copyright Law specifically only refer to the economic rights (Article 10 (5) to (17) Chinese Copyright Law) and stipulate that owners may authorize others to exercise such or fully/partially transfer the rights; conversely this means that the rights stipulated in Article 10 (1)-(4) Chinese Copyright Law are non-transferrable.

This provision clarifies that the copyright in a work cannot be licensed or transferred as a whole which is very close to the German system. However, the German system does not allow a transfer at all but only a "usage right". The U.S. allows for a full transfer.

Therefore, the Chinese system seems to be a mix of both the unassignability of personal rights as in German Law and the whole or partial transfer of the economic rights as in the American Law.

5. Conclusion and Criticism

As it has been shown in the above, it is very difficult to categorize the Chinese Copyright Law into one of the known existing copyright systems – the Anglo-American System or the European Droit d'Auteur systems.

China has picked some parts from the European system and other parts from the Anglo-American system. Especially with reference to the underlying objective of the Chinese Copyright Law, it is not possible to concretely classify the system as economically driven like the U.S. or creativity driven like in Germany.

[676] *U.S. Copyright Act* (1995), 17 U.S.C. §§ 101 et seq.

When looking at the fact that the Chinese copyright framework is a mixture of the different systems, it becomes clear once again that the copyright legislation is a transplant and not a law that has grown and flourished historically in China. Even if the legislation is somewhat advanced in the books following China's accession to the WTO, this does not automatically mean that it is being properly applied. The numerous problems regarding enforcement of copyright in China are discussed critically in the following section.

Summarizing the above, it can be concluded that the current Chinese Copyright Law can be best described as a hybrid between the Anglo-American copyright and the European droit d'auteur with an own socialist touch.[677]

III. State Authorities and the Enforcement of the Copyright Law

In order to fully understand the copyright system in China it is very important to look at the different authorities responsible for copyright protection as well as analysing the enforcement system in China.

1. State Authorities

First, the state authorities and their different tasks concerning the protection of copyright in China are discussed.

a) National People's Congress and Its Standing Committee

According to Article 57 of the Constitution, the NPC is the highest state organ in China and the Standing Committee of the NPC is the permanent legislative body in China operating directly under the NPC. The NPC has the legislative competence to amend the Constitution and enact the fundamental laws.[678] Since the NPC only meets once a year[679], the Standing Committee has the power to enact all the other laws (法律 fǎlǜ) and partially to amend laws of the NPC as long as they are not conflicting with the

[677] See also Enders and Steiner, "Urheberrechtsreform und Urheberrechtsdurchsetzung" *ZChinR* 17, 2 (2010), 95.
[678] The legislative competence is given to the NPC by Article 62 (1), (3) *Constitution PRC* (1982/2018 version).
[679] Article 61 ibid.

main principles of the law.[680] Also, the Standing Committee has the duty – according to Article 67 (6) of the Constitution – to supervise the work of the State Council as well as the work of the Supreme People's Court.

The Copyright Law of the People's Republic of China of 1990 is a law passed by the Standing Committee. The complete process of passing a law is discussed in more detail in the *Chapter 4* concerning the creation of the new copyright law.

b) State Council

According to Article 85 of the Constitution, the State Council is the highest executive state organ and therefore responsible for the administration of the state. The State Council has the authority to release administrative regulations (行政法规 xíngzhèng fǎguī) that enhance the enforcement of laws.[681] Examples are the reformed Implementing Regulations released by the State Council in 2002 and amended in 2013.[682]

c) National Copyright Association of China

The National Copyright Association of China (NCAC) is an administration department under the State Council and is responsible for the administration of copyrights in China.[683] It was introduced in 1985 to strengthen the protection of copyrights by preparing copyright legislation, helping owners of copyrights, by administrating compulsory licences concerning foreign works and by resolving any other problems of international dimension.[684]

680 Article 67 (2), (3) ibid.; Article 7 *Legislation Law PRC* (2000/2015 version).

681 The legislative competence is given to the State Council by Article 89 (1) and to the ministries under the State Council by Article 90 (2) *Constitution PRC* (1982/2018 version).

682 *Regulations for the Implementation of the Copyright Law of the People's Republic of China* (2013 - issued 2 August 2002, effective 15 September 2002, amended 8 January 2011, amended 30 January 2013, effective 1 March 2013), State Council of the People's Republic of China.

683 Matthew Murphy, "III. Specific Fields and Topics of Law - Chapter 10.4. - Copyright" in *Doing Business in China*, ed. Michael J. Moser and Fu Yu (Huntington, NY, U.S.A.: Juris Publishing Inc., 2014), §10.04.05.

684 Peter Ganea, Thomas Pattloch, and Christopher Heath, *Intellectual Property Law in China* (The Hague, The Netherlands: Kluwer Law International, 2005), 209.

Article 7 of the current Copyright Law states that the copyright administration department is a subdivision of the State Council and is responsible for the nationwide administration and that the administrative departments under the local governments are responsible in their respective province, autonomous region or municipality. Shortly after the copyright law was introduced, the NCAC promulgated the regulations on the implementation of the copyright law.[685] Chapter II of these Implementing Regulations dealt with the administrative authorities of copyright in the People's Republic of China. Article 7 of the Implementing Regulations stated that the National Copyright Administration is the administrative department under the State Council and has to fulfil the duties laid out in Article 7 of the Copyright Law. Article 7 of the first Implementing Regulations of 1991stated that the NCAC is responsible for

- implementing the law and regulations related to copyright,
- dealing with the infringement cases of nationwide character,
- approving the creation of collective copyright administration and other copyright agencies,
- dealing with the administration of external copyright relations,
- organizing State copyrights,
- guiding the local copyright departments and
- fulfilling the duties assigned by the State Council.[686]

However, these Regulations were abrogated once new regulations on the implementation of copyright were promulgated in 2002 (amended 2013) after China's accession to the WTO.[687] These specify in Article 37 that the

685 *Regulations for the Implemenation of the Copyright Law of the People's Republic of China* (1991 - 24 May 1991, promulgated 30 May 1991, effective 1 June 1991), National Copyright Administration of the People's Republic of China; see also Li, "The Sky is High and the Emperor is Far Way" *Bol Mex Derecho Comp* 36, 108 (2003), 967.

686 Article 7 *Regulations for the Implemenation of the Copyright Law of the People's Republic of China* (1991 - 24 May 1991, promulgated 30 May 1991, effective 1 June 1991), National Copyright Administration of the People's Republic of China.

687 *Regulations for the Implementation of the Copyright Law of the People's Republic of China* (2013 - issued 2 August 2002, effective 15 September 2002, amended 8 January 2011, amended 30 January 2013, effective 1 March 2013), State Council of the People's Republic of China.

administrative department under the State Council is responsible for handling nationwide infringement cases and that the administrative departments under the local governments are responsible for infringements in their respective regions.[688]

d) The Judicial Authorities

The structure of the Chinese People's Courts is made up of four trial levels:[689]

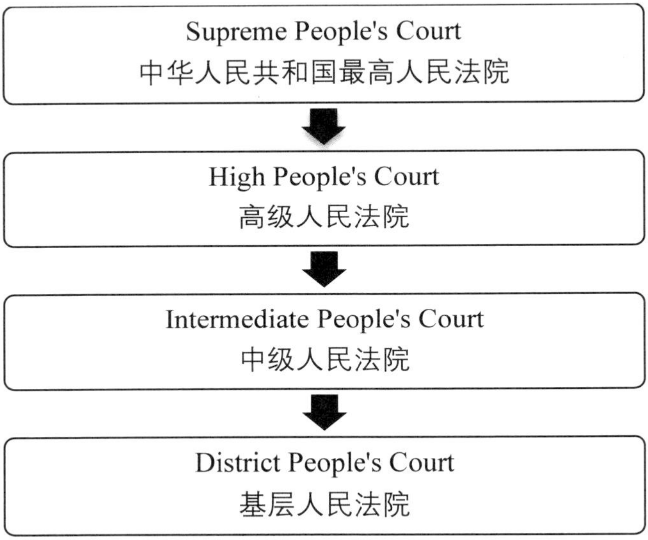

[688] Article 37 ibid.

[689] Naigen Zhang, "Intellectual Property Law in China: Basic Policy and New Developments" *Annual Survey of Int'l & Comp Law* 4, 1 (1997), 14.

Each of these courts is made up of four trial divisions:[690]

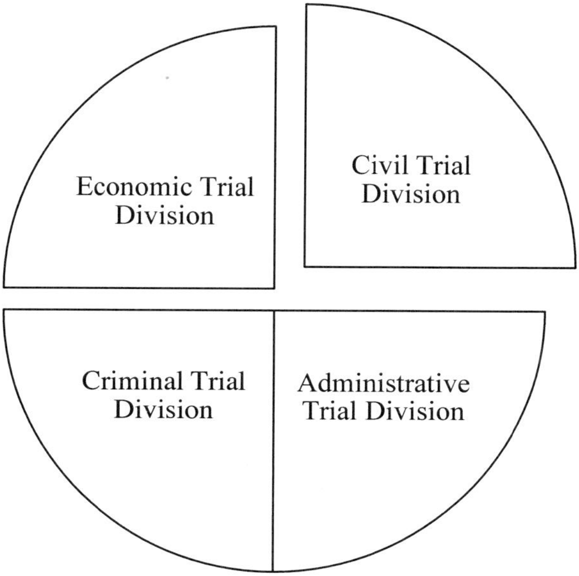

Copyright cases were usually dealt with in the civil trial divisions.[691] Cases involving intellectual property issues demand a high level of judicial professionalism because the law is very complex and international parties are often involved.[692]

The problem of the judicial track at the time of implementation of the intellectual property laws in China was that most of the expert personnel was

690 Ibid.

691 Ibid.

692 Guoqiang Lu, "15: Recent Developments in Judicial Protection for Intellectual Property in China" in *Volume 25 of IIC Studies in Industrial Property and Copyright Law - New Frontiers of Intellectual Property Law: IP and Cultural Heritage - Geographical Indications - Enforcement - Overprotections*, ed. Christopher Heath and Anselm Kamperman Sanders (Portland, USA and Oxford, Great Britain: Hart Publishing, 2005), 323.

working for the administrative track.[693] Following that, the system needed to be amended.

To improve the judicial enforcement, specialised intellectual property divisions, that can be seen as a combination of the civil and economic trial divisions, have been introduced to some High People's Courts[694] as early as 1993 and also, to some Intermediate People's Courts[695] in the same regions and to Special Economic Zones in the jurisdiction of the High People's Courts as well as to some District People's Courts[696].[697] The reason for setting up the specialised divisions in these regions were the industries in those regions and therefore, the faster development in those specific regions that gave rise to more intellectual property disputes than in less developed areas.[698] Up until the end of 2013, in total 410 intellectual property divisions had been established within Chinese courts.[699]

In 2014, the Standing Committee of the National People's Congress passed a decision by which three intellectual property courts ("IP Courts") were established at the end of 2014 in Beijing, Shanghai and Guangzhou.[700]

---

693 Mingde Li, "Special intellectual property courts in China" in *Governance of Intellectual Property Rights in China and Europe*, ed. Nari Lee, Niklas Bruun, and Mingde Li (Cheltenham, UK: Edward Elgar Publishing Limited, 2016), 304.
694 Namely Beijing, Shanghai, Tianjin and in the Provinces of Guangdong, Fujian, Jiangsu and Hainan.
695 Namely Beijing, Shanghai, Tianjin, Guangzhou, Shenzhen, Zhuhai, Haikou, Dalian, Xiamen, Haidian and Shantou.
696 Namely Beijing, Shanghai, Guangdong Province, Huangpu and Dalian.
697 Murphy, "III. Specific Fields and Topics of Law - Chapter 10.4. - Copyright" (2014), §10.04.05[02]; Zhang, "Intellectual Property Law in China: Basic Policy and New Developments" *Annual Survey of Int'l & Comp Law* 4, 1 (1997), 15.
698 Lu, "15: Recent Developments in Judicial Protection for Intellectual Property in China" (2005), 323.
699 See Li, "Special intellectual property courts in China" (2016), 304. I Acc. to Li the data is taken from the Intellectual Property Tribunal of the Supreme Court of China.
700 *Decision of the Standing Committee of the National People's Congress on Establishing Intellectual Property Right Courts in Beijing, Shanghai and Guangzhou* (31 August 2014), Standing Committee of the National People's Congress (provided by PKU Law); also see Li, "Special intellectual property courts in China" (2016), 303; for more detailed information see Nari Lee and Liguo Zhang, "Specialised IP courts in China - judicial governance of intellectual property rights" *IIC* 48, 8 (2017); Intellectual propery courts are also

With regard to copyright cases, the three IP courts are responsible for administrative actions regarding copyrights made by a department of the State Council or a local government at or above county level and in civil or administrative cases involving computer software.[701] The IP courts are also competent for administrative cases refusing to accept a ruling or decision of the department of the State Council regarding the granting, the confirmation and the compulsory license for an intellectual property right as well as any other act involving granting or confirmation of an intellectual property right.[702] Further, they are responsible for appeal copyright cases against judgments by lower courts in their region.[703]

The IP courts do not have China-wide jurisdictions – cases emerging outside the territory of the IP courts will be dealt with by the competent courts in their regions.[704]

In addition to the IP courts, specialised IP tribunals were established in several provinces in China.[705] By September 2019, further IP tribunals have been set up so that there are currently the three IP courts Beijing, Shanghai and Guangzhou and 20 IP tribunals across China, namely in Shenzhen, Chengdu, Nanjing, Suzhou, Wuhan, Hefei, Hangzhou, Ningbo, Fuzhou, Jinan, Qingdao, Tianjin, Zhengzhou, Changsha, Xi'an, Nanchang, Changchun, Lanzhou, Urumqi and Haikou.[706]

---

laid down in Article 15 *Organic Law of the People's Courts PRC* (1979/2018 version).

[701] Article 1 (1) and (2) *Provisions of the Supreme People's Court on the Jurisdiction of the Intellectual Property Courts of Beijing, Shanghai and Guangzhou over Cases* (27 October 2014), Supreme People's Court of the People's Republic of China (provided by chinacourt.org); see also Lee and Zhang, "Specialised IP courts in China - judicial governance of intellectual property rights" *IIC* 48, 8 (2017), 916.

[702] Article 5 *Provisions of the Supreme People's Court on the Jurisdiction of the Intellectual Property Courts of Beijing, Shanghai and Guangzhou over Cases* (27 October 2014), Supreme People's Court of the People's Republic of China.

[703] Article 6 ibid.; see also Lee and Zhang, "Specialised IP courts in China - judicial governance of intellectual property rights" *IIC* 48, 8 (2017), 916.

[704] Lee and Zhang, "Specialised IP courts in China - judicial governance of intellectual property rights" *IIC* 48, 8 (2017), 916.

[705] Ibid., 917.

[706] The Supreme People's Court of The People's Republic of China "The status of judicial protection of intellectual property in Chinese courts (2018)"

In these tribunals not only civil cases but also IP administrative and criminal cases are heard.[707]

Furthermore, on 18 August 2017 an "internet court" has been established in Hangzhou that is competent to deal with cases involving disputes that are internet-related, including copyright and infringement cases.[708] According to a press release from August 2018, the Hangzhou Internet Court had concluded more than 9,600 cases by that time.[709] In 2018, two further "internet courts" were established in Beijing and Guangzhou.[710] By the autumn 2019 more than 80,000 cases were heard at the "internet courts".[711]

In 2018, an intellectual property tribunal was set up directly at the SPC which commenced work on 1 January 2019 and acts as an appellate-level tribunal with a central jurisdiction over appeals on technology-related intellectual property disputes.[712]

Furthermore, the SPC can issue judicial interpretations that are necessary for filling in the loopholes in the legislation. As previously explained, these interpretations have a 'semi-legislative character' and take effect as secondary law.[713]

(19 April 2019), at 54-55; The Supreme People's Court of the People's Republic of China, "Hainan sets up tribunals for foreign-related civil and commercial, IP cases", 27 September 2019 (http://english.court.gov.cn/2019-09/27/content_37514175.htm, accessed: 6 March 2021).

[707] Lee and Zhang, "Specialised IP courts in China - judicial governance of intellectual property rights" *IIC* 48, 8 (2017), 917.

[708] The Supreme People's Court of the People's Republic of China, "China first internet court handles over 10,000 cases", 20 August 2018 (http://english.court.gov.cn/2018-08/20/content_36798243.htm, accessed: 6 March 2021).

[709] Ibid.

[710] The Supreme People's Court of the People's Republic of China, "Online courts ease access to legal services", 6 December 2019 (http://english.court.gov.cn/2019-12/06/content_37528117.htm, accessed: 6 March 2021).

[711] Ibid.

[712] The Supreme People's Court of The People's Republic of China "The status of judicial protection of intellectual property in Chinese courts (2018)" (19 April 2019), at 52.

[713] Keith and Lin, "Judicial Interpretation of China's Supreme People's Court as "Secondary Law"" *China Information* 23 (2009), 224.

Summarizing, it can be said that there has been much movement within the last years, which especially shows that China is adapting to the technological development. This is further discussed in the next paragraph relating to the enforcement of rights in China.

2. Enforcement Proceedings

Secondly, emphasis is put on the enforcement of copyright in China. TRIPS has introduced specific provisions concerning the enforcement of intellectual property rights; none of the earlier treaties had provided rules on that particular issue; the ultimate aim of TRIPS is an effective protection of intellectual property rights across borders to strengthen and increase international trade.[714] According to Article 41 (4) TRIPS, parties shall have an opportunity for review by a judicial authority of final administrative decisions. Furthermore, Article 61 TRIPS stipulates that members have to provide criminal sanctions in the case of wilful copyright infringement.

Intellectual Property Right holders can enforce their right in two different ways in China with the first being the administrative path and the second being the judicial path.[715] This system is called 'two channels, coordinated operation'.[716] This mechanism of a dual enforcement has been shown to be a good solution for the society and the legal traditions in China; also, the possibility of administrative enforcement has lessened the case load of courts and decreased the financial burden; however, it should be monitored carefully so that the judicial track is not weakened in its functioning.[717]

[714] See Preamble and Part III - Article 41 - 61 *TRIPS Agreement* (1994), 1869 UNTS 299; 33 ILM 1197 (Annex 1C of the Marrakesh Agreement establishing the World Trade Organization, signed in Marrakesh, Morocco on 15 April 1994, 33 I.L.M. 1125); see also Difan Qu and Yahong Li, "The Challenges for the Enforcement against Copyright Violations in China under the TRIPS Agreement" *Frontiers L. China* 7, 2 (2012), 248.
[715] Thomas I. Ross, "Enforcing Intellectual Property Rights in China" *China Bus. Rev.* (2012), 25.
[716] Feng and Huang, "International Standards and Local Elements" *J. Copyright Soc'y U.S.A.* 49 (2001-2002), 940.
[717] Ibid.

Most right holders that decide to follow the administrative track are Chinese citizens; foreign investors mainly choose the judicial track.[718]

The enforcement of copyright protected material at customs has also gained importance because many of the Chinese 'quality copies' go across the borders; hence, stricter custom mechanisms can be of great help in the fight against copyright infringement in the People's Republic of China.[719] The cooperation with customs and hence, a greater border control could be a good alternative to the two main enforcement tracks in China.[720]

a) Legal Claims

The situations where legal claims against an infringer arise have been discussed in the previous section.

An infringer can be held liable under civil law in the situations described in Articles 46 and 47 Chinese Copyright Law. The possibility of criminal liability is given by Article 47 Chinese Copyright Law in connection with Articles 217 and 218 Chinese Criminal Law. In the following the administrative enforcement and the judicial enforcement as well as the possible customs measures are discussed and critically assessed.

b) Administrative Enforcement

In the following paragraph, the enforcement competences given to the administrative organs under the 2010 Copyright Law are discussed.

The possibility of enforcing copyright through the administrative track is stipulated in Section V of the Copyright Law. According to Articles 47 and 48, copyright infringers can be sanctioned by the administrative authorities in cases where a copyright has been infringed or damage has been done to the public interest; penalties include actions such as prohibiting the infringing conduct, confiscating the profit gained, confiscating and destroying the infringing product and imposing specific fines upon the infringers. Depending on the severity of the infringement the administrative agencies can

[718] Ross, "Enforcing Intellectual Property Rights in China" *China Bus. Rev.* (2012), 25.
[719] Murphy, "III. Specific Fields and Topics of Law - Chapter 10.4. - Copyright" (2014), §10.04.05.
[720] Enders and Steiner, "Urheberrechtsreform und Urheberrechtsdurchsetzung" *ZChinR* 17, 2 (2010), 108.

also confiscate the machinery and materials used for producing the infringing copy.

In comparison to the law of 1990, the power of the administrative agencies has been strengthened with the right to confiscation and destruction of the infringing goods as well as the tools used for making the copies. In 2002, the State Council published the Regulations for the Implementation of the Copyright Law (amended 2013)[721] that further specify the duties of the different copyright agencies. As stated above, according to Article 37 of these Regulations the copyright departments of the local governments should generally deal with the infringing acts and investigate in the specific regions whereas the copyright department under the State Council is obligated to deal with and investigate the infringing conduct which has an effect onto the whole nation.

aa) Competences and Process

According to Article 7 Copyright Law, the administrative department of the State Council has the competence for copyright administration in the whole nation and the administrative departments of the provinces, municipalities and autonomous regions are responsible for the administration in their administrative sectors. Article 56 Copyright Law stipulates the rights of the parties to a copyright conflict. If a party is not satisfied with the outcome of an administrative process it can take legal action in a People's Court within three months from the date of the authority's decision; contrary to that, the administrative department can enforce an action in front of a People's Court if the party does not implement the decided penalties in the given time and does not take legal action itself.[722]

If the authority in the respective city or province can relate to the right holder's complaint, it starts investigations on the alleged infringer.[723] The

[721] *Regulations for the Implementation of the Copyright Law of the People's Republic of China* (2013 - issued 2 August 2002, effective 15 September 2002, amended 8 January 2011, amended 30 January 2013, effective 1 March 2013), State Council of the People's Republic of China.
[722] Article 37 ibid.
[723] Ross, "Enforcing Intellectual Property Rights in China" *China Bus. Rev.* (2012), 25.

administrative authorities have the right to make use of the police in order to ensure the compliance with the respective orders.[724]

Some provinces and municipalities have introduced special intellectual property right bureaus and committees to better coordinate between the different authorities.[725]

bb) Criticism

A huge advantage of the administrative enforcement possibility is that it is less cost and time consuming compared to the judicial enforcement.[726] However, intellectual property right holders face the problem with the administrative track that agencies have no power to impose damages upon the infringer and have no way to appeal in the administrative track; if claimants are unsatisfied with the outcome, they have to pursue the judicial track afterwards.[727] However, at least the results obtained in the administrative proceedings can be used as evidence in the litigation.

The actual enforcement difficulties are discussed in greater detail below.

c) Judicial Enforcement

Judicial enforcement is possible before the civil courts and before the criminal courts.

aa) Civil Proceedings

Before 1986, copyright cases were only dealt with by administrative authorities and judicial enforcement was not at all set in place yet.[728] The General Principles of Civil Law, which were introduced in 1986, can be seen as the first foundation of judicial enforcement of copyright in the People's Republic of China.[729] Article 2 of the *Interpretations of the Supreme*

---

[724] Ibid.

[725] Andreas Blume, "Produkt- und Markenpiraterie in der Volksrepublik China " *China Analysis* 33 (2004), 25.

[726] Also see Barbara Grüneis, "Produktpiraterie in China - Durchsetzung geistiger Eigentumsrechte vs. wirtschaftliche Entwicklung " (Dissertation submitted to the Technical University of Munich, Germany, 2010), 77.

[727] Ross, "Enforcing Intellectual Property Rights in China" *China Bus. Rev.* (2012), 25.

[728] Article 56 *Copyright Law PRC* (1990/2010 version).

[729] Articles 94 and 118 *General Principles of the Civil Law PRC* (1986); Ganea, Pattloch, and Heath, *Intellectual Property Law in China* (2005), 209.

People's Court Concerning Several Issues in Application of Law in Hearing Correctly the Civil Copyright sets out that the civil copyright disputes have to be held at the Intermediate People's Court or a higher court. The local jurisdiction depends on the place where the infringement is committed, where the pirated goods are stored or confiscated as set out in Article 46 of the Chinese Copyright Law (2010) or at the place where the defendant has his/her residence. As outlined above, specialized IP tribunals have been established in some regions that are responsible for IP civil cases as well as IP administrative and criminal cases.[730]

Article 49 Chinese Copyright Law stipulates that compensation has to be paid in the amount of the losses suffered and in cases where such loss is not determinable, compensation is based on the illegally gained revenue.

bb) Criticism

Contrary to the U.S. system, there is no real discovery procedure in a Chinese court case which makes it very difficult for the plaintiff and the judge to specify a certain amount for damages, especially because no insight into the profits and sales numbers has to be provided.[731] However, the SPC has published its *Several Provisions on Evidence in Civil Litigation* on 25 December 2019, which are effective from 1 May 2020 onwards.[732] These new provisions include general rules on the disclosure of documentary evidence which will give the parties the possibility to apply to the court to order disclosure of documentation and if the order is not adhered to by the other party, the court can decide on the partial evidence that the applying party was able to gather; adapting these to intellectual property cases could mean that if the right holder applies for the disclosure of financial records to prove damage claims and the infringer does not disclose these upon request

[730] Lee and Zhang, "Specialised IP courts in China - judicial governance of intellectual property rights" *IIC* 48, 8 (2017), 917.

[731] Ross, "Enforcing Intellectual Property Rights in China" *China Bus. Rev.* (2012), 25.

[732] *Several Provisions on Evidence in Civil Litigation* (2019 - adopted 14 October 2019 amending version of 6 December 2001, effective 1 May 2020), The Supreme People's Court of the People's Republic of China (provided by court.gov.cn).

of the court, the right holder might be granted damage compensation without further proof based on the documents submitted with the claim.[733] This provision greatly enhances the possibilities of the right holder and are a good sign on the road to effective enforcement. However, it still has to be seen whether these rules will be enforced in practice.

Further, judges who are members of the CCP can be in a conflict because as party members they have the duty to promote the regional economy, whereas as a judge they have to decide on an objective and legal basis.[734] Additionally, the requirements for the admissibility of evidence are set very high in judicial proceedings; for example, evidence from abroad can only be used in a trial if it is notarized, which is a very costly matter.[735]

However, a huge advantage of choosing the judicial track is the possibility of awarding damages to the copyright holder.

The actual enforcement difficulties are discussed in greater detail below.

cc) Criminal Proceedings

The lack in criminal enforcement was also part of the WTO dispute between China and the U.S.. The U.S. complained that the hurdles to pursue criminal proceedings were too high and therefore not aligned with Article 61 TRIPS.[736] However, the panel did not see enough proof of that and did not allow the claim.[737] A criminal claim can be made by the victim or along with a civil proceeding.[738]

---

[733] Grace Guo and Stefaan Meuwissen, "China: looking back at 2019's main IP developments and looking forward at what 2020 may bring", 13 April 2020 (https://www.jdsupra.com/legalnews/china-looking-back-at-2019-s-main-ip-93099/, accessed: 6 March 2021).

[734] Enders and Steiner, "Urheberrechtsreform und Urheberrechtsdurchsetzung" *ZChinR* 17, 2 (2010), 110.

[735] Grüneis, "Produktpiraterie in China - Durchsetzung geistiger Eigentumsrechte vs. wirtschaftliche Entwicklung " (2010), 75.

[736] Enders and Steiner, "Urheberrechtsreform und Urheberrechtsdurchsetzung" *ZChinR* 17, 2 (2010), 113.

[737] Peter Ganea, "Internationales - WTO-Panel veröffentlicht Ergebnisse zum Streit zwischen den USA und China wegen Defiziten im chinesischen Immaterialgüterrechtsschutz" *GRUR Int.* (2009), 275.

[738] Enders and Steiner, "Urheberrechtsreform und Urheberrechtsdurchsetzung" *ZChinR* 17, 2 (2010), 113.

In 2004, the People's Court and the Public Prosecution gave a statement and introduced threshold levels for infringements to become criminally relevant. In relation to copyright infringements, criminal liability should only start in cases where the amount of infringed goods exceeds 50,000 Yuan or the illegal gains of the infringer mount up to a minimum of 20,000 Yuan.[739]

dd) Criticism

Administrative authorities rarely want to forward cases to the criminal authorities because once a criminal proceeding starts, infringers do not have to pay the administrative penalties to the authorities but rather have to pay the fines when they are sentenced in court.[740]

Furthermore, the rule of evidence is very strict in Chinese criminal courts and formal obstacle often make it very difficult for infringed right holders to initiate criminal proceedings.[741]

d) Custom Measures

Enforcement of intellectual property rights can also be carried out through custom protective measures. The first regulation regarding the authorization of customs authorities in relation to intellectual property rights were the *Regulations on the Protection of Intellectual Property Rights by Customs* in 1995. Article 4 of the Regulations read:

> *"The Customs Offices of the People's Republic of China shall protect intellectual property rights relating to goods entering or leaving the territory, and shall exercise the relevant powers stipulated under the Customs Law of the People's Republic of China."*[742]

[739] Grüneis, "Produktpiraterie in China - Durchsetzung geistiger Eigentumsrechte vs. wirtschaftliche Entwicklung " (2010), 74-75.
[740] Ibid., 75.
[741] Ibid.
[742] Article 4 *Regulations on the Protection of Intellectual Property Rights by Customs* (1995 - promulgated 5 July 1993, effective 1 October 1995), State Council of the People's Republic of China (provided by WIPO).

Such regulations were politically motivated by the bilateral agreement between China and the United States in the same year – the MoU 1995.[743]

aa) Competences and Process

These first regulations set out that right holders needed to register their right with customs to receive protection at the borders by customs.[744] These were repealed by the new Regulations that were promulgated in 2003 and took effect in 2004.[745] Following the amendment, customs could not only act by an application of the right holder but also "ex officio", if they suspected infringing goods.[746] This does not mean that customs can seize the products "ex officio" but they can detain them and inform the right holder of the suspected infringing goods who then has to decide whether the goods are infringing the rights and whether he/she wants to file an application.[747]

The Regulations were amended again in 2010 and 2018.[748]

The border seizure application is valid for ten years and can be renewed for another ten-year term; if the application is not renewed or the protection of the intellectual property right expires, the application at customs becomes invalid.[749]

If the custom authority finds goods that might be infringing intellectual property rights, they have to immediately inform the right holder;[750] the right holder needs to present a customs application according to Article 13

[743] Blume, "Produkt- und Markenpiraterie VR China" *China Analysis* 33 (2004), 33.
[744] Article 6 and 8 *Regulations on the Protection of Intellectual Property Rights by Customs* (1995 - promulgated 5 July 1993, effective 1 October 1995), State Council of the People's Republic of China.
[745] *Regulations on Customs Protection of Intellectual Property Rights* (2003 - promulgated 2 December 2003, effective 1 March 2004), State Council of the People's Republic of China (provided by WIPO).
[746] Peter Ganea, "Volksrepublik China - Neue Zollbestimmungen zum Schutz des geistigen Eigentums" *GRUR Int.* (2004), 532.
[747] Ibid., 533.
[748] *Regulations on Customs Protection of Intellectual Property Rights* (2018 - promulgated 2 December 2003, effective 1 March 2004, amended 24 March 2010, amended 19 March 2018), State Council of the People's Republic of China (provided by gov.cn).
[749] Article 10 ibid.
[750] Article 16 ibid.

of the Regulations within three working days and has to provide a security according to Article 14 of the Regulations. If all of these requirements are fulfilled, customs have to detain the goods and send a receipt to the consignor or consignee notifying such of the detention.[751] Following that, customs have a period of thirty days to determine whether the goods are infringing; if no infringement can be determined or no court proceeding has been initiated within fifty days of detention the goods need to be released.[752] If customs determine that the goods in fact infringe intellectual property rights, customs have to confiscate them according to Article 27 of the Regulations.

Furthermore, Article 26 stipulates that the custom authorities shall transfer the case to the relevant prosecutor in cases of suspected criminal offences.

bb) Criticism

The custom seizure procedure is an affordable and easy way for intellectual property right holders to improve enforcement of their rights. Also, customs authorities are seen to be cooperative and independent.[753]

Although applications to customs are not obligatory anymore and customs can act "ex officio", it is recommended to have such application in place because customs, in practice, tend to only intervene in cases where an application has been filed beforehand; this can be explained due to the fact that they do not have enough information on the intellectual property rights without an application.[754]

Another point of criticism is that the right holder has to pay a deposit when ordering customs to seize the goods. According to Article 14 of the Regulations, the security, which is calculated in relation to the value of the detained goods and has the purpose of compensating the consignor or consignee in cases, where infringement cannot be determined and cover the

[751] Article 16 ibid.
[752] Articles 20 and 24 (2) ibid.
[753] Grüneis, "Produktpiraterie in China - Durchsetzung geistiger Eigentumsrechte vs. wirtschaftliche Entwicklung " (2010).
[754] Ibid., 77; Blume, "Produkt- und Markenpiraterie VR China" *China Analysis* 33 (2004), 43.

arising costs in terms of storage, maintenance and disposal of the goods. These costs lead to the deterrence of some right holders.[755]

e) Actual Enforcement and Difficulties

As it can be seen, China has shaped its law substantially during the last decades to keep up with international requirements. The difficulties in enforcing intellectual property rights, in particular copyright, are discussed in the following.

aa) Problems in the Administrative Track

First, obstacles in the administrative track also have an effect on the proper enforcement of intellectual property rights in China.

(1) Lack of Coordination, Training and Sufficient Salaries

The People's Republic of China is a very large country with many provinces and regions. China does not only have the National Copyright Administration (NCAC) but also many smaller regional copyright authorities spread all over China.[756] The large population of China and the uneven development of the country in the various regions result in laws and enforcement being handled differently.[757] Some agencies are more ambitious and act effectively whereas others do not see the importance and take action relatively slowly.[758]

Furthermore, many officials are missing adequate training in enforcing intellectual property issues which leads to less enforcement of more complex intellectual property cases.[759] Production sites are changed often and the officials are missing legal as well as technical knowledge.[760]

[755] Blume, "Produkt- und Markenpiraterie VR China" *China Analysis* 33 (2004), 33-34.
[756] Lina Wang, "Intellectual Property Protection in China" *International Information & Library Review* 36, 3 (2004), 259.
[757] Ibid.
[758] Ibid.
[759] Ibid.
[760] Li, *Urheberrecht in Deutschland und der Volksrepublik China - ein Rechtsvergleich* (2015), 148.

Also, a monetary incentive for officials to act more ambitiously is not provided since the salaries for such are quite low.[761]

(2) The Problem of Local Protectionism

During the Open Door Policy in the 1970s the government around Deng Xiaoping made the decision to decentralise the power from the federal to the local and provincial levels.[762] The decentralisation resulted in the problem of the so-called protectionism because regional and provincial government gained more power and became autonomous in some ways so that the central government in Beijing steadily lost its influence.[763] It can be said that local protectionism is "a corollary of decentralization"[764].

The administration is not only responsible for the enforcement of intellectual property rights but also involved in approval procedures and in the management of registries.[765] Administrative authorities often have an intensive relationship to the industries in their regions including companies that produce counterfeit or pirated products.[766] Cities and provinces are even proprietors of formerly state-owned enterprises, that nowadays operate as production sites of infringing products[767] or at least hold stakes in local companies.[768] All of these occurrences lead to the assumption that such administrative authorities cannot be independent and impartial in making their decisions.[769]

---

[761] Wang, "Intellectual Property Protection in China" *International Information & Library Review* 36, 3 (2004), 259.
[762] Berkman, "Intellectual Property Rights in the PRC" *Pacific Basin L.J.* 15, 1 (1996), 17.
[763] See ibid.
[764] Yiqiang Li, "Evaluation of the Sino-American Intellectual Property Agreements: A Judicial Approach to Solving the Local Protectionism Problem" *Colum. J. Asian L.* 10 (1996), 399.
[765] Grüneis, "Produktpiraterie in China - Durchsetzung geistiger Eigentumsrechte vs. wirtschaftliche Entwicklung " (2010), 83.
[766] Ibid.
[767] Ibid.
[768] Stanley Lubman, "Bird in a Cage: Chinese Law Reform after Twenty Years" *Nw. J. Int'l L. & Bus.* 20, 3 (1999-2000), 395.
[769] Grüneis, "Produktpiraterie in China - Durchsetzung geistiger Eigentumsrechte vs. wirtschaftliche Entwicklung " (2010), 83.

Another explanation for the weak enforcement, especially in the more rural areas, is that those production sites generate many jobs in the respective areas and a possible closure of a production site would lead to the loss of many jobs and hence, poverty in the region.[770] Linked to this is the dependency on the economic volume generated by the illegal businesses; the provinces of Zhejiang, Fujian, Guangdong, Jiangsu and Anhui are especially concerned.[771] Those businesses also have a positive effect on the other industries in the respective areas such as hotels, restaurants and the like that benefit from a much frequented area and hence, better consumer behaviour.[772]

In summary, officers in the respective administrative bureaus often face a conflict of interests. On one hand, they want to enforce the legislation and hence, improve the legal certainty, on the other hand they want to fulfil all the requirements of boosting the economy in their regions.[773] If an officer wants to be promoted to a better position, his/her decisions need to be in line with the superior with the main aim of promoting economic development.[774] Corruption is one of the main obstacles.

In achieving their aims, the local administrations use their power to pressurize the local courts to decide in favour of local companies rather than companies from another region or from abroad or to prevent execution of a judgement that is non-favourable to local businesses; courts mostly will

---

770 Keith E. Maskus, "Intellectual Property Rights in the WTO Accession: Assessing China's Reforms" in *China and the WTO - Accession, Policy Reform, and Poverty Reduction Strategies*, ed. Deepak Bhattasali, Shantong Li, and Will Martin (Washington D.C., USA: The World Bank and Oxford University Press, 2004), 56; Marcus Ring, *China und das Recht des geistigen Eigentums - Die Vereinbarungen mit der WTO und ihre Umsetzung*, Reihe China Band 17 (Hamburg: Diplomica Verlag GmbH, 2008), 20; Grüneis, "Produktpiraterie in China - Durchsetzung geistiger Eigentumsrechte vs. wirtschaftliche Entwicklung " (2010), 83.

771 Blume, "Produkt- und Markenpiraterie VR China" *China Analysis* 33 (2004), 38.

772 Grüneis, "Produktpiraterie in China - Durchsetzung geistiger Eigentumsrechte vs. wirtschaftliche Entwicklung " (2010), 84.

773 Ibid.

774 Li, "Evaluation of the Sino-American Intellectual Property Agreements: A Judicial Approach to Solving the Local Protectionism Problem" *Colum. J. Asian L.* 10 (1996), 400.

obey to the conditions because they are financially dependent on the local authorities.[775]

According to Transparency International, China is still on rank 78 out of 180 with a corruption score of 42 (with 0 meaning “highly corrupt” and 100 meaning “very clean”).[776] In comparison to that, Germany is on rank 9 with a score of 80 and the United States of America are on rank 25 with a score of 67.[777]

The current ranking shows that corruption is still a problem in China and needs to be eliminated to improve the work of the enforcement authorities.

bb) Problems in the Judicial Track

Secondly, obstacles in the judicial track are discussed.

(1) Judicial Independence and Corruption

One major problem of the Chinese judicial system is the lack of an independent judiciary.[778] The Chinese Judges Law states in Article 7 that administrative organs, public organizations or individuals must not interfere with the work of the judges.[779] However, they can still be controlled by the

[775] Lubman, "Bird in a Cage: Chinese Law Reform after Twenty Years" *Nw. J. Int'l L. & Bus.* 20, 3 (1999-2000), 395-396; Yuanshi Bu, *Einführung in das Recht Chinas*, Schriftenreihe der Juristischen Schulung / Ausländisches Recht, Band 191 ed. (München: Verlag C.H. Beck, 2009), 17 (§13,11); For more details and statistics look at: Cheryl Xiaoning Long and Jun Wang, "Judicial local protectionism in China: An empirical study of IP cases" *International Review of Law and Economics* 42 (2015).

[776] China's score has not changed significantly during the last years: 2019: 41, 2018: 39, 2017: 41, 2016: 40, 2015: 37; see Transparency International, "Corruption Perceptions Index 2020" (https://www.transparency.org/en/cpi/2020/index/nzl, accessed: 16 March 2021).

[777] Ibid.

[778] Bu, *Einführung in das Recht Chinas* (2009), §3.10 (p. 17).

[779] *Judges Law of the People's Republic of China* (1995/2019 version) (provided by npc.gov.cn).

People's Congress[780] and by the public prosecutors[781].[782] According to Articles 38 to 42 Judges Law, a judge is evaluated annually and based on the evaluation, can be dismissed. It can be argued that due to the evaluation mechanism lower-ranked judges are less independent because they have to satisfy their supervisors to avoid negative evaluations.[783] This hierarchy/corruption is of great concern in judicial proceedings, especially in courts at the lower or intermediate level.[784]

The judges' independency can also be questioned when reading the yearly reports published by the SPC on the protection of intellectual property in Chinese courts. For example, in the report for 2018 it is written in the section on the enhancement of judicial capabilities:

> *"Intellectual property judges must appreciate the full importance of the Party's political development to the People's Courts' developments, uphold the absolute leadership of the party, and stay determined and unwavering in their political belief. They must develop greater political awareness, improve on their political qualities and capabilities, and strengthen their political conviction, and they must adhere strictly to political discipline and political rules."*[785]

This shows again that there is no separation of powers in China and that the Chinese judiciary is depending on the political leadership.

---

780 Carried out by the Standing Committee; Article 67 (6) *Constitution PRC* (1982/2018 version).

781 Articles 20 et seq. *Organic Law of the People's Procuratorates of the People's Republic of China* (1979/2018 version) (provided by npc.gov.cn).

782 Bu, *Einführung in das Recht Chinas* (2009), §3.10 (p.17), §16.14-15 (p.28), §16.27 (p.30).

783 Also see ibid., §3.16 (p.18).

784 Ibid., §3.16-17 (p.18).

785 The Supreme People's Court of The People's Republic of China "The status of judicial protection of intellectual property in Chinese courts (2018)" (19 April 2019), at 85.

(2) Judges' Qualifications

Many judges are missing the correct legal training and knowledge to understand complex legal issues in copyright cases, which leads to ineffective enforcement.[786] This can be traced back to the era of Mao Zedong. During the reign of Mao, no proper education for judges, prosecutors and lawyers was available and any personnel decisions were made based on political fear and motivation rather than academic education.[787] The judicial reform in 2002 led to the introduction of an entrance examination for judges, prosecutors and lawyers that consists of substantive and material civil, criminal and public law (uniform national bar exam).[788] Everyone who has obtained a bachelor's degree in any kind of subject[789] and a certificate of good conduct can take the examination to qualify.[790] Article 12 Judges Law stipulates all the requirements needed for becoming a judge. Besides Chinese citizenship, endorsement of the Constitution, political and professional quality and good health, a future judge needs to have worked in law for at least five years[791] independent of the university degree obtained as long as professional knowledge of law is present.[792] The entrance examination is only a precondition for becoming a judge because according to Articles 14 to 17 Judges Law, a strict examination and appraisal of potential candidates is required.[793]

---

[786] Amy Rosen, "China vs. United States: A Cosmopolitan Copyright Comparison" *J. Technol. Law Policy* 15, Fall 2014 (2014), 19-20.

[787] Li, *Urheberrecht in Deutschland und der Volksrepublik China - ein Rechtsvergleich* (2015), 144-145.

[788] Bu, *Einführung in das Recht Chinas* (2009), §2.10-11 (p.12); Zhiwen Yang, "A Commentary on the Selection of Judges in China: From the Perspective of Judicial Professionalization" *US-China Law Review* 14 (2017), 253-254.

[789] Not necessarily in legal sciences.

[790] Bu, *Einführung in das Recht Chinas* (2009), §2.11 (p.12).

[791] If an applicant holds a Master of Law or a Doctor of Law degree, such time frames can be reduced.

[792] Article 12 (1)-(7) *Judges Law of the People's Republic of China* (1995/2019 version).

[793] For this selection a national civil service exam an appraisal of the applicant are carried out; also see Yang, "A Commentary on the Selection of Judges in China: From the Perspective of Judicial Professionalization" *US-China Law Review* 14 (2017), 255.

As mentioned previously, at the end of 2014 specialised IP courts were established – these IP courts have established a selection committee that is said to improve the impartiality.[794] Only judges that have enough experience in the respective sector are chosen for the specialised IP courts.[795]

In the yearly reports published by the SPC, it can be seen that the enhancement of judicial capabilities is one of the goals of the SPC, e.g. in 2018, many trainings in intellectual property law at the National Judge's College and the local courts took place.[796]

Since the beginning of the 21st century the system has been improved significantly but there is still much work needed to build a well working judiciary, especially by improving the selection and continuous training of judges.[797]

(3) Cost Issues

Another problem are the costs for initiating court proceedings. The costs of a court proceeding are very high compared to the salary of the Chinese citizens.[798] Another obstacle of pursuing litigation is the difficulty of finding an attorney who is specialised in intellectual property law.[799] Furthermore, right holders have to incur many different costs before actually filing a claim in front of the court. Since there is no discovery procedure carried out by the court, all documents have to be notarized in order to be valid before court and all investigations have to be carried out privately (e.g. by engaging a private investigator, buying infringing goods as proof et

794 Lee and Zhang, "Specialised IP courts in China - judicial governance of intellectual property rights" *IIC* 48, 8 (2017), 917.
795 Ibid.
796 The Supreme People's Court of The People's Republic of China "The status of judicial protection of intellectual property in Chinese courts (2018)" (19 April 2019), at 86.
797 For more details, see Yang, "A Commentary on the Selection of Judges in China: From the Perspective of Judicial Professionalization" *US-China Law Review* 14 (2017), 251-269.
798 Rosen, "China vs. United States: A Cosmopolitan Copyright Comparison" *J. Technol. Law Policy* 15, Fall 2014 (2014), 20.
799 Ibid.

cetera).[800] All these different cost matters lead to the deterrence of right holders in pursuing their claims in a judicial proceeding.

cc) Pressure from the Outside and Cultural Peculiarities

As previously explained in the historical chapter, intellectual property rights are still a pretty new construct in the Chinese legal world. The first copyright laws in China were promulgated in earlier times but were either repealed at the beginning of a new dynasty or never seriously enforced. The need for China to start formulating intellectual property laws only arose during the Open Door Policy and pressure from the outside, especially by the United States.[801] China started to develop legislation quite heavily from the 1980s onwards with the aim of becoming a market attractive to foreign investors.[802]

The Chinese population does not have much knowledge in the field of intellectual property rights which can be traced back to the 'Confucian Way of Thinking' and hence, the perception of monopolistic rights in general.[803] It can be argued that the education of the masses and by that, an improvement of the awareness of intellectual property rights will eventually result in better enforcement.[804]

dd) China's Latest Efforts

The State Council reported at the end of 2019, that 25 IP protection centres were established all across the country to enhance the efficiency of intellectual property applications as well as the dispute resolutions for patents, trademarks and copyrights.[805] By that, it will hopefully be easier and less costly for right holders to enforce their rights.

---

[800] Grüneis, "Produktpiraterie in China - Durchsetzung geistiger Eigentumsrechte vs. wirtschaftliche Entwicklung " (2010), 75.

[801] Naigen Zhang, "Intellectual Property Law Enforcement in China: Trade Issues, Policies and Practices" *FORDHAM INTELL. PROP. MEDIA & ENT. L.J.* 8, 1 (1997), 72.

[802] Also see Li, *Urheberrecht in Deutschland und der Volksrepublik China - ein Rechtsvergleich* (2015), 143.

[803] See *Chapter 2 I. 2.* of this dissertation.

[804] Wang, "Intellectual Property Protection in China" *International Information & Library Review* 36, 3 (2004), 259.

[805] CGTN, "China intensifies IP protection with 25 centers set up nationwide", 23 December 2019

f) Current Opinions of Representatives of the Business World

One example to show the view of foreigners investing in China is the Business Confidence Survey of the European Chamber of Commerce in China in cooperation with the consultancy company Roland Berger that is released every year.

The 2019 survey summarizes that half of the European companies (52%) think that China's intellectual property laws are adequate[806] and only 7% are of the opinion that they are excellent.[807] With reference to the enforcement of the law, around 35% think that the authorities are actually enforcing the law adequately. This number has improved significantly over the last years[808], which is a good indicator that the enforcement is in fact improving. However, the majority (42%) still believes that the law enforcement is inadequate[809].[810] Furthermore, it can be seen in the report that according to the European companies, IPR infringement is still happening but that the numbers are decreasing.[811] In the 2019 survey, 67% of the asked companies answered that their companies had not suffered and infringement of their rights in China, whereas 33% answered that they suffered infringements (25% rarely and 8% frequently).[812]

However, these numbers need to be read carefully as only around 550 companies participate in the survey each year.

(http://english.www.gov.cn/news/videos/201912/23/content_WS5dfff70dc6d0bcf8c4c19417.html, accessed: 6 March 2021).

806 The number has not significantly changed in the last couple of years: 2012: 49%, 2013: 47%, 2014: 55%, 2015: 53%, 2016: 54%, 2017: 50%, 2018: 53%

807 European Chamber of Commerce in China (in cooperation with Roland Berger) "European Business in China - Business Confidence Survey 2019" (2019), 47.

808 The numbers have increased steadily in the last couple of years, unfortunately, the strong increase in 2018 was not repeated in 2019: 2012: 16%, 2013: 13%, 2014: 18%, 2015: 24%, 2016: 25%, 2017: 29%, 2018: 34%.

809 This number has decreased significantly from 2012-2019: 2012: 70%, 2013: 69%, 2014: 65%, 2015: 56%, 2016: 59%, 2017: 52%, 2018: 51%.

810 European Chamber of Commerce in China (in cooperation with Roland Berger) "European Business in China - Business Confidence Survey 2019" (2019), 47.

811 Ibid., 48.

812 Ibid.

Another depiction of the current view on intellectual property law enforcement in China is the China Business Climate Survey Report of the American Chamber of Commerce in China in cooperation with the consultancy company Deloitte. The 2019 Report[813] contains a section on "Innovation and IPR" of which some results are shown in the following:

According to the 2019 survey, the top five business challenges for U.S. companies are (1) inconsistent regulatory interpretation and unclear laws and enforcement, (2) rising labour costs, (3) rising tensions in US-China relations, (4) increased competition from privately owned Chinese companies and (5) shortage of qualified employees.[814] Interestingly, Chinese protectionism that was ranked third in 2017 and fifth in 2018 is not listed in the top five business challenges anymore.

With reference to the protection of intellectual property rights, respondents are of the opinion that the lack of sufficient intellectual property protections is the major barrier preventing the increase of innovation in China; further, vague policies and lack of detailed implementation guidelines are also regarded as hindering.[815] Positively to note is, that 59% of the respondents answered that they see an improvement of the enforcement of intellectual property rights in China; 37% answered that enforcement remained the same and only 4% answered that it deteriorated.[816]

Regarding copyright laws and regulations, 52% of the respondents concluded in 2018[817] that such are effective.[818] It is interesting to note that the number has decreased compared with 2016 when 56% were of the opinion that the laws are effective.[819] 20% stated that the laws were ineffective – this number has decreased significantly in comparison to the previous survey as in which 44% stated that the laws were ineffective; however, it must be noted that a new answer category "Don't know" was introduced in

[813] American Chamber of Commerce in China (in cooperation with Deloitte) "2019 China Business Climate Survey Report" (2019).
[814] Ibid., 39.
[815] Ibid., 57.
[816] Ibid., 60.
[817] Please note that the report compares the years 2018 and 2016.
[818] American Chamber of Commerce in China (in cooperation with Deloitte) "2019 China Business Climate Survey Report" (2019), 61.
[819] Ibid.

2018.[820] A similar picture can be seen when looking at the question of enforcement of copyright laws and regulations: 43% answered that enforcement was effective whereas 27% answered that it was ineffective and 23% chose the answer "Don't know".[821] Furthermore, the members were asked what the most important IP challenge is for them. Around a third answered that the biggest challenges are legal challenges, namely difficulties in the prosecution of IP infringement in court and at the administrative level (39%) and insufficient protection offered by text of IP-related laws and regulations (26%).[822]

In summary, it can be said that these two surveys show the view of the business world in the last years pretty precisely. The foreign firms are still sceptical on the enforcement of their rights which might eventually lead to less investments in China and steer foreign investors to other countries where more emphasis is put on their rights.

g) Case Statistics

The following part provides an overview of statistics from the last years to see how the enforcement of copyrights has developed over the years.

aa) Administrative Track

The NCAC publishes statistics of copyright enforcement for every year. The NCAC does not publish the number of copyright complaints received but rather provides statistics on the conducted actions such as the number of seized copies/pirated goods and the amount of the imposed fines.

---

[820] Ibid.
[821] Ibid.
[822] Ibid., 63.

The first graph shows the total number of copies/pirated goods seized by the authorities between 2014 and 2019:[823]

It can be seen that the number of seized products infringing copyrights has decreased from 2014 being 16,665,890 to 7,303,778 in 2019.

[823] NCAC "Statistics on National Copyright Law Enforcement in 2014" (30 October 2015); NCAC "National Copyright Enforcement Status in 2015" (18 January 2017); NCAC "2016 National Copyright Enforcement Table" (11 May 2018); NCAC "Statistics Related to Copyright Enforcement in 2017" (10 October 2018); NCAC "Statistics on National Copyright Enforcement in 2018" (14 January 2020); NCAC "Statistics on National Copyright Enforcement in 2019" (29 January 2021).

The second graph shows the number of fines imposed on the copyright infringers (in Yuan) between the years 2014 to 2019:[824]

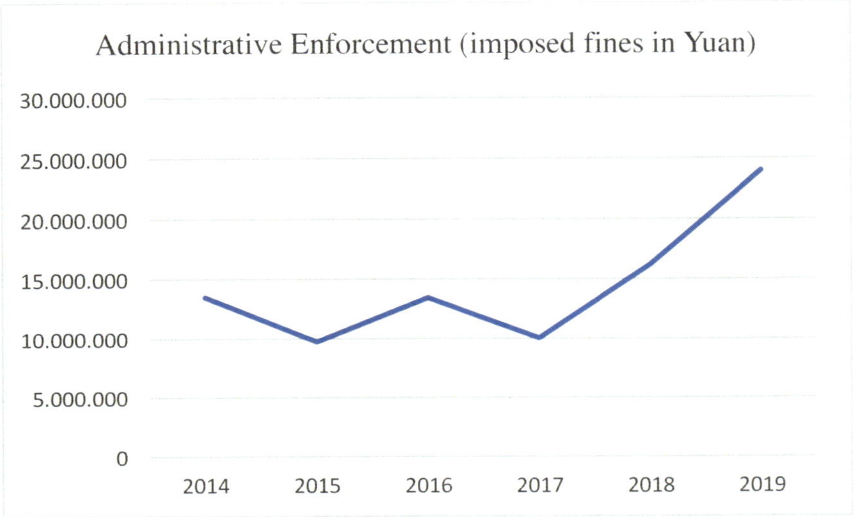

Here, it can be seen that the fines imposed in 2019 were the highest at a value of 23,995,277 Yuan compared to previous years, although the number of the seized copied was the lowest in 2019.

bb) Judicial Track

The SPC publishes statistics of intellectual property cases for every year.

[824] NCAC "Statistics on National Copyright Law Enforcement in 2014" (30 October 2015); NCAC "National Copyright Enforcement Status in 2015" (18 January 2017); NCAC "2016 National Copyright Enforcement Table" (11 May 2018); NCAC "Statistics Related to Copyright Enforcement in 2017" (10 October 2018); NCAC "Statistics on National Copyright Enforcement in 2018" (14 January 2020); NCAC "Statistics on National Copyright Enforcement in 2019" (29 January 2021).

The first diagram shows the development of first instance civil copyright cases, administrative copyright cases and criminal copyright cases brought before Chinese courts in the years from 2014 to 2019:[825]

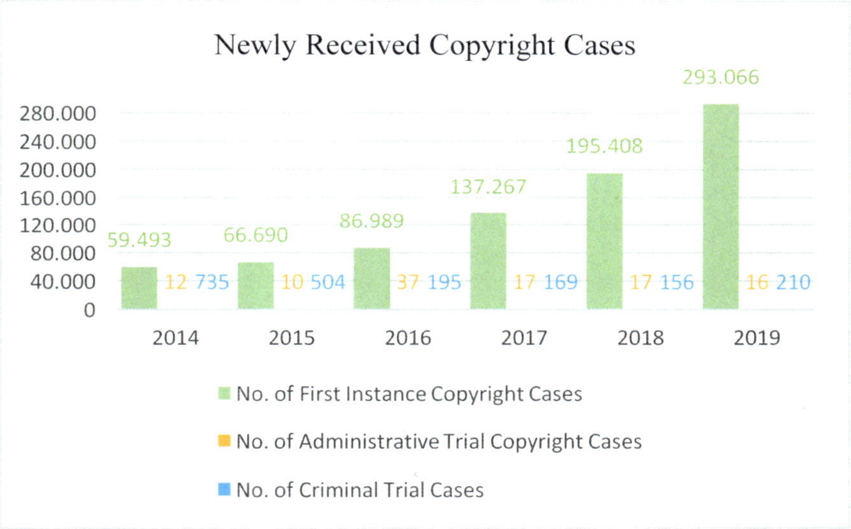

As it can be seen in the diagram, the total number of newly received civil and administrative cases has steadily increased during the last years – up 12.09 % from 2014 to 2015, up 30.47 % from 2015 to 2016 and up 57.75 %

[825] The Supreme People's Court of The People's Republic of China "The status of judicial protection of intellectual property in Chinese courts (2014)" (20 April 2015); The Supreme People's Court of The People's Republic of China (April 2016) "The status of judicial protection of intellectual property in Chinese courts (2015)" (14 December 2018); The Supreme People's Court of The People's Republic of China "The status of judicial protection of intellectual property in Chinese courts (2016)" (27 April 2017); The Supreme People's Court of The People's Republic of China "The status of judicial protection of intellectual property in Chinese courts (2017)" (19 December 2018); The Supreme People's Court of The People's Republic of China "The status of judicial protection of intellectual property in Chinese courts (2018)" (19 April 2019); The Supreme People's Court of The People's Republic of China "Intellectual Property Protection by Chinese Courts in 2019" (21 April 2020).

from 2016 to 2017, another 42.35 % up from 2017 to 2018 and a further 49.97 % from 2018 to 2019.

Additionally, the total number of concluded cases at first instance in the civil courts is interesting to see. Unfortunately, the publication of the SPC does not distinguish between the different types of intellectual property rights with these numbers so that the following diagram shows the IP cases concluded that have been concluded in the first instance in the years 2014 until 2019; for the years 2014 to 2016 the numbers published by the SPC also included the number of foreign-related cases:[826]

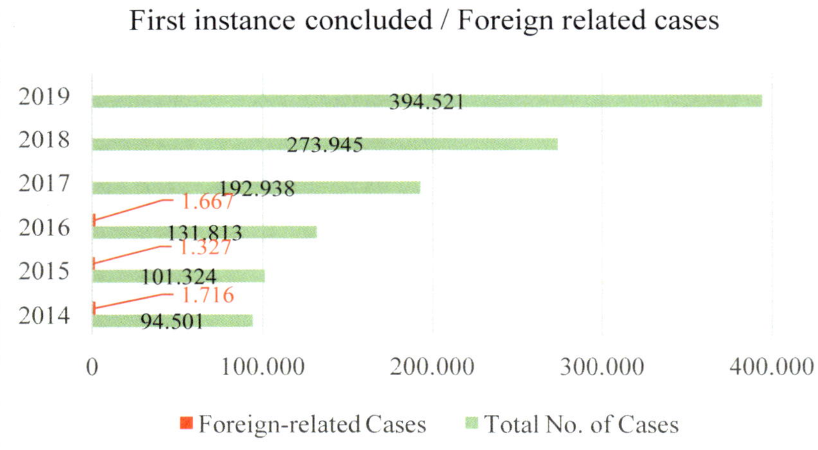

[826] The Supreme People's Court of The People's Republic of China "The status of judicial protection of intellectual property in Chinese courts (2014)" (20 April 2015); The Supreme People's Court of The People's Republic of China (April 2016) "The status of judicial protection of intellectual property in Chinese courts (2015)" (14 December 2018); The Supreme People's Court of The People's Republic of China "The status of judicial protection of intellectual property in Chinese courts (2016)" (27 April 2017); The Supreme People's Court of The People's Republic of China "The status of judicial protection of intellectual property in Chinese courts (2017)" (19 December 2018); The Supreme People's Court of The People's Republic of China "The status of judicial protection of intellectual property in Chinese courts (2018)" (19 April 2019); The Supreme People's Court of The People's Republic of China "Intellectual Property Protection by Chinese Courts in 2019" (21 April 2020).

As it can be seen, the number of cases concluded at first instance has been steadily increasing from 2014 to 2019, namely by 417%.

For the years from 2014 to 2016, the diagram shows that the foreign-related IP cases only represent a fraction of the total concluded civil IP cases – namely 1.8 % of all concluded cases in 2014, only 1.3 % of all concluded cases in 2015, even lower in 2016 with only 1.26 % of all concluded cases. Unfortunately, these numbers are not published for the following years so that the development cannot be further tracked.

However, it is reported in the press in January 2020 that for example the IP Court in Beijing has in total concluded 20.7% of foreign-related case since its establishment in 2014.[827] This is a very promising development.

cc) Evaluation and Criticism

With reference to the administrative track, the development does not look very promising because of the decreasing number of seized copies, especially when taking into account that the copyright registrations per year are vastly increasing over the years. It is hard to believe that the infringing actions have actually decreased.

However, positive to note is that the amount of the fines is actually increasing and in 2018, is the highest amount compared to the lowest number of seized copies. In return, this leads to the assumption that the individual penalties have been increased which is a good sign because higher penalties will hopefully lead to greater deterrence.

In contrast to the administrative track, the cases in the Chinese courts have been constantly increasing over the years which is very positive.

When comparing the development of cases in the administrative track and the judicial track it could be argued that more copyright holders choose the

[827] DEQI Intellectual Property Law Corporation, "Beijing Intellectual Property Court: Foreign-related Intellectual Property Cases Increasing Year by Year", 20 January 2020 (https://www.lexology.com/library/detail.aspx?g=62f25070-8679-4b84-bf67-202b3109e949&utm_source=Lexology+Daily+Newsfeed&utm_medium=HTML+email+-+Body+-+General+section&utm_campaign=Lexology+subscriber+daily+feed&utm_content=Lexology+Daily+Newsfeed+2020-01-22&utm_term=, accessed: 6 March 2021).

judicial track – maybe because damage compensation can be claimed in court.

However, the numbers of cases need to be read carefully. The fact that the number of copyright cases in Court has increased significantly does not necessarily mean that the copyright protection has improved as well.[828]

In order to get a full picture, it would be necessary to evaluate the actual number of infringements taking place in China to see whether enforcement has improved because if the number of infringement cases rose as steadily as the number of cases brought to administrative authorities/court, there is, in fact, no better protection taking place.[829] However, such number is unknown so that no relative comparison of the numbers can be made.

IV. Summary

From 1990 until now, the Chinese Copyright Law and the respective regulations and interpretations have evolved significantly and the recognition as well as the protection of copyright works have been majorly improved. The steady update of the law and the regulations over the last decades show that China has understood the importance of a strong copyright legislation, in particular, to stay attractive to foreign investors and provide the Chinese people with incentives to create copyright material. However, due to the vast amount of regulations it has become quite difficult to understand/interpret the law correctly. A more structured and unified law would lead to improved transparency and better understanding of the law for everyone.

Further, having good laws in the "books", does not necessarily mean that these will be effectively enforced. As it has been shown, China is still lacking adequate enforcement of the law and due to the vast amount of regulations it is not very transparent for the right holders. The introduction of specialized IP courts and tribunals in the economically relevant regions has been a very important step sending a signal to the world that China is slowly building a stronger intellectual property regime.

---

[828] Rosen, "China vs. United States: A Cosmopolitan Copyright Comparison" *J. Technol. Law Policy* 15, Fall 2014 (2014), 13.
[829] Ibid.

CHAPTER 4 – THE ONGOING REFORM OF THE COPYRIGHT LAW OF THE PEOPLE'S REPUBLIC OF CHINA

This chapter aims at explaining the ongoing reform of the Chinese Copyright Law by chronologically depicting the process of the reform as well as showing the influences of various organizations and countries in shaping the reformed legislation.

I. Legislation Process in China – Short Overview

The legislation process for national laws in China can be divided into five phases:

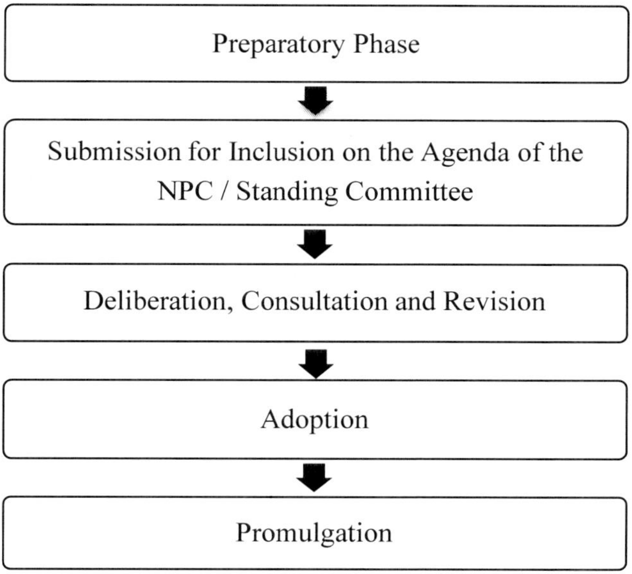

The preparatory phase is the phase prior to the formal legislative process in which the law is drafted. Furthermore, according to Article 5 Legislation Law, the public needs to be able to participate in the legislative activities for example by publishing the drafted law and requesting public comments; this requirement is also stipulated in Article 37 Legislation Law regarding the legislative procedures for the Standing Committee.[830]

[830] *Legislation Law PRC* (2000/2015 version).

The following may introduce a bill to the NPC or the Standing Committee:

- Presidium of the NPC (to NPC)[831],
- Chairmen's Meeting (to Standing Committee)[832],
- Standing Committee (to NPC)[833],
- State Council, Central Military Commission, Supreme People's Court, Supreme People's Procuratorate and specialized committees of the NPC (to NPC or Standing Committee – Presidium/Chairmen's Meeting decides whether bill is put on the NPC's agenda)[834],
- a delegation or a group of thirty or more co-signing deputies (to NPC – Presidium decides whether bill is put on the NPC's agenda)[835] or
- a group of ten or more co-signing members of the Standing Committee (to NPC or Standing Committee) delegation or group of thirty or more co-signing deputies[836].

Once a bill has been brought onto the agenda of the NPC or the Standing Committee, the proposer of the new bill provides an explanation; following that, deliberation shall be conducted in several sessions in which the bill shall be revised as necessary.[837]

Following successful deliberation and revision, the law will be adopted by a simple majority and then signed and issued by an order of the President and signed by the President.[838]

[831] Article 14 paragraph 1 ibid.
[832] Article 26 paragraph 1 ibid.
[833] Article 14 paragraph 2 ibid.
[834] Article 14 paragraph 2 and Article 26 paragraph 2 ibid.
[835] Article 15 ibid.
[836] Article 27 ibid.
[837] Articles 17-23 (for NPC) and Articles 28-40 (for Standing Committee) ibid.
[838] Article 25 and 41 (for adoption) and Article 25 and 44 (for promulgation) ibid.

II. Developing Process

First, the whole developing process and the introduction of the first drafts are discussed.

1. First Draft of the NCAC – 2012

The NCAC published a first draft on its website to gather various public opinions on 31 March 2012.[839] The draft tried to comprise the copyright provisions from various regulations into one document and was approximately one third longer in volume than the current 2010 Chinese Copyright Law. It increased the number of articles from 61 to 88 and from six chapters to eight chapters.

a) Explanation by the NCAC regarding the First Draft

In its explanation, the NCAC pointed out that the previous two revisions of the Chinese Copyright Law in 2001 and 2010 were only minimum amendments in order to access the WTO and to satisfy the findings of the Sino-US copyright dispute of 2009.[840] The NCAC called the former changes being "passive and partial" that did not lead to an "active and complete" amendment of the legislation.[841] Furthermore, it emphasized that an improved legislation would lead to an increase of innovation and hence, stimulate the development and flourishing of the Socialist culture.[842] The NCAC also stated that it is important to find a good balance between protecting the individual and the creation and guaranteeing the use and dissemination of the work.[843] The NCAC had established two groups – the Copyright Law Revision Leading Small Group and the Copyright Law Re-

---

[839] *Copyright Law of the People's Republic of China "First Revision Draft"* (March 2012 - posted on 31 March 2012, updated on 8 April 2012), National Copyright Administration of China (provided by China Copyright and Media).

[840] *"A Brief Explanation concerning the 'Copyright Law of the People's Republic of China' (Revision Draft)"* (March 2012 - posted on 31 March 2012, updated on 4 October 2012), National Copyright Administration of China (provided by China Copyright and Media). at "I. The Basic Situation of our Country's Copyright Law".

[841] Ibid. at "I. The Basic Situation of our Country's Copyright Law".

[842] Ibid. at "II. The Necessity of Revising the Copyright Law".

[843] Ibid. at "III. The Basic Line of Thought for Copyright Law Revision".

vision Work Expert Committee – that were responsible for bringing forward the revision.[844] Such groups had been formed with people from various fields such as education, culture, technology industry, from the Supreme Court and the like.[845] Concerning the content of the revision, the groups defined a method on how to approach a revision of the law and figured out four important points that should be considered:

- The legislation should be comprised of all basic principles including the principles that are laid down in the regulations, namely the Implementing Regulations, the Computer Software Protection Regulation and the Regulations on the Protection of Right of Dissemination via Information Network;
- The legislation needs to be fully compliant with the international treaties, especially by adding provisions on author's and performer's rental rights, technological protection measures and rights management information;
- The legislation needs to reflect the judicial interpretations that have been proven to be efficient;
- The legislation needs to be better applicable in the business world.[846]

b) Public Opinion

Since the first draft had been long delayed, the interest for it was huge at the time of publication. In the following, the opinion of the bloggers and representatives of the music industry as well as the comments of the American Bar Association are described in some detail.

aa) Blogger and Music Producers

Article 47 and 48 of the draft were of particular interest to bloggers and music producers.[847] Article 47 stipulated that a producer can make recordings of musical works without authorization of the owner if the music had

---

[844] Ibid. at "IV. The Basic Process of Copyright Law Revision".
[845] Ibid. at "IV. The Basic Process of Copyright Law Revision".
[846] Ibid. at "V. The Main Method and Content of Copyright Law Revision".
[847] Lu Na, "New copyright law amendment under fire", 6 April 2012 (http://www.china.org.cn/arts/2012-04/06/content_25077760.htm, accessed: 6 March 2021).

been published for three months or longer and if the requirements of Article 48 have been met.[848] Article 48 set out that individuals or corporations who want to make use of certain works have to contact the NCAC, specify the work to be used (including information on author and source) and submit a usage fee within one month of use to the copyright collective administration organization which will then be transferred to the relevant parties.[849]

These two provisions led to major outrage between famous artists who feared that such regulations would have a negative impact on original music producers, especially because the suggested time frame was set very low.[850] A representative from the music industry[851] feared that as a consequence of such provisions, record companies would stop investing in advertisement which will eventually be detrimental to producers of original content.[852] Moreover, copyright in such songs will be less desired because record companies will not invest in a copyright if the monopolistic control is lost so quickly.[853] Furthermore, the stipulations in Article 48 would strengthen the Music Copyright Society of China and harm the record companies; an artist could be deprived of his/her earnings if the Society abuses its monopolistic position.[854]

bb) Comments of the American Bar Association from 8 June 2012

The Section of Intellectual Property Law and the Section of International Law of the American Bar Association (ABA)[855] gave a joint statement on the draft concerning the revision of the Chinese Copyright Law that was made available to the public with a request for comments on 31 March 2012 by the National Copyright Administration of China.

---

848 Ibid.
849 Ibid.
850 Ibid.
851 Yaping Zhou, CEO of Beijing New Run Entertainment Co., Ltd (6 April 2012).
852 Na, "New copyright law amendment under fire", 6 April 2012 (http://www.china.org.cn/arts/2012-04/06/content_25077760.htm, accessed: 6 March 2021).
853 Ibid.
854 Ibid.
855 In the following abbreviated as “The ABA”.

(1) Executive Summary

The ABA's executive summary started off by rewarding the efforts of the NCAC to draft a new copyright legislation, that would provide an increase in legal certainty for copyright holders as well as for users of copyright protected works.[856] However, the ABA also critically discussed the first draft and summarized some of the major points in the executive summary before going into more detail in respect to specific articles in its general comments.[857]

The ABA identified the need to provide more definitions in the new legislation (e.g. with regard to orphan works) and would have welcomed it, if the Chinese legislation would use international accepted terms (e.g. with regard to related rights).[858]

Furthermore, the ABA advised the legislators to create a law that can keep up with the vast technological development by using a language that covers the existing technologies but that leaves enough room for future technologies (e.g. with regard to new broadcasting technologies in contrast to traditional television and radio).[859] The ABA was of the opinion that the draft was missing some more detail on the exceptions to copyrights so that loopholes for commercial use will be prevented.[860] In relation to the transfer of copyright and the responsibilities of service providers, the ABA saw the need for more explanation, so that – in relation to transfers – parties know exactly which clauses to include and if omission of certain clauses is possible and – in relation to service providers – the providers exactly know what they have to do in the event of infringing activities of their users and how such responsibilities will be enforced.[861] Also, clarifications were needed in relation to computer programs.[862]

---

[856] American Bar Association "Joint Comments of the American Bar Association Section of Intellectual Property Law and Section of International Law on the Draft Amendments to China's Copyright Law " (8 June 2012), 2.
[857] Ibid.
[858] Ibid.
[859] Ibid.
[860] Ibid.
[861] Ibid.
[862] Ibid.

In other areas, the ABA saw the need for the introduction of certain safeguards to decrease potential abuse (i.e. in the area of collective management) and in general, to revise the provision on damages.[863]

In summary, it can be said that the ABA majorly criticized the lack of definition and clarification in some of the provisions and urged the NCAC to improve in these fields so that right holders and users of works are better protected.

(2) General Comments to the Draft

Following the executive summary, the ABA closely explained specific articles where it feared misinterpretation or saw the need for a general revision. The most substantive recommendations are briefly summarized in the following:

"Works" – Article 3 of the Copyright Draft
The ABA feared that the protection scope is hard to define if the law does not clarify that the fixation of a work must have some form of persistence and cannot only be transitory; further to that, it proposed that the work terms should be better defined.[864]

"Related Rights" – Article 5 of the Copyright Draft
Article 5 was very unclear and leads to confusion. Especially international right holders who want to conduct business in China could not depict which laws and regulation are superior to the Chinese Copyright Law. This provision needed to be further clarified and the process of reviewing and supervising works by the State needed to be more transparent as well as some kind of a more specific remedy against State decisions should be introduced.[865]

"Attribution and Integrity Rights" – Article 26 of the Copyright Draft
Concerning the term of protection, the first draft would have granted an eternal right. The ABA suggested that the right of integrity should not be inheritable to avoid complications because an eternal right would greatly affect the possibilities of using a work in the future.[866]

[863] Ibid.
[864] Ibid., 3.
[865] Ibid., 4.
[866] Ibid., 8.

"Duration of Copyright" – Article 27 of the Copyright Draft

The Berne Convention requires a minimum duration of copyright works of natural persons of the life of the author plus fifty years after the death; this length was originally decided upon with the intention of providing protection for the following two generations of the author.[867] Since the lifespan of humans has internationally risen, many countries including the U.S. and Germany have raised the protection to the life of the author plus seventy years.[868] In order to prevent confusion between the countries and enhance harmonisation it would be wise for China to raise the duration of protection as well.[869]

Article 27 also dealt with joint works and the proposed regulation. In the opinion of the ABA, it faced some problems because of the separation of a work in respective portions of the co-authors.[870] Especially in the music sector, where many people work on one piece, it could be harmful to a work because parts of it would lose protection earlier than others.[871] In the U.S. and the EU such joint works are called unitary joint works and the protection is granted based on the death of the last surviving author.[872]

A similar problem occurs when looking at the term of protection of audiovisual works, as China set the protection to a maximum of fifty years either starting from the day of publication or creation. Both the U.S. and the EU having a much higher protection term (from 70-120 years) – China should align to international standards in order to prevent confusion.[873]

"Publishers" – Article 29 and 30 of the Copyright Draft

The ABA was of the opinion that Article 29 should clarify the distribution term including electronic distribution as well as concerning the page format design to make sure that not only the single page formats are protected under the law but also the whole format of the book.[874] The same needed to be included in Article 30 dealing with the publisher's rights and it should

867 Ibid.
868 Ibid.
869 Ibid.
870 Ibid., 9.
871 Ibid.
872 Ibid.
873 Ibid., 10.
874 Ibid., 11.

be laid out that also a page design/book design under the Berne Convention has to be protected for at least fifty years after the author's death if it qualifies as a creative work.[875]

"Radio and Television Stations"- Article 37 of the Copyright Draft
In Article 37, the ABA would have welcomed an update of the definition of radio and television programs to include webcasts, because nowadays, many works are first broadcasted on the web via web broadcasters and podcasters.[876]

"Limitations on Rights" – Article 40 of the Copyright Draft
The ABA highly recommended emphasizing in the Copyright Law that certain exceptions to copyright are only for personal or non-profit use.[877] Furthermore, the provisions need to be more carefully drafted with regard to digitizing analogue works in order to prevent downstream infringement.[878] The exception in Article 40 (11) (translation into a minority language) may limit the authors rights in cases where the author intends to publish the work in the minority language himself/herself, so that the limitation should only be applicable in cases where the author has no own intention.[879]

"Computer Programs" – Article 41 of the Copyright Draft
Concerning the use of computer programs in Article 41, it should be clarified, that these rules only apply if the license agreement does not include these issues because the parties should be given contractual autonomy.[880] In relation to the creation of a back-up copy, it should be limited to one copy in order to prevent abuse.[881]

"The Exercise of Rights" – Articles 50-55 of the Copyright Draft
Concerning the licensing of copyright, it needed to be clarified whether the license agreements need to include all the terms set forth in Article 50 in order to be enforceable and what the consequences are if one of the terms

[875] Ibid.
[876] Ibid., 14.
[877] Ibid., 14-15.
[878] Ibid.
[879] Ibid., 15.
[880] Ibid., 15-16.
[881] Ibid., 16.

is left out – if the requirement is as strict as it seems it is very impractical because an invalid contract (with clauses missing) could result in problems concerning the control and use of licenses.[882] Concerning the republication of a book, it should be clarified that the author has the right to terminate the contract and not the copyright holder because the copyright can be assigned to the publisher, also the term should not be fixed.[883] It should rather include a regulation similar to the one in the U.S. and Europe that the author can set a deadline when a work is out of print.[884] Similar to the license agreement in Article 50, the stipulation in Article 55 concerning transferring rights should also be more flexible in order to achieve better enforceable contracts.[885]

"Collective Copyright Management" – Articles 59-63 of the Copyright Draft

Collective Copyright Management was dealt with in Articles 59-63. When establishing this system, it should be ensured that the right holders enjoy a reasonable remuneration, licenses are not exceeded and downstream infringement is prohibited.[886] Also, the system of Collective Copyright Organizations should be carefully planned to avoid corruption and right holders should get an audit right against CMOs.[887]

"Technological Protection/Rights Management Information" – Article 65-67 of the Copyright Draft

With regard to Articles 65 and 66, the ABA criticised that the draft contained the subjective element "wilfully" in connection with the circumvention of technical measures because this places a huge burden on the injured party to prove wilful conduct; the ABA referred to the WIPO Treaties that do not include such a strict requirement.[888] Furthermore, the exceptions to such prohibition should be clearly stated and the exceptions in Article 67

[882] Ibid., 17.
[883] Ibid., 18.
[884] Ibid.
[885] Ibid.
[886] Ibid., 19-20.
[887] Ibid.
[888] Ibid., 21-22.

should only be given to non-profit teaching and research that is non-commercial.[889]

"Computer Programs" – Article 71 of the Draft
Article 71 should be deleted completely because it discriminates creators and right holders of computer programs since the proof of knowledge concerning users of computer program reproductions is very difficult; also, the provision in the Draft is contrary to the provisions set out in TRIPS and other international copyright treaties.[890]

(3) Summary

The ABA has made many valid points with regard to the revision of the Chinese Copyright Law. It is shown in the following whether the legislators have taken (some of) these comments into account when revising the first draft.

2. Second Draft of the NCAC – 2012

The second draft for the revision of the Copyright Law was published by the NCAC in May 2012 and also open for public comments.[891]

a) Explanation by the NCAC regarding the Second Draft

Again, the NCAC published an explanation along with the second revision draft of the Copyright Law. The first part of the explanation dealt with the opinion seeking process of the first draft by explaining that – additionally to the draft being publicly available online – letters were sent to relevant departments as well as State Council ministries and commissions to gather opinions.[892] Statistics have shown that the NCAC had received more than

---

[889] Ibid.
[890] Ibid., 26.
[891] *Copyright Law of the People's Republic of China "Second Revision Draft"* (July 2012 - posted on 7 July 2012, updated on 18 June 2014), National Copyright Administration of China (provided by China Copyright and Media).
[892] *"A Brief Explanation concerning the Revision and Perfection of the 'Copyright Law of the People's Republic of China' (Second Revision Draft)"* (July 2012 - posted on 7 July 2012, updated on 5 October 2012), National Copyright Administration of China (provided by China Copyright and Media). at "I. The Basic Situation of the Opinion-seeking Draft".

1,600 letters from various people, departments of Chinese or foreign governments, associations and the like by 31 May 2012.[893] Following the opinion-seeking process that formally ended on 30 April 2012, the NCAC called in the "legislative revision expert committee" as well as the legislative and judicial departments for a third expert meeting that dealt with the various opinions and formed a new revision draft.[894] The revision was quite substantive as three articles were deleted, three were added and 27 articles were modified in terms of content.[895]

b) Public Opinion

It could be seen in the second draft that the legislators took the comments of the public into account and amended some parts of the law accordingly. For example, the "droit de suite" that was introduced in the first draft (Article 11 second paragraph (13) first draft) has been weakened to a right to remuneration (see Article 12 second draft) in the case the original work is transferred for the first time.

A detailed description of all the modifications made is omitted because comments on the second draft led to the formulation of the third draft that is discussed later on.

3. Influence of the Beijing Treaty

As mentioned previously, the Beijing Treaty was adopted in June 2012 which is the first international treaty in the area of intellectual property law that has been established in China. In the following, it is outlined which parts of the Chinese Copyright Law need to be amended to adhere to the Beijing Treaty provisions and what has already been included in the revision drafts:

a) The Scope of Performance Works

The concept of performance works is not clearly defined in the Chinese Copyright Law. In Article 5 (6) Implementing Regulations it is stipulated

---

[893] Ibid. at "I. The Basic Situation of the Opinion-seeking Draft".
[894] Ibid. at "I. The Basic Situation of the Opinion-seeking Draft".
[895] Ibid. at "II. The Main Content of this Revision and Perfection".

that performers are actors, performance units or other persons who perform literary or artistic works.[896]

This is a substantial difference to the Beijing Treaty because this specifically includes the performances of works of folklore in Article 2 (a) of the Treaty.[897] Since China has many resources in this field, the law needs to be amended to include folklore to achieve greater protection and by that enhancing prosperity and development of folklore.[898]

This has already been taken into account when formulating the first draft of the new Copyright Law as Article 31 included "*folk literature and art works*"[899]. The current version in the third draft now reads

> "*Performers as named in this law, refers to natural persons performing literary or artistic work, or folk literature and art expressions through declamatory, singing, instrumental performance or other methods.*"[900]

Additionally, it is interesting to note that in contrast to the 2010 Copyright Law and the first draft of the ongoing revision, performers are only defined as "*natural persons*". Previously, also performing groups/work units were included in the definition. Hence, it can be seen that the Chinese legislators have already applied the Beijing Treaty provisions to the draft text.

---

[896] *Regulations for the Implementation of the Copyright Law of the People's Republic of China* (2013 - issued 2 August 2002, effective 15 September 2002, amended 8 January 2011, amended 30 January 2013, effective 1 March 2013), State Council of the People's Republic of China.
[897] Also see Liu and Huang, "On the Beijing Treaty on Audivisual Performances and the Upgrading of China's Copyright Law (English Title)" *Journal of Shaoyang University - Social Science Edition* 3, 4 (2014), 21.
[898] Also see ibid., 21-22.
[899] *Copyright Law of the People's Republic of China "First Revision Draft"* (March 2012 - posted on 31 March 2012, updated on 8 April 2012), National Copyright Administration of China.
[900] Article 33 *Copyright Law of the People's Republic of China "Third Revision Draft, Submission Version"* (June 2014 - posted on 6 June 2014, updated on 18 June 2014), National Copyright Administration of China (provided by China Copyright and Media).

b) The Right to Rent

The 2010 Chinese Copyright Law only specifies the rental rights of copyright holders without regulating rental rights concerning the neighbouring rights of performers.[901] The right of rental is stipulated in Article 9 (1) of the Beijing Treaty and states that performers

> *"shall enjoy the exclusive right of authorizing the commercial rental to the public (...) fixed in audiovisual fixations (...), even after distribution of them by, or pursuant to, authorization by the performer".*[902]

The legislators have already included a right of rental for performers in the first draft and Article 34 (5) of the current third draft now reads

> *"permitting other persons to reproduce, distribute or* ***rent*** *records of their performances or reproductions of the said records".*[903]

Again, this inclusion of a rental right for performers shows that the legislator is already trying to include the provisions of the Beijing Treaty.

c) The Right to Broadcast

In Article 11 of the Beijing Treaty, it is stipulated "*performers shall enjoy the exclusive right of authorizing the broadcasting and communication to the public of their performances fixed in audiovisual fixations.*"[904] Article 11 (2) and (3) of the Treaty provide certain possibilities of exemption to that provision.

[901] Liu and Huang, "On the Beijing Treaty on Audivisual Performances and the Upgrading of China's Copyright Law (English Title)" *Journal of Shaoyang University - Social Science Edition* 3, 4 (2014), 22.
[902] Article 9 (1) *Beijing Treaty* (2012), TRT/BEIJING/001.
[903] Article 34 (5) *Copyright Law of the People's Republic of China "Third Revision Draft, Submission Version"* (June 2014 - posted on 6 June 2014, updated on 18 June 2014), National Copyright Administration of China.
[904] Article 11 (1) *Beijing Treaty* (2012), TRT/BEIJING/001.

China has no mechanism for the collective management of performers and no mechanism for the negotiation of the pay standard with television stations in place.[905] To discuss every license and its conditions individually will impose a huge burden on the radio and television stations; also, the financial resources of stations are very limited so that it will be a huge financial burden for them to pay rewards.[906]

Because of that situation in China, it is not likely that China will include the right to broadcast including remuneration because China has also exempted from the almost identical Article 15 of the WPPT.[907]

d) The Transfer of Rights

The provision regarding the transfer of performer's rights is one of the main aims of the Beijing Treaty and leaves a lot of flexibilities for the countries to implement it.[908] The current 2010 Chinese Copyright Law does not contain any special provisions on the transfer of rights of performers, but from judicial practice it can be seen that the transfer of rights in film and television works is granted to the producer (filmmaker), whereas the performance rights in a video are granted to the performer himself/herself.[909]

The lack of a clear legal system for the transfer of performer rights is not helpful in reducing the incurring transaction costs and will impede the dissemination of audiovisual products.[910]

Prior to the Treaty's conclusion, Article 33 of the first revision draft stipulated that the performer's rights are subject to agreements in writing and can either belong to the producers (normal case) or the performers.[911] However, after the conclusion of the Treaty, Article 36 of the second revision

---

[905] Liu and Huang, "On the Beijing Treaty on Audivisual Performances and the Upgrading of China's Copyright Law (English Title)" *Journal of Shaoyang University - Social Science Edition* 3, 4 (2014), 22.
[906] Ibid.
[907] Ibid.
[908] Ibid.
[909] Ibid.
[910] Ibid.
[911] Article 31 *Copyright Law of the People's Republic of China "First Revision Draft"* (March 2012 - posted on 31 March 2012, updated on 8 April 2012), National Copyright Administration of China; Liu and Huang, "On the Beijing

draft stipulated that the performer's rights are vested in the producer. This amendment to the revision draft of the copyright law shows that China is moved from the protection of performers to the protection of producers, hence from the pursuit of equity to the pursuit of efficiency.[912] The better protection of producers might lead to dissatisfaction of the performers and might hinder the enthusiasm and the creativity of audiovisual performers.[913]

In the third draft, the legislator had again amended the provision on the rights enjoyed by the producer/performer. Article 37 of the third draft stated that the property rights according to Article 34 (5) and (6) need to be agreed upon between the parties and in absence of an agreement or lack of clarity these economic rights are enjoyed by the producer whereas the performer enjoys the right to sign a name and a share in the profits.

This weakening of the provision shows that the legislator has taken note of the problems that could occur when the rights of the producers are strengthened too severely which could deter performers from creating new performances.

e) Summary

Summarizing, it can be said that the legislators have already started to include the provisions adopted in the Beijing Treaty into the draft copyright legislation. The adaptation to the internationally agreed provisions within the ongoing legislation process is a promising sign that the importance of intellectual property legislation and hopefully also the enforcement will be increasing in China to keep the Chinese market attractive.

Treaty on Audivisual Performances and the Upgrading of China's Copyright Law (English Title)" *Journal of Shaoyang University - Social Science Edition* 3, 4 (2014), 22.

912 Liu and Huang, "On the Beijing Treaty on Audivisual Performances and the Upgrading of China's Copyright Law (English Title)" *Journal of Shaoyang University - Social Science Edition* 3, 4 (2014), 22.

913 Ibid.

4. Third Draft by the State Council – 2014

The draft of the NCAC was submitted to the State Council Legal Affairs (SCLAO) Office for further review.[914] The SCLAO published the third draft of the law in June 2014 for public comment before it should be sent to the National People's Congress for further reading.[915]

a) Explanation by the State Council Legal Affairs Office regarding the Third Draft (Submission Version)

The State Council's explanation started off with explaining the general need to revise the Chinese Copyright Law.[916] In summary, the State Council was of the opinion that the current law does not reflect the substantive changes that have taken place in China's economy as well as in the Chinese society during the last decades.[917] The State Council saw an "urgent need" to reform the copyright legislation in order to keep up with the technological progress, the flourishing of the Chinese culture and the general economic development.[918]

At the end of the explanation, the State Council emphasized that this submission draft had been created in cooperation with the public as well as all relevant departments by opening the previous two drafts to the public for comment that were used by the NCAC to amend and improve the first draft; the NCAC also participated in and organized several conferences that aimed at analysing and applying the public opinion.[919]

---

[914] China IPR, "State Council Legislative Affairs Office Releases NCA Draft of Copyright Law for Public Comment", 9 June 2014 (https://chinaipr.com/2014/06/09/state-council-legislative-affairs-office-releases-nca-draft-of-copyright-law-for-public-comment/, accessed: 6 March 2021).

[915] *Copyright Law of the People's Republic of China "Third Revision Draft, Submission Version"* (June 2014 - posted on 6 June 2014, updated on 18 June 2014), National Copyright Administration of China.

[916] *"Explanation of the 'Copyright Law of the People's Republic of China' (Submission Version of the Revision Draft)"* (June 2014 - posted on 18 June 2014), State Council Legal Affairs Office (provided by China Copyright and Media). at "Concerning the Necessity of the Revision".

[917] Ibid. at "Concerning the Necessity of the Revision".

[918] Ibid. at "Concerning the Necessity of the Revision".

[919] Ibid. at "III. Concerning the Situation of Opinion Solicitation".

The State Council defined four objectives for the improvement of the law which is further explained in the following.

aa) "Encouraging Creation, Integrating the Rights System"

In order for the system to work efficiently the terms must be best defined to prevent misinterpretation.[920] The revision draft included the definition of work terms that have previously been defined in the Implementing Regulations and restructured the content of the rights to improve applicability.[921] In relation to ownership, the new draft places an emphasis on the contractual autonomy by giving priority to agreements between the parties in some situations.[922] Furthermore, the term of protection and the limitations to copyright were adjusted to meet international standards.[923]

bb) "Stimulating Use, Adjusting, Authorization Mechanisms and Market Transaction Rules"

The State Council pointed out that major focus of the revision is the balancing of giving enough respect to the creators and providing sufficient ways for users to lawfully use the works.[924] Therefore, copyright registrations systems had been introduced: on one hand, for owners to prove ownership more easily and on the other hand, in relation with copyright transfers to provide more security to the transfer parties.[925]

Furthermore, the rules on statutory licensing had been amended to match related international treaties and to include the opinions that have been collected in the drafting process.[926] The revision draft also included provisions

---

[920] Ibid. at "III. Concerning the Situation of Opinion Solicitation, (1) Encouraging Creation, Integrating the Rights System, 1.".
[921] Ibid. at "III. Concerning the Situation of Opinion Solicitation, (1) Encouraging Creation, Integrating the Rights System, 2.".
[922] Ibid. at "III. Concerning the Situation of Opinion Solicitation, (1) Encouraging Creation, Integrating the Rights System, 3.".
[923] Ibid. at "III. Concerning the Situation of Opinion Solicitation, (1) Encouraging Creation, Integrating the Rights System, 4.-5.".
[924] Ibid. at "III. Concerning the Situation of Opinion Solicitation, (2) Stimulating, Adjusting Authorization Mechanisms and Market Transaction Rules".
[925] Ibid. at "III. Concerning the Situation of Opinion Solicitation, (2) Stimulating, Adjusting Authorization Mechanisms and Market Transaction Rules, 1.-2.".
[926] Ibid. at "III. Concerning the Situation of Opinion Solicitation, (2) Stimulating, Adjusting Authorization Mechanisms and Market Transaction Rules, 3.".

simplifying the use of work in the digital network in cases of unknown owners by providing a mechanism where users can apply to a certain body and pay a usage fee.[927] Also, the system of collective copyright management had been improved in the revision draft so that right holders have a better "support system" in handling and protecting their rights.[928]

cc) "Strengthening Protection, Perfecting Relief Measures"

The scope of civil infringement is expanded and the civil liability of network service providers has been included in the Copyright Law.[929] The revision draft also stipulated that right holders can choose between the different ways of compensation and the whole damage system has been improved (i.e. addition of punitive damages).[930] Fines had also been increased when it comes to the administrative system and a regulation concerning the mediation of administrative copyright dispute had been added.[931]

dd) "Scientific Standards, Perfecting Layout and Structure"

In this section, the State Council referred to China's other intellectual property laws as well as other foreign laws and the need of the Copyright Law to get an improved structure.[932] Therefore, some chapters were added, some names were adjusted and the order was changed in some parts to improve understanding of the law.[933] Furthermore, linkages to other laws had been clarified.[934] The State Council also informed the reader that a plan

[927] Ibid. at "III. Concerning the Situation of Opinion Solicitation, (2) Stimulating, Adjusting Authorization Mechanisms and Market Transaction Rules, 4.".
[928] Ibid. at "III. Concerning the Situation of Opinion Solicitation, (2) Stimulating, Adjusting Authorization Mechanisms and Market Transaction Rules. 5.".
[929] Ibid. at "III. Concerning the Situation of Opinion Solicitation, (3) Strengthening Protection, Perfecting Relief Measures, 1.-2.".
[930] Ibid. at "III. Concerning the Situation of Opinion Solicitation, (3) Strengthening Protection, Perfecting Relief Measures, 3.".
[931] Ibid. at "III. Concerning the Situation of Opinion Solicitation, (3) Strengthening Protection, Perfecting Relief Measures, 4.-5.".
[932] Ibid. at "III. Concerning the Situation of Opinion Solicitation, (4) Scientific standards, perfecting layout and structure".
[933] Ibid. at "III. Concerning the Situation of Opinion Solicitation, (4) Scientific standards, perfecting layout and structure, 1.-3.".
[934] Ibid. at "III. Concerning the Situation of Opinion Solicitation, (4) Scientific standards, perfecting layout and structure, 4.".

exists to abolish the Computer Software Regulations as well as the Regulations on International Copyright Treaties as they had been merged into the new revision draft and would be redundant now.[935]

ee) Comment on the State Council's Explanation

The explanation by the State Council on the 2014 revision draft clearly showed that the legislator saw the importance of improving the law. The State Council repeatedly named the alignment with international treaties or international standards in general as the reasons for certain changes to the existing copyright law. Also, by integrating existing regulations into the Copyright Law and adjusting the structure, the interpretation and applicability of the law would have been highly improved. In particular, the reference to the adherence to international standards showed that China had finally seen the need to send a strong signal that the protection of rights in China will not be different to other countries anymore.

b) The New Structure of the Law

Taking the form of the third draft published in 2014, the copyright legislation would have changed quite substantially in quantity and structure.

The third draft contained 90 articles, whereas the "old" Copyright Law only consists of 61 articles.

The 2014 draft was structured into eight chapters whereas the "old" Copyright Law only has six chapters. The structure is depicted in the following:

- **Chapter I**: General Principles
- **Chapter II**: Copyright
    - Section I: Copyright Holders and their Rights
    - Section II: Copyright Entitlement
    - Sections III: The Term of Copyright Protection
- **Chapter III**: Related Rights
    - Section I: Publishers
    - Section II: Performers
    - Section III: Audio Producers
    - Section IV: Radio Stations and Television Stations
- **Chapter IV**: The Limitation of Rights

[935] Ibid. at "III. Concerning the Situation of Opinion Solicitation, (4) Scientific standards, perfecting layout and structure, 5.".

- **Chapter V**: The Exercise of Rights
    - Section I: Copyright and Related Rights Contracts
    - Section II: Collective Copyright Management
- **Chapter VI**: Technological Protection Measures and Rights Management Information
- **Chapter VII**: The Protection of Rights
- **Chapter VIII**: Supplementary Provisions

c) Integrations of Regulations

Since one of the goals of the reform was to improve the structure of copyright law by reducing the regulations and including the major provision into one unified law, it is shown where the newly integrated provisions originate from – the legislators have tried to integrate many provisions from other legislation such as regulations for the purpose of improving the autarky of the Chinese Copyright Law. Especially, the following regulations have been integrated:

- Implementing Regulations (2013),
- Regulations on Computer Software Protection (2013),
- Regulations on the Protection of Right of Dissemination via Information Network (2013) and
- Regulations on Copyright Collective Administration (2004, amended 2013).

d) The Origin of the Provisions of the Third Draft

The following table shows each article of the third draft (first column). The middle column shows the content of each article in a simplified/shortened form making reference to the changes whereas the third column identifies the source of the provision, also showing which Article of the current 2010 Copyright Law is reflected in such.

The following abbreviations are used:

- Current Chinese Copyright Law (2010) – CRL
- Implementing Regulations – IR
- Regulations on Computer Software Protection – RCSP
- Regulations on the Protection of Right of Dissemination via Information Network – RIN
- Regulations on Copyright Collective Administration – RCCM

Article Draft	**Content (summarized) & Changes/Additions**	**Origin of the Provision / Comments**
1	Object of the Law - flourishing the economy has been added	Article 1 CRL
2	General Scope of Application - the term "Chinese citizens" is changed to "Chinese natural persons"	Article 2 CRL
3	Extended Scope - protection of page format designs, performances, audio works and radio or television programs (related rights) – mirroring the provision in Article 2	Partially Article 36/Article 26 IR New provision
4	Extended Scope - protection of works of applied art from foreigners and stateless persons under the condition that Chinese right holders are granted protection in the country of residence or nationality	New provision
5	Work Forms and Requirements - work does not only need to be fixed in some form but also requires originality ("intellectual expression") - definitions are included for all work forms (each has its own paragraph, in total 15 different works) o further work forms included: applied arts and solid works o cinematographic works are now "audiovisual works"	Article 3 CRL Article 2 IR Article 4 IR & Article 3 (1) RCSP

	- stipulated that copyright exists from date of creation and no formality is required	Partially Article 6 IR
6	<u>Related Rights and Requirements</u> - definitions included for all four related rights - stipulated that copyright exists from the date of publication/first performance/completion of productions/first transmission and no formality is required – mirroring Article 5 paragraph 2	 Article 26 IR New provision
7	<u>Exclusion of Protection</u> - no violation of Constitution - State responsible for supervision and management - inclusion of reference to related rights	Article 4 CRL
8	<u>Copyright Registration Mechanism</u> - copyright holders may register rights - registration documents are preliminary evidence for verification - fees shall be paid for registration	New provision
9	<u>Scope of Protection</u> - no protection of ideas - no protection of processes, principles, mathematical concepts, operational methods etc. - list of three categories to which the law is not applicable o term "news on current affairs" is changed to "simple factual information" and further defined	 New provision New provision Article 5 CRL

10	Rules regarding Folk Literature and Art Expression - reference to both literature and art folklore expressions is made	Partially Article 6 CRL
11	Responsibilities of State Council / local authorities - reference to related rights is included	Article 7 CRL
12	Copyright holders	Article 9 CRL
13	Copyright Scope - heading "Personal rights" included: Article 13 paragraph 1 (1)-(3) o alteration right and right of integrity are joined - heading "Property rights": Article 13 paragraph 2 (1)-(10) o right of presentation is included in the right of performance o right of adaptation includes producing audio-visual products from written, music, dramatical and other such works and right of compilation - paragraph 3 states that separate regulations are formulated for information network dissemination and right of pursuit	Partially Article 10 CRL
14	Special Right regarding Original Pieces - original pieces of fine art, photographic work or manuscripts of literary or musical works	New provision

	- if transferred for the first time, authors/heirs/legatees have the right to a share if owner sells piece through auction with added value; - separate regulations will be formulated	
15	<u>Copyright Entitlement</u> - further definition of works organized or invested in by legal persons	Article 11 CRL
16	<u>Derivative works</u> - the term "derivative works" is included for works created by adaptation, translation etc. - the use of derivative works requires both permission of copyright holder in original and in derivative work	Partially Article 12 CRL New provision
17	<u>Joint works</u> - cooperative works that cannot be divided must be used unanimously by the co-creators; no single party may obstruct the other without reason and the income generated from use must be shared - lawsuit can be raised by each co-author but compensation must be shared	Article 13 CRL Article 9 IR New provision
18	<u>Compilations</u> - the use of a compilation requires both permission of copyright holder in original and in compilation	Article 14 CRL New provision
19	<u>Audiovisual Works using Pre-existing Works</u> - movie producers using novels, music, dramatical or other works	Article 15 CRL New provision

	need to obtain permission of copyright holder	
	- copyright holders of the already existing works hold exclusive right over the use of the audiovisual works – a user must obtain permission acc. to Article 16 paragraph 2	New provision
	- division of property rights is agreed upon by the producer and the creators – if no agreement is concluded, copyright is enjoyed by the producer but creators have right to sign their name and to a share in profit	Partially Article 15 paragraph 1 CRL
	- creators can use right on their own but may not hamper regular use of the audiovisual work	Partially Article 15 paragraph 2 CRL
20	Professional Works	Article 16 CRL
	- the term "works created in the course of employment" is changed to "professional works"	
	- work needs to be created during work hours	New provision
	- copyright entitlement needs to be agreed upon by parties	New provision
	- in absence of agreement copyright is enjoyed by the employee	New provision
	o except in cases of engineering design drawings, maps, computer programs as well as works created in the course of reporting duties (newspaper, radio, television)	Partially Article 16 paragraph 2 CRL
	o but: the creator has the right to sign a name	

	- if works belongs to employee, work unit may use the work in their professional scope free of charge and exclusively for two years - if works belong to work unit, employee shall receive a reward on the basis of quantity and quality	Article 16 paragraph 1 CRL New provision
21	<u>Commissioned/Entrusted Work</u> - ownership of work needs to be agreed upon by parties - in absence of agreement, copyright is enjoyed by party accepting the entrustment and entrusting side may use work within professional scope free of charge - if no agreement on scope exists, entrusting party may use within the scope of the specific objective the work was created upon	Partially Article 17 CRL New provision New provision
22	<u>Original Piece of Fine Art</u> - ownership transfer of original piece is not a transfer of the copyright but owner of the original may display the work - right of exhibition is not infringed even if not previously published - buy-back option of artist if owner wants to destroy/substantially change the work	Article 18 CRL New provision New provision
23	<u>Inheritance of Authorship and Integrity Right</u>	Article 15 IR
24	<u>Inheritance of Right to Publish of Unpublished Works</u>	Article 17 IR
25	<u>Inheritance of Property Rights</u>	Article 19 CRL

	- term "property rights" is used (as it is now defined Article 13)	
26	<u>Inheritance in Cases of Co-Authors;</u> - term "property rights" is used (as it is now defined Article 13)	Article 14 IR
27	<u>Works of Unknown Authors</u>	Article 13 IR
28	<u>Protection Term for Authorship and Integrity Right</u>	Article 20 CRL
29	<u>Protection Term for Publication Rights and Property Rights</u> - general: lifetime of author plus fifty years - term "property rights" is used (as it is now defined Article 13) - photographic works are now included in general protection term being lifetime of author plus fifty years instead of fifty years from publication - audiovisual works are integrated in provision on works of legal entities and professional works and protected for fifty years starting from publications - regulation on applied art works added with protection term of twenty-five years - photographic works that might have already expired previously are not protected anymore although they would still be valid under the new regime - special right regarding original pieces are now included in general	Article 21 CRL New provision New provision New provision New provision New provision

	protection term being lifetime of author plus fifty years	
30	<u>Protection Term of Works of Unknown Authors</u>	Article 18 IR
	<u>Publisher's Rights</u>	
31	- definition of publishing - definition of page format design	Article 58 CRL New provision
32	- publishers have right to permit others to use page format design and protection term of page format design is ten years	Article 36 CRL
	<u>Performer's Rights</u>	
33	- definition of a performer - inclusion of folk literature and art expressions - performing through declamatory, singing, instrumental performance and other methods	Article 5 (6) IR New provision New provision
34	- list of performer rights (1)-(6) - rental right included - protection for personal rights is unlimited; protection term for economic rights is fifty years - permission of copyright holder needs to be obtained (reference to remuneration is deleted)	Article 38 CRL New provision Article 39 CRL Partially Article 38 paragraph 2 CRL
35	- duty of organizer of performance to obtain permission of the copyright holder (reference to remuneration is deleted)	Article 37 para 1 CRL
36	- definition of professional performances	New provision – mirroring Article 20 of the Draft

	- ownership to be agreed between parties - in absence ownership is enjoyed by the performers but rights of collective professional performances are enjoyed by performance work unit - units may use performance free of charge - performers shall be granted rewards	
37	- producers employing performers to produce audiovisual works shall sign written agreements and pay remuneration - property rights need to be agreed upon; in absence producer enjoys rights except for authorship right and share in profits	New provision
	<u>Rights of Audio Producers</u>	
38	- term "audio products" is used for sound and video recordings - definition of audio products	Article 5 (2), (3) IR
39	- list of rights of audio producers (1)-(4) and protection term is fifty years - anyone who is authorized to reproducing, distributing etc. shall obtain permission from copyright holder and performer (reference to remuneration is deleted)	Article 42 CRL Partially Article 42 paragraph 2 CRL
40	- provision regarding the remuneration in cases of openly broadcast-	Article 42 paragraph 2 CRL

	ing and disseminating audio products through technological equipment	
41	Rights of Radio and Television Stations - definition of radio and television programs	New provision
42	- list of rights of radio and television stations: permits others to relay, record or reproduce (new: right to reproduce is separated now) - protection term is fifty years - where persons have been permitted to use the work, performance or audio product they shall obtain permission of copyright holders, performers and producers	Partially Article 45 CRL New provision
43 (1) (2) (9) (10) (13) last sentence	Limitation of Rights – General - "self-entertainment" is deleted - clarification that cited part may not constitute main or substantial part - included that no economic benefits must be gained in any way - included that reproducing, disseminating or broadcasting is allowed unless it is reproduced in the identical manner exhibited or openly disseminated - open provision "other circumstances" - use may not influence regular use of work and harm copyright holder	Article 22 CRL New provision New provision Article 21 IR

	<u>Limitation of Rights – Computer Programs</u>	
44	- limitations for lawfully authorized users of computer programs: installing, producing back-up alterations, conducting necessary alterations and not providing third parties with devices or components used for such alterations	Article 16 RCSP
45	- use of the computer program for the purpose of research and study	Article 17 RCSP
	- provides open list "or by other means"	New provision
46	- limitations for lawfully authorized users of computer program: partial reproduction and translation for obtaining compatibility	New provision
	- the use objective of computer program compatibility may not be exceeded (may not be used to develop, produce or sell virtually similar computer programs and may not be used for any activity infringing copyright)	New provision
	<u>Limitation – Compulsory Education and Publication in Newspapers or Periodicals</u>	
47	- copying of already published works for the compilation in a text book for compulsory education (reference to nine years deleted) in accordance with Article 50	Partially Article 23 CRL
	- stipulation that only "short portions" can be copied	New provision
	- author's right to oppose in advance was deleted	

48	- reprinting or republishing works or materials that have been published in newspapers or periodicals in accordance with Article 50 - newspaper and periodical publishers enjoy exclusive right if work includes indication that reprinting and republishing is prohibited	Article 33 para 2 CRL
49	- radio and television stations may rebroadcast already published work in accordance with Article 50 but when rebroadcasting audiovisual works, the permission of the holder needs to be obtained (reference to remuneration is deleted) - provision regarding unpublished works has been deleted - provision applies to Chinese and foreign copyright holders whose work is created in China	Article 43 para 2 and 44 CRL New provision
50	- the use of already published works (Article 47-49) must conform to some conditions: applying/filing to copyright management organization before first use, indicating full name of creator and source, paying usage fees directly to right holders or via copyright management organizations - management organizations shall timely publish filing information and establish work use situation consulting systems - management organizations must transfer the usage fee to the right	Partially 27 RCCM Partially Articles 23, 33 paragraph 2, 44 CRL New provision Partially Article 29 RCCM

	holder within a reasonable time period	
51	<u>Limitation – Works of Unknown/Unreachable Authors</u> - users may use the work in digital form after applying with the competent authority in cases where the right holder cannot be found or it is impossible to establish contact; separate regulations will be formulated	New provision
	<u>Exercise of Rights – Copyright and Related Rights Contracts</u>	
52	- exercise of property rights through permission, transfer, establishment of pledges and other permitted manners	Partially Article 10 paragraphs 2 and 3 CRL
53	- for use, a permission of use contract shall be concluded in cases where permission is required; contract contains: name of work, right categories and use methods, specification if exclusive right, geographical scope, remuneration method, liability for breach, others - requirement to include name of work	Partially Article 24 CRL
	- compensation payment is agreed by the parties, otherwise remuneration is paid according to market price or remuneration standards	Article 28 CRL
54	- exclusive contracts need to be in written form	Article 23 IR
	- in cases, where the exclusiveness is unclear, it shall be assumed that	New provision

	the contract grants non-exclusive rights	
	- in cases, where the method has been agreed but the content of the exclusive rights has not been agreed upon/is unclear, it shall be assumed that the person permitted can exclude any person including the holder to use the work in a similar way	Article 24 IR
	- in cases of newspaper and periodical publishers, in absence of an agreement on the period, the exclusive rights last for one year	New provision
55	- in absence of concrete content exclusive publishing rights in book publishing contracts shall be considered to be exclusive publication right of original and revised edition of the similar written language within the agreed geographical scope and during agreed term	Partially Article 31 CRL
56	- in cases of reprinting and republishing, publishers need to notify the holder and pay remuneration	Article 32 paragraph 3 CRL
	- in cases of refusal to reprint/republish after the book is sold out, holder can terminate the contract (two unfulfilled orders within six months)	Article 29 IR
57	- copyright transfer contracts need to be in written form and contain: name of work, right categories, transfer sum, day and method of payment, liability for breach, other	Article 25 CRL and Article 10 para 3 CRL

58	- rights not clearly permitted to use or transferred may not be exercised by the person receiving permission or the transferee - third parties may not be permitted by transferee to exercise the same right unless the holder has agreed	Article 27 CRL Partially Article 24 IR
59	- exclusive license and transfer contracts can be registered; rights that are not registered cannot be used in opposition against third parties of good will - fees shall be paid for registration, fee collection standards shall be formulated	Partially Article 25 IR New provision
60	- pledging of copyright must be registered - included that fees shall be paid - fee collection standards shall be formulated	Partially Article 26 CRL
61	Collective Copyright Management - definition of collective copyright management organizations (CMOs) as non-profit social organizations - CMOs may advocate rights under their own name and may act as a party in litigation or arbitration and mediation activities - inclusion of mediation	Article 8 paragraph 2 CRL and Article 4 RCCM Article 8 paragraph 1 CRL and Article 2 RCCM New provision
62	- CMOs shall provide use fee standards on the basis of the rights they manage and need to be announced	Partially Article 8 paragraph 2 CRL and Article 13 RCCM

	in media. Where there is objection, a special committee will adjudicate - the committee is composed of judges, officials, lawyers etc.	 New provision
63	- CMOs may represent the whole body of right holders in exercising copyrights and related rights for the dissemination to the public through self-service-song-selection systems as well as other methods and the transfer of the use fee shall be carried out equally among the right holders	New provision
64	- the right of remuneration stipulated in Article 14 and 40 shall be exercised through the CMOs	New provision
65	- where two CMOs obtain usage fees for the same use method or the same user, uniform use fees must be formulated jointly and then divided accordingly	Article 26 RCCM
66	- the State Council administrative copyright management department is in charge of nationwide collective copyright management work; responsible for examination, approval, supervision etc. - other State Council controlling departments conduct supervision and management over CMOs within their scope	Partially Article 5 RCCM New provision

67	- CMOs establishment method, business scope, rights and duties etc. are separately provided for by the State Council	New – Referral to the RCCM
68	Technological Protection Measures and Rights Management Information - definition of technological protection measures - definition of digital management information - inclusion broadcasting programs	Article 26 RIN
69	- permission of owner to adopt technological protection measures - no one must wilfully avoid or destroy such measures; may wilfully produce, import or provide public with installations that help to destroy or avoid such measures	Article 4 RIN
70	- prohibitions: wilful deletion or change of rights management information, providing works to the public that deleted or altered information if known or where it should be known	Article 5 RIN
71	- list of limitations: provision of works, performances, audio products or radio and television programs to small numbers of teachers or researchers for classroom teaching or scientific research, provision to blind people by unique methods with no aim of profit, if state organs use it to implement their duties, if bodies with security monitoring qualifications	Partially Article 12 RIN

	are testing the security of computers/systems/ networks, if research is done on encryption or reverse engineering - inclusion of research on encryption and reverse engineering	 New provision
72	The Protection of Rights - civil responsibility to cease infringements, cancel influence, make formal apology, compensate damage, etc. in cases of copyright infringement or violation of technological protection measures and rights management information	Partially Article 47 CRL, Article 23 RCSP and Article 18 sentence 1 RIN
73	- no duty to examine for infringement for network service providers if they only provide storage, search, linking and other purely technological network services - after notification by right holder network provide must adopt necessary measures and if not, it bears joint responsibility with the infringer for the expanded part of damage - if providers know or should have known of infringement and do not adopt measures, they bear joint responsibility - if providers instigate or assist infringement, they bear joint responsibility - provisions of paragraph 1 do not apply in cases, where the provider provides other person's work, performances or audio products to the public through networks	Partially Articles 20 and 21 RIN Partially Articles 14, 15, 22 (5) and 23 RIN Article 23 RIN New provision Partially Article 11 RIN

74	- where users pay remuneration to CMOs and a lawsuit is raised by a non-member right holder for the same right and method, users shall cease use and compensate damage according to the use fee standards - exceptions: where users know of objection, where users have been notified and where users have ceased use but use it again	New provision New provision
75	- where users have a computer program reproduction and do not know/should not know that such is infringing, they do not bear responsibility for compensation, but have to cease use and destroy infringing copy or obtain permission from the holder	Article 30 RCSP
76	- compensation for right holders can be calculated on the basis of (1) actual loss, (2) unlawful income or (3) a reasonable multiple of the rights transaction fee or (4) up to 1 Million Yuan - type of damage calculation can be chosen - if conduct is wilful, compensation can be two or three times the amount (determined by court) - the court must include the right holder's costs for ceasing infringing acts and his/her reasonable expenses - the court can oblige the infringer to provide ledgers and materials related to the infringing act; if	Updated Article 49 para 1 and para 2 CRL -> raised maximum New provision New provision Article 49 paragraph 1 sentence 2 CRL New provision

	such cannot be obtained or are false, the court may determine the compensation based on the right holder's position	
77	- infringing activities where the administrative department may order cessation, issue a warning, confiscate unlawful income, confiscate or destroy infringing goods and reproductions	Partially Article 48 CRL
	- if the illegal business value is higher than 50,000 Yuan a fine might be imposed from one time to less than five times the amount of illegal business value and a fine of 250,000 Yuan or less in cases below 50,000 Yuan	Article 36 IR
	- in the case of serious infringement, the materials can be confiscated; where the conduct constitutes a crime, criminal responsibility is investigated	Article 48 paragraph 1 last sentence CRL
(1)	- without permission of the holder, reproducing, distributing, renting, exhibiting, performing, transmitting, disseminating through networks - renting is added	Article 48 (1) CRL
(2)	- without permission of the performer, transmitting or recording their performances, reproducing, distributing or renting audio products through networks - renting is added	Article 48 (3) CRL
(3)	- without permission of the audio producer, reproducing, distributing, renting or disseminating	Article 48 (4) CRL

	their audio products through networks - renting is added	
(4)	- without permission of radio or television stations, relaying, recording or reproducing their programs - recording and relaying added	Article 48 (5) CRL
(5)	- using works performances etc. when others hold exclusive rights	New provision
(6)	- using works in violation of Article 50	New provision, partially Article 48 (2) CRL
(7)	- using copyrights or related rights that are hard to exercise or to control without permission, except under circumstance laid out in Article 74	New provision
(8)	- producing or selling works passing off another person's signature	Article 48 (8) CRL
78	- infringing activities where the administrative department may impose a warning, confiscate unlawful income and confiscate the devices or components used in avoiding or destroying technological measures	Partially Article 48 CRL, Article 19 RIN
	- if the illegal business value is higher than 50,000 Yuan a fine might be imposed from one time to less than five times the amount of illegal business value and a fine of 250,000 Yuan or less in cases below 50,000 Yuan, where the conduct constitutes a crime, criminal responsibility is investigated	Article 48 paragraph 1 last sentence CRL, Articles 18 and 19 RIN

(1)	-	without permission, wilfully avoiding or destroying technological protection measures	Article 48 (6) CRL, Article 18 (2) RIN
(2)	-	without permission, wilfully producing, importing or providing devices or components to avoid or destroy protection measures; or wilfully providing technology or services for such	Article 19 (1) RIN
(3)	-	without permission, wilfully deleting or changing digital management information	Article 49 (7) CRL, Article 18 (3) RIN
(4)	-	without permission, reproducing, distributing etc. works where it is known or should be known that the rights management information is deleted or changed	Article 18 (3) RIN
79	-	the administrative copyright management departments can conduct investigations and prosecution and inquire related parties, etc. and may seal up or detain venues or suspicious products	Partially Article 37 IR
	-	the parties have to grant support and cooperation in these investigation activities; the ones refusing, obstructing or delaying may be subject to warning and in grave circumstances, the materials can be confiscated; where it constitutes a crime, criminal responsibility is investigated	New provision Article 48 paragraph 1 CRL
80	-	the punished party can apply for administrative redress with the related government organ within 60 days of the day of receiving the	Partially Article 56 CRL

	administrative punishment or raise a lawsuit within three months; if no opposition is raised, the administrative department may apply for implementation of its verdict with the court	
	- possibility of administrative redress is added	New provision
81	- circumstances, under which a user shall bear civil and administrative legal responsibility regarding publishers, producers, network users, renters and distributors - regulation is better structured by listing four scenarios	Partially Article 53 CRL
82	- holders can apply for preservation of activities, assets and evidence according to Civil Procedure Law	Article 51 paragraph 1 CRL
83	- the court may confiscate unlawful income, infringing goods and reproductions and devices used for such from the infringers	Article 52 CRL
84	- parties in copyright disputes may apply for arbitration with an administration organ according to Arbitration Law	Article 55 paragraph 1 CRL
85	- copyright departments may establish copyright dispute mediation committees; provisions in Civil Procedure Law apply and composition, mediation procedures will be provided separately by State Council departments	New provision

86	- holders may apply to customs to investigate and prosecutes works that are imported or exported and suspected of infringing; rules are provided separately by the State Council	Articles 3, 4 and 7 Customs Regulations
	Supplementary Provisions	
87	- copyright (zhùzuòquán) and author's right (bǎnquán) refers to the same	Article 57 CRL
88	- the provisions of this law relating to copyright and related rights also apply to the limits and exercise of corresponding rights	New provision
89	- the rights as provided in this Law, where they have not already exceeded the term of protection provided in the new law, will be protected according to it	Article 60 para 1 CRL
90	- effective date	Article 61 CRL

e) Major Changes / Developments

In the following, the major changes in the 2014 draft are depicted and the benefits and downsides of the new proposed provisions are explained.

aa) Definitions of Copyrightable Works

The 2014 draft lifted up the two main requirements for a work to be protected by copyright law. According to Article 5 of the 2014 draft, copyright protection is given to

- intellectual expressions that
- have originality and
- can be fixed in some form.

This was previously dealt with in Article 2 of the Implementing Regulations. Lifting this provision up to the main Copyright Law showed China's ambition to improve the coherency of the law. Also, the requirement of the form being "tangible" had been deleted stipulating that "some form" must be possible. This change enhanced the scope of protected works.

Furthermore, the list of examples of copyrightable works was expanded from eight examples to fifteen examples. However, this change did not mean that there were seven new copyrightable works. The legislators had decided to split up the groups (i.e. musical, dramatic, qǔyì, choreographic and acrobatic works) each having its own paragraph. Only one work example had been added to the non-exhaustive list being (9) applied artworks that were formally seen as a sub-category of works of fine art.[936] "Applied artworks" were defined to be two- or three-dimensional works that have a "practical function" as well as an "aesthetic significance".[937]

Further, the legislators had decided to include the definitions of the various work forms. These were formally stipulated in Article 4 of the Implementing Regulations and, with regard to computer programs, in Article 3 (1) Computer Software Regulation. The inclusion of the definitions of the various work forms that are protected by Copyright Law would have improved the understanding of the law.

The term of "*cinematographic and works created by a process analogous to cinematography*"[938] had been changed to "*audiovisual works*" in Article 5 (12) of the 2014 draft. Further, the new provision named examples of audiovisual works such as "*films and television dramas*". This is a great example to show that China is adopting to the internationally used terminology as the term "*audiovisual works*" is used in the United States as well as in the Beijing Treaty.[939]

936 See Wan Hui Da Intellectual Property Agency (Chao Feng and Paul Ranjard), "Final draft of proposed PRC Copyright Law amendment released by NCAC", 7 January 2013 (https://www.lexology.com/library/detail.aspx?g=eb127dd5-03cc-43ed-b0ba-4c3b6974e9b8, accessed: 6 March 2021), 1-2.

937 Article 5 (9) *Copyright Law of the People's Republic of China "Third Revision Draft, Submission Version"* (June 2014 - posted on 6 June 2014, updated on 18 June 2014), National Copyright Administration of China.

938 Article 3 (6) *Copyright Law PRC* (1990/2010 version).

939 See Wan Hui Da Intellectual Property Agency (Chao Feng and Paul Ranjard), "Final draft of proposed PRC Copyright Law amendment released by NCAC",

Another good development was the unification of the term for computer related works. In contrast to the current law, the draft did not include computer software but the much broader term "computer programs" meaning

> *"works that are expressed as source code or object code used as commands for electronic computers and other information processing equipment"*[940].

Additionally, the new provision emphasized that object and source code constitutes the identical work in Article 5 (15) of the 2014 draft. This definition had been taken from Article 3 (1) of the new Computer Software Regulation. This upgrade of "computer programs" to be included in the Copyright Law also significantly improved the interpretation of the law by the public.[941]

It can be concluded that the legislators had upgraded the provision on the copyright subject matter quite extensively which would improve the public's understanding of copyright protected work.

bb) Emphasizing Related Rights

Article 6 of the 2014 draft defined the term "related rights" as being publisher's, performer's, audio work producer's as well as radio and television stations' rights. This provision was new to the Copyright Law as related rights had been included but its definition was only included in Article 26 Implementing Regulations. The inclusion of the definition as well as the better placement of the related rights (in the new Chapter III) put emphasis on related rights. This could be seen as a very good sign for China's international relations and also reflects the agreements of the Beijing Treaty.

---

7 January 2013 (https://www.lexology.com/library/detail.aspx?g=eb127dd5-03cc-43ed-b0ba-4c3b6974e9b8, accessed: 6 March 2021), 2; *Beijing Treaty* (2012), TRT/BEIJING/001.

[940] Article 5 (15) *Copyright Law of the People's Republic of China "Third Revision Draft, Submission Version"* (June 2014 - posted on 6 June 2014, updated on 18 June 2014), National Copyright Administration of China.

[941] See Wan Hui Da Intellectual Property Agency (Chao Feng and Paul Ranjard), "Final draft of proposed PRC Copyright Law amendment released by NCAC", 7 January 2013 (https://www.lexology.com/library/detail.aspx?g=eb127dd5-03cc-43ed-b0ba-4c3b6974e9b8, accessed: 6 March 2021), 2.

cc) Copyright Registration

Article 8 of the 2014 draft was a completely new provision that opened up the possibility of copyright owners to have their rights registered. Such registration should act as preliminary evidence for verification in copyright disputes. The law further explained that separate regulations would be formulated for this. Although the registration of copyrights had been possible before, it demonstrated that China planned on strengthening the rights of copyright owners by stipulating in the law that a registration can be used as preliminary evidence in copyright disputes. As you can see from the statistics in *Chapter 3 I. 2. c)*, copyright registrations in China are increasing extensively over the last years. This can on the one side, be interpreted as more creativity taking place in China. However, on the other side, it can be argued that the need for right holders to register their copyrights means that more copying is actually taking place and registration is needed to better enforce the rights in court. In this regard, the statistic on the increase of copyright cases in *Chapter 3 III. 2. g)* speaks for itself.

dd) Copyright Ownership and Contractual Agreements

The 2014 draft also strengthened the rights of copyright creators by providing them with the possibility of contractually agreeing on the ownership of the copyrights of a work (more room for contractual autonomy). Additionally, the provisions set rules for cases where no agreement has been concluded between the parties so that the ownership does not have to be decided in court.

(1) Strengthening of Copyright Owners of Audiovisual Works

The draft significantly strengthened the rights of the owners of already existing works when producing an audiovisual work. Article 19 paragraph 1 clarified that movie producers who use pre-existing works (e.g. novels) need to obtain the permission from the copyright holder of such pre-existing works; users of such audiovisual works need to obtain permission both from the producer as well as from the owner of the original work (see Article 19 paragraph 2 and Article 16 paragraph 2 2014 draft). This statutory exclusive usage right could be overcome in cases where the parties have concluded an agreement on the usage rights.

With regard to the ownership distribution between producers of audiovisual works and the individual creators such as directors, screenwriters and the like, Article 19 of the 2014 draft stipulated in paragraph 4 that the individual rights need to be agreed upon by the various parties and that in absence of an agreement the property rights and interests are granted to the producer whereas the individual creators remain with the authorship right (= statutory right of authorship) as well as the right to a share in profits.[942] The current Copyright Law saw this "back-up" option as the standard leaving no room for contractual autonomy. This change significantly upgraded the rights of the individual creators.

(2) Clarifying the Provision on Professional Works

The same contractual freedom was provided for works created by employees during their work duties and hours. Article 20 of the 2014 draft stipulated that the copyright entitlement between the employer and the employee has to be agreed upon. Only in cases missing such an agreement the copyright is directly granted to the creating employee and the employer is granted an exclusive free-of-charge usage right for two years in the professional scope (Article 20 paragraph 3). Similar to the previous provision in Article 16 of the "old" Copyright Law, there are some occasions in which the copyright vests in the work units (i.e. maps, product design drawings, works created in the scope of reporting duties).

Article 20 paragraph 4 of the 2014 draft set out that the work units have to pay a reward based on the quantity and quality of the work to the employee and the employee then retains the right to use such work in the creation of compilations.

This much more detailed provision clarified the relationship between employees and their work units extensively and would hopefully lead to more autonomy of the employees.

ee) Protection Period

Not much changed with regard to the protection period of the different works. However, one important change was the extension of the protection period of photographic works as it was not listed in the shortened protection period (Article 29 paragraph 2) of fifty years anymore but was part of the general protection period meaning life of the author plus another fifty years after his/her death (see Article 29 paragraph 1). Although China is in line with the minimum protection period stipulated in Article 7 of the

[942] See ibid., 3.

Berne Convention, it would have been welcomed if China harmonizes its law with the majority of the industrial countries that grant a protection period of the life of the author plus seventy years (e.g. United States or European Union).

The newly included applied works were granted a protection period of twenty-five years for the right of publications (Article 29 paragraph 3).

With regard to works of unknown identity, the protection period was fifty years from first publication but shifted to the general protection period if the author can be determined (Article 30). This was formally only stipulated in the Implementing Regulations.

ff) Limitations to Copyright

The current Copyright Law as well as the first drafts of the copyright revision included an exhaustive list of possible limitations to copyrights. After the publication of the first draft in March 2012, the public was disappointed that the limitations to Chinese copyright were supposed to remain limited to the exceptions named in the law. This would be contradictory to the purpose of limitations of balancing the public interest with the rights of the copyright owners.[943] This was adhered to in the further drafting process as the second and the third drafts included a number (13) in Article 43 being “other circumstances”. This addition was changing the nature of the limitations list to a non-exhaustive list leaving more room for exceptions. Here, China followed the U.S. model.[944] It is unclear what other circumstances would fall under this open term. It will be up to the judges to interpret this.

Although the list was open-ended in the 2014 draft, it still contained problematic provisions on the different case scenarios.

First, the private use exception is discussed. The first draft of the provision on the exception of personal use contained the restriction of one copy (see Article 40 (1) first draft).[945] After consultation with the public this was changed to the allowed reproduction of extracts of works. The new provi-

[943] Hong Xue, "A User-Unfriendly Draft: 3rd Revision of the Chinese Copyright Law" *JICTL* 7, 4 (2012), 351.
[944] Wenqi Liu, "Reform of China's Copyright Legislation" *J. Copyright Soc'y U.S.A.* 59 (2011-2012), 856.
[945] Xue, "A User-Unfriendly Draft: 3rd Revision" *JICTL* 7, 4 (2012), 351.

sion still remained disturbing as the use is restricted to the act of reproduction.[946] This should be adjusted to also include translation and adaptation making sure that this exception is applicable to all forms of private use.[947] This restriction led to an unreasonable discrimination of the public interests.

Secondly, the 2014 draft had also not changed the restriction of use for classroom education and scientific research that does not include students as fair users.[948] The 2014 draft had not addressed this still existing problem that students might be subject to copyright license and payment even though their teachers are exempted from such.[949]

Another major change was the inclusion of the three-step-test that was formally only included in Article 21 Implementing Regulations. The last paragraph of Article 43 of the 2014 draft read that the exceptions are only allowed if the use of the copyright protected work does not influence the regular use and unreasonably harms the rights of the copyright holder. This upgrade from the Implementing Regulations to the Copyright Law reduced the uncertainty of the importance of the three-step-test clarifying that all limitation scenarios also need to pass the three-step-test in order to be legally allowed.[950]

gg) Computer Programs

As previously mentioned, the 2014 draft contained many provisions that have been previously contained in separate regulations. This was also true for the Computer Software Regulation and the Regulation on Information Network. The upgrade of the major provisions from the regulations to the main Copyright Law emphasized the importance of such rights.

---

946 Hong Xue, "One Step Ahead, Two Steps Back: Reverse Engineering the Second Draft for the Third Revision of the Chinese Copyright Law" *Am. U. Intl'l L. Rev.* 28, 1 (2013), 302.

947 Ibid.

948 Xue, "A User-Unfriendly Draft: 3rd Revision" *JICTL* 7, 4 (2012), 351.

949 Xue, "One Step Ahead, Two Steps Back" *Am. U. Intl'l L. Rev.* 28, 1 (2013), 302.

950 Liu, "Reform of China's Copyright Legislation" *J. Copyright Soc'y U.S.A.* 59 (2011-2012), 855-856.

Chapter IV of the 2014 draft dealt with the limitations to copyright and included three articles on limitations (fair-use) of computer programs. Articles 16 and 17 of the Computer Software Regulation dealing with the fair use of an owner of a legal reproduction (i.e. installation of software, back-up copy and necessary modifications) and the fair use with regard to learning and studying were inserted as Articles 44 and 45 in the 2014 draft. In Article 44 (3) of the 2014 draft, it was additionally stipulated that the owner of the legal reproduction must not provide third parties with the altered programs as well as the devices or components that have been used to carry out such alterations. Here, reference can be made to Article 19 (1) Regulations on Information Network which prohibits the provision of others with devices or components that are mainly used for the circumvention of technical measures.[951]

A new provision was added regarding the allowed reproduction and translation of the part related to the compatibility information to obtain such information (Article 46 of the 2014 draft).

Further to that, Article 30 of the Computer Software Regulations had been inserted into Article 75 of the 2014 draft dealing with the case in which a protected software is unknowingly reproduced by a third party. Here, the third party is exempted from paying compensation but has to cease the use and destroy the reproduction or, in some cases, can apply for permission by the right holder.

hh) Technological Protection Measures

Further, the 2014 draft intensified the protection for technological protection measures which can be compared to the protection in the United States.[952]

The 2014 draft even extended the technological measures to broadcasting programs that have not been included in Article 26 of the Regulations on Information Network before. Broadcasting programs are not included in any international agreements and could be an obstacle to open licensing if

[951] See Wan Hui Da Intellectual Property Agency (Chao Feng and Paul Ranjard), "Final draft of proposed PRC Copyright Law amendment released by NCAC", 7 January 2013 (https://www.lexology.com/library/detail.aspx?g=eb127dd5-03cc-43ed-b0ba-4c3b6974e9b8, accessed: 6 March 2021), 4.

[952] Xue, "One Step Ahead, Two Steps Back" *Am. U. Intl'l L. Rev.* 28, 1 (2013), 303-304.

the media industry uses technological protection measures on its works.[953] According to Article 78 (1) of the 2014 draft, the circumvention or destruction of technological protection measures would lead to significant penalties by administrative as well as criminal enforcement authorities.

The 2014 draft also provided for an extended scope of fair use with regard to the avoidance of technological protection measures by adding research on encryption and research on reverse engineering to the exception circumstances listed in Article 71 of the 2014 draft. Although this provision had been extended to further exceptions, it is still not understandable why Article 71 of the 2014 draft did not refer to the exceptions stipulated in Article 43 of the 2014 draft. It was uncertain from the proposed version whether technological measures could be prevented in cases of private use (Article 43 (1) of the 2014 draft).[954] It is feared that right holders could exclude their works from the private use limitation by adding technological protection.[955]

Here, it can be said that the legislators had not improved the law but rather failed to create a new law that balances the interest of the right holders as well as the public.

ii) Inclusion of Provision on Collective Copyright Management

The "old" Copyright Law only contains one provision regarding collective copyright management in Article 8. This provision generally allows collective copyright management and stipulates that a collective copyright administration organization can exercise the rights in its own name and participate in disputes. Clarifying regulations are formulated separately.

In contrast to that, the 2014 draft had a whole section designated to collective copyright management (Chapter V – Section II).

The first draft of the proposed new Copyright Law led to an outrage when it was published in March 2012 because it gave much power to the collecting societies as it opened up the possibility of the societies to represent all right holders (including non-members) unless they have specifically opposed such representation (see Article 60 of the first draft).[956] Right holders

953 Ibid.
954 Ibid., 307.
955 Ibid., 305.
956 Ibid., 306.

who were not fond of the collective management system strongly opposed to these provisions.[957] This led to a reassessment in the subsequent two drafts in which the collective management of non-members had been limited to only one case, namely the public communication of already published musical and audiovisual works through self-service-song-selection systems ("Karaoke") as well as other methods (see Article 63 of the 2014 draft).

This extended collective management system can be compared to the system used in the Nordic countries, where it is quite successful because the right holders as well as the collective management organizations in the Nordic countries are well organized.[958] It is not clear how this system would work in China. Article 74 of the 2014 draft set out that bona-fide users who have paid to a collective management organization need to cease the use and pay compensation in the amount of the fee standards in cases where the right holder, who is a non-member, raises a lawsuit.

Further, the strengthening of the collective management organizations might have been harmful to the advancement of open licensing (= creative commons).[959] It remained unclear what right holders have to do if they want their work to be in open licensing.

jj) Enforcement

It is very encouraging to see that the proposed revision of the copyright law enhanced the scope of civil remedies as well as administrative punishment possibilities.[960]

(1) Inclusion of Duties and Obligations of Network Service Providers

The duties and obligations of web service providers were previously only part of the Regulations on Information Network. The 2014 draft included Article 73 that clarified the most important issues. In paragraph 1 it was stipulated that network service providers do not bear any monitoring re-

---

957 Ibid.

958 Liu, "Reform of China's Copyright Legislation" *J. Copyright Soc'y U.S.A.* 59 (2011-2012), 859-860.

959 Xue, "A User-Unfriendly Draft: 3rd Revision" *JICTL* 7, 4 (2012), 353; Xue, "One Step Ahead, Two Steps Back" *Am. U. Intl'l L. Rev.* 28, 1 (2013), 306.

960 Xue, "A User-Unfriendly Draft: 3rd Revision" *JICTL* 7, 4 (2012), 353.

sponsibilities in cases where they only provide purely technological network services. If they adopt necessary measures in a timely manner following a notification of a right holder, they do not bear responsibility for compensation in relation to the infringement (see paragraph 2).

The providers only have joint responsibility in cases, in which they do not adapt measures in a timely manner, know or should know of the infringing activities of their users or they have instigated or assisted them in carrying out their infringing activities (see paragraph 3 and 4).

Unfortunately, the new provision did not deal with the personal data protection issue that arises if the network service provider forwards the personal information to the authorities (this is stipulated in Article 13 Regulations on Information Network).[961]

(2) Freedom of Choice for Damage Calculation

According to Article 76 of the 2014 draft, there are four different ways of damage calculation:

- real damage,
- unlawful income of the infringer,
- reasonable multiple of the rights transaction fee or
- a semi-statutory damage[962] of 1 Million Yuan or less.

In comparison, the current law does not leave any room for freedom of choice and has a rigid provision on how damages have to be calculated. This was a huge change compared to the current 2010 Copyright Law and enhanced the possibilities of the right holders tremendously. Also, the possibility to calculate damages on the basis of a reasonable transaction fee (meaning royalties) was a new addition to the Chinese Copyright Law. Further, the maximum damages are increased from 500,000 Yuan to 1 Million Yuan.

In cases of wilful repeated infringement, the damages could be increased by doubling or tripling the damage (see Article 76 paragraph 2 of the 2014

[961] See Xue, "One Step Ahead, Two Steps Back" *Am. U. Intl'l L. Rev.* 28, 1 (2013), 308.
[962] See ibid., 307.

draft). By that, China introduced the system of punitive damages.[963] The raise of damages would hopefully lead to a stronger deterrence of infringers.

The determination of damages has to be carried out by the court that also has to add the right holder's costs of approaching the infringement as well as reasonable expenses (see Article 76 paragraph 3 of the 2014 draft). Furthermore, Article 76 paragraph 4 of the 2014 draft gave the court the power to order the infringer to hand over materials and the like for the purpose of calculating the damage in cases where the right holder has exhausted all possibilities to obtain evidence. If such are not provided, the court may decide on the basis of the right holder's position. This shift of the burden of proof was a major development and would strengthen the position of copyright holders.

All of these amendments would have improved the enforcement possibilities of the infringed right holders considerably.

(3) Emphasizing Fines

The 2014 draft also included a provision on the calculation of administrative fines. This was previously stipulated in Article 36 Implementing Regulations and Article 19 of the Regulations on Information Network and was upgraded to Article 77 and 78 of the 2014 draft. This upgrade also showed that China is emphasizing the enforcement by administrative authorities.

(4) Improving Administrative Punishments and the Rights of the Authorities

Another major amendment was the insertion of an investigation right of the administrative authorities in Article 79 of the 2014 draft. This investigation right has been included in Article 37 Implementing Regulations before but the provision was very general and did not specify the exact powers that the administrative authorities shall have when conducting investigations. The new investigation right, that had been upgraded to the Copyright Law, gives the authorities the power to

- interrogate related parties,

963 See Liu, "Reform of China's Copyright Legislation" *J. Copyright Soc'y U.S.A.* 59 (2011-2012), 861; Xue, "One Step Ahead, Two Steps Back" *Am. U. Intl'l L. Rev.* 28, 1 (2013), 307.

- investigate situations that are linked to suspected infringement activities,
- inspect locations and objects of the suspects' activities,
- consult and reproduce contacts, invoices, accounts and other materials related to the infringing activities and
- seal up and detain venues or products that are suspicious.

Further, Article 79 paragraph 2 stipulated that the involved parties "shall grant support and cooperation". If parties oppose to the investigation activities by refusing cooperation or obstructing and delaying the investigations without a legal reason, the authorities can pose a warning and in serious cases, confiscate materials and equipment. Further, the opposing party should be held criminally liable if its conduct constitutes a crime.

This comprehensive investigation right showed that China wanted to improve the enforcement of copyright infringement as a stronger enforcement regime would hopefully have a deterrent effect on infringers.

(5) Customs Enforcement Measures

A new provision was added to the 2014 draft in Article 86 stipulating that right holders can make an application to customs to investigate suspicious products at import and export. This was formerly only dealt with in the Regulation on Customs Protection of Intellectual Property Rights, in particular Articles 3, 4 and 7.[964]

5. Summary

Summarizing, it can be said that the 2014 draft included many necessary and useful amendments improving the coherency and transparency of the Chinese Copyright Law. The inclusion of the main regulations into the law emphasized the importance of the relevant topics such as computer program protection or protection of works by technological measures. The improved enforcement possibilities as well as the raised fines and damages

[964] *Regulations on Customs Protection of Intellectual Property Rights* (2018 - promulgated 2 December 2003, effective 1 March 2004, amended 24 March 2010, amended 19 March 2018), State Council of the People's Republic of China.

would hopefully result in a deterrent effect for the infringers and eventually lead to a decrease of copyright infringement in China

The law would have been easier for the Chinese population to be understood and would hopefully also have led to a better enforcement of the rights of the owners of copyright protected works.

However, it could also be seen that the draft still had some weaknesses such as the private use provisions which could have led to major hindrances in the educational paths. It was hoped that these weaknesses would be taken care of in the further deliberation of the draft before adoption and promulgation of the law.

III. Current Status of the Reform and Further Developments between China and the U.S.

1. Standstill from 2014 to 2019

The first draft was published by the NCAC in March 2012 and, following collection of the public opinion and several discussions, the second draft was then made available to the public in May 2012. At first, it seemed that the reform of the copyright legislation was evolving quite fast but following the publication of the revised second draft in May 2012 not much happened until summer 2014 when the third (submission) draft was finally published by the SCLAO. In many speeches, Chinese authorities emphasized the need for an update of the intellectual property legislation and stated that improving the legislation is a priority.

- For example, the State Council issued a White Paper titled "China and the World Trade Organization" in June 2018 with the aim of showing the WTO China's commitments since the accession in 2001.[965] The White Paper highlights China's efforts in improving trade and the protection of intellectual property rights. In relation

[965] The State Council of The People's Republic of China, "White Paper: China and the World Trade Organization", 28 June 2018 (http://english.www.gov.cn/archive/white_paper/2018/06/28/content_281476201898696.htm, accessed: 6 March 2021).

to Copyright Law the State Council emphasized that China is currently revising the Copyright Law to build a "full-fledged legal system on IPR protection" and that several measures have been conducted to strengthen the enforcement such as the introduction of the IP courts and campaigns to strengthen the administrative enforcement.[966]

- Also, in an executive meeting of the State Council in July 2019, the importance of stronger intellectual property protection was again highlighted by Premier Li Keqiang and General Secretary of the CCP and President of China Xi Jinping.[967] It was further discussed that "campaigns against violations of IPR-related law" shall be carried out and higher fines/damages shall be imposed/awarded to deter infringers; specific reference was also made to the revision of the Copyright Law and it was stated that it will be advanced.[968]
- In November 2019, the General Offices of the CCP Central Committee and the State Council jointly published a directive titled "The Guideline on Strengthening Intellectual Property Rights Protection" which again highlights the need for a strong IP protection to "*boost China's economic competitiveness*".[969] It further states that "*by 2025, social satisfaction with IPR protection in China will reach and maintain a high level*".[970] The directive further includes the statement that the introduction of a system for punitive damages in copyright infringement will be advanced.[971]

It was hoped, that China would actually pursue the abovementioned goals that it set itself. Since some years had passed from the submission of the

---

[966] Ibid., at I. 4.
[967] Zhang, "China to enhance IPR protection to improve business climate, boost tech innovation", 17 July 2019 (http://english.www.gov.cn/premier/news/201907/17/content_WS5d2fdfb2c6d00d362f668704.html, accessed: 6 March 2021).
[968] Ibid.
[969] Xinhua, "China issues guideline for enhancing IPR protection", 24 November 2019 (http://english.www.gov.cn/policies/latestreleases/201911/24/content_WS5dda789bc6d0bcf8c4c17bd4.html, accessed: 6 March 2021).
[970] Ibid.
[971] Ibid.

third draft, a newer draft would have to go through further revisions, in particular, to adapt to the technological developments.

2. U.S.-Chinese Relations

The dispute between the U.S. and China has been going on for years and has and is still influencing the development of copyright law in China. In the following the current status is depicted.

a) Initiation of Section 301 Investigations in 2017

On 14 August 2017, the U.S.T.R. was instructed by the President to conduct investigations into "*China's law, policies, practices, or actions that may be unreasonable or discriminatory and that may be harming American intellectual property rights, innovations, or technology development*".[972] A particular focus of the investigations was laid on the technology and IP transfer regime in China.[973] Amongst others, the U.S.T.R. found that China's intellectual property protection including the enforcement mechanisms are inadequate.[974] At the end of the investigations in 2018, the U.S.T.R. found that several conducts by China related to technology transfer, intellectual property rights and innovation are "*unreasonable or discriminatory, and burden or restrict U.S. commerce*".[975] The U.S.T.R. recommended to impose additional tariffs on Chinese products and to initiate further dispute settlement processes at the WTO.[976]

In March 2018, the U.S. again made use of the DSB of the WTO and requested consultations with China regarding "*certain Chinese measures pertaining to the protection of intellectual property rights*" and arguing that China discriminates against foreign patent holders/imported foreign

[972] The United States Trade Representative "Findings of the Investigation into China's Acts, Policies, and Practices related to Technology Transfer, Intellectual Property, and Innovation under Section 301 of the Trade Act of 1974" (22 March 2018), 4.
[973] Ibid., 5-7.
[974] Ibid., 179-180.
[975] The United States Trade Representative, "Section 301 Investigation Fact Sheet", June 2018 (https://ustr.gov/about-us/policy-offices/press-office/fact-sheets/2018/june/section-301-investigation-fact-sheet, accessed: 6 March 2021).
[976] Ibid.

technology (WT/DS542/14).[977] The DSB was joint by several other countries but upon request by the U.S. and agreement by China the Panel has suspended its work with effect from 8 June 2020.[978]

Over the last years extensive tariffs were imposed on various Chinese products which started a trade war between China and the U.S. with China also imposing tariffs on U.S. products.[979]

b) 2019 Special 301 Report by the U.S.T.R.

The U.S.T.R. has kept China on the Watch List for IP Issues for several years. The Special 301 Report is published by the U.S.T.R. every year and contains results on the status of the protection and enforcement of intellectual property rights around the world; in particular, it focusses on trading partners of the U.S. in which the protection and enforcement has declined or in general, can be regarded as inadequate.[980]

In the report of 2019, the U.S.T.R. (again) devotes a large section to China, one of the largest trading partners of the U.S.[981] For the 15th consecutive year China has been placed on the Priority Watch List.[982] According to the U.S.T.R. China has failed,

> *"to make fundamental structural changes to strengthen IP protection and enforcement, open China's market to foreign investment, allow the*

[977] WTO "China - Certain Measures Concerning the Protection of Intellectual Property Rights - Request for Consultations by the United States" (2018), WT/DS542/1 (18-1799).

[978] The U.S. had already requested several suspensions of the work of the Panel from 14 June 2019 onwards due to ongoing negotiations with China. Article 12.12 DSU states that the work may be suspended for a period not exceeding 12 months and if the period is longer, the authority for establishment of the Panel shall lapse – *DSU* (1994), 869 UNTS 401; 33 I.L.M. 1226 (Annex 2 of the Marrakesh Agreement establishing the World Trade Organization, signed in Marrakesh, Morocco on 15 April 1994 , 33 I.L.M. 1125).

[979] For further information, see Daniele and da Costa Palumbo, Ana Nicolaci, "Trade war: US-China trade battle in charts", 10 May 2019 (https://www.bbc.com/news/business-48196495, accessed: 6 March 2021).

[980] The United States Trade Representative "2019 Special 301 Report" (April 2019), 5.

[981] Ibid., 6.

[982] Ibid., 11.

> *market decisive role in allocating resources, and refrain from government interference in private sector technology transfer decisions."*[983]

Furthermore, the U.S.T.R explicitly emphasizes the "stalled legal reform" is one of the severe business challenges for U.S. persons/ companies and that the statements of Chinese government officials on the importance of IP protection and innovation cannot compensate the lack in real structural changes in any way.[984]

The U.S.T.R. positively notes that China has reorganized the ministries and agencies responsible for IP protection to further centralize the administration and enforcement of which the actual impact still has to be seen in the future and also welcomes the introduction of the appellate IP tribunal at the SPC but highlights that independency of the judiciary is a key factor to improve enforcement in China.[985] In the following, the U.S.T.R.'s main findings on copyright protection and enforcement in China are summarized:

- In relation to e-commerce and online piracy, the U.S.T.R. states that there have been positive developments but that IP right holders still fear ineffective takedown procedures and sufficient measures for deterring infringers.[986] Furthermore, the U.S.T.R. argues that in the development of the E-Commerce Law China has disregarded the concerns by the U.S. that the law stipulates "burdensome requirements" on right holders; China needs to make sure that the new law will not lead to the weakening of the existing legal framework, namely the Regulations on Protection of the Right to Network Dissemination.[987] Additionally, China has not improved the possibilities for content from abroad to enter the market which further enhances online piracy of such content.[988]

---

[983] Ibid., 40.
[984] Ibid.
[985] Ibid., 41.
[986] Ibid., 43.
[987] Ibid.
[988] Ibid., 44.

- In relation to the advancement of copyright legislation in China, the U.S.T.R. negatively notes that albeit indications by the authorities of further progress, no new draft for the reform has been published.[989]

The 2019 Report of the U.S.T.R. again shows that China still has severe inefficiencies in the protection and enforcement of intellectual property rights including copyright.

c) U.S.-China Trade Deal of January 2020

To de-escalate the ongoing trade war between the U.S. and China both countries finally signed an agreement on 15 January 2020 named the "Economic and Trade Agreement" ("Phase One") which also takes up on the protection of intellectual property rights and covers the main issues of the abovementioned Section 301 investigation.[990]

In relation to intellectual property rights, Article 1.2. of the Agreement stipulates the following.

> *"The Parties shall ensure fair, adequate, and effective protection and enforcement of intellectual property rights. Each Party shall ensure fair and equitable market access to persons of the other Party that rely upon intellectual property protection."*[991]

In the following, the specific agreements in relation to copyright protection are shown:

- Section E of the Agreement is devoted to piracy on e-commerce platforms and stipulates that China should improve the enforcement procedures for right holders by easing the hurdles for right holders in the notice and takedown system.[992] Furthermore, it is agreed that the Parties must take effective actions against major

[989] Ibid., 45.
[990] U.S. and China "Economic And Trade Agreement Between The Government Of The United States Of America And The Government Of The People's Republic Of China" (15 January 2020).
[991] Ibid., 1-1.
[992] Ibid., 1-8.

platforms that do not adopt the necessary steps to prevent IP infringement.[993]

- Section G generally deals with the need for effective actions against the manufacture and export of pirated goods, in particular with regard to goods that might impair the public health or personal safety – effective measures include the destruction of retained/seized goods and border enforcement actions as well as the improvement of judicial orders against infringers to pay profits from the infringement or adequate damages to the right holder.[994]
- Section I contains general agreements on the judicial enforcement and procedure in intellectual property cases. In particular, Chinese administrative authorities shall be instructed to initiate criminal proceedings if there is a "reasonable suspicion" and the penalties for infringement shall be increased to deter future infringement.[995] Furthermore, final judgments should be rigorously enforced.[996] In relation to the enforcement of copyrights, Article 1.29 facilitates the burden for right holders to prove their right and shifts the burden of proof to the infringer that the use of the work was authorized in any way.[997] In Article 1.30 it is agreed that in civil proceedings no formalities to authenticate evidence shall be required if they can be proven in another way (e.g. by witness testimony) and in general, the notarization process shall be improved.[998]
- Section J provides for the strengthening of the bilateral cooperation.[999]
- Lastly, in Section K Article 1.35 it is agreed that China will present an Action Plan to strengthen IP protection.[1000]

It will be interesting to see whether China will adhere to the various measures agreed in the U.S.-China Trade Deal. It is very likely that the

[993] Ibid., 1-8 - 1-9.
[994] Ibid., 1-10 - 11-14.
[995] Ibid., 1-15 - 11-17.
[996] Ibid., 1-15 - 11-16.
[997] Ibid., 1-16.
[998] Ibid., 1-16 - 11-17.
[999] Ibid., 1-17.
[1000] Ibid., 1-18.

Trade Deal will have an impact on the further advancement of the revision of the Chinese copyright legislation.

3. 2020-2021 Promotion Plan

On 20 April 2020, CNIPA released the "2020-2021 Implementation of the 'Opinions on Strengthening the Protection of Intellectual Property' Promotion Plan".[1001] It can be argued that this Promotion Plan is China's commitment under Article 1.35 of the Trade Deal with the U.S. that provides for China to present an IP Action Plan within 30 days.[1002]

The Promotion Plan consists of 133 sections split up in eight chapters. The chapters deal with the following issues:

- Formulation and amendment of laws and regulations,
- strengthening administrative and judicial enforcements,
- improving the construction of large-scale IP protection mechanisms,
- optimizing key links for fast protection of IP,
- expanding foreign exchange and cooperation,
- strengthening the protection of resources,
- promoting IP protection and cultural construction and
- strengthening the IP organisations.

The plan includes several references to copyright and related rights. In the following, the key sections are depicted:

- Section 2 sets out that the revision and review of the Copyright Law will be promoted including the raise of the punitive damages. Unfortunately, no timeline is provided.
- Section 7 deals with the revision of the E-Commerce Law and further strengthening of IP protection.
- Section 15 sets out an update of the provisions to transfer administrative cases to criminal authorities.

[1001] CNIPA "2020-2021 Implementation of the 'Opinions on Strengthening the Protection of Intellectual Property' Promotion Plan" (20 April 2020).

[1002] The process was probably delayed by a month due to the worldwide Corona pandemic.

- Section 22 stipulates that guidelines shall be promulgated for the enforcement of copyright and related rights before the end of October 2020 and Section 23 lies out that measures for the protection of folk literary and artistic works shall be formulated before the end of December 2021.
- Section 46 provides for a special operation to combat online infringement and piracy.
- Section 57 emphasizes the strengthening of the cooperation between administrative and criminal authorities.
- Section 63 highlights the strengthening of the supervision of NPC and timely inspections of enforcement in accordance with the revision of the Copyright Law.
- Section 97 aims at improving multilateral and bilateral IP rights cooperation and coordination.
- Section 98 highlights the cooperation with WIPO, WTO and the like.
- Section 112 deals with the strengthening of customs enforcement by training personnel.
- Section 122 to 126 provide for the promotion of publicity of IP protection such as IP events, regular reports et cetera.

All of these plans sound very promising and take up many issues addressed in the U.S.-China Trade Deal of January 2020.

However, it needs to be noted that the Promotion Plan is issued by the CNIPA whereas the Guidelines issued in November 2019 were issued by the CCP Central Committee and the State Council who have much more authority. The Promotion Plan can be more regarded as a recommendation for action rather than a concrete act implementation.

It will be interesting to see if and how China fully implements the plan.

4. NPCSC Deliberation and Promulgation of the Amendment

a) First Round of NPCSC Deliberation – April 2020

From 26 April until 29 April 2020, the NPC Standing Committee held its 17th legislative session in Beijing. Following the session, a new draft was published for public consultation.[1003]

Contrary to expectations, the new draft did not build up on the previous 2014 draft but rather on the currently effective 2010 Copyright Law. The draft looked more like a small amendment to the existing Copyright Law rather than a substantial revision, especially when considering the drafts of 2012 and 2014. A detailed description of the first draft by the NPCSC is omitted because the third and final draft is discussed in more detail in the following.

b) Second Round of NPCSC Deliberation – August 2020

In August 2020, the Standing Committee published a second draft with some further slight amendments of the wording and requested comments before finalising the legislation.[1004] A detailed description of the second draft by the NPCSC is omitted because the third and final draft is discussed in more detail in the following.

c) Third (Final) Round of NPCSC Deliberation – November 2020

On 11 November 2020, the NPC Standing Committee held its 23rd meeting of the 13th National People's Congress and finally decided on the amendments to the Copyright Law of the People's Republic of China which will come into force on 1 June 2021.[1005]

[1003] *Amendment to the Copyright Law of the People's Republic of China (Draft)* (26 April 2020), NPC Standing Committee (provided by NPC Observer).

[1004] *Amendment to the Copyright Law of the People's Republic of China (Draft) (Second Review Draft)* (8 August 2020), NPC Standing Committee (provided by NPC Observer).

[1005] *Decision of the Standing Committee of the National People's Congress on Amending the "Copyright Law of the People's Republic of China"* (11 November 2020 - Adopted at the 23rd Meeting of the Standing Committee of the 13th National People's Congress), NPC Standing Committee (provided by npc.gov.cn).

The 2020 Amendment[1006] contains 67 articles, whereas the "old" Copyright Law only consists of 61 articles. The structure of the legislation has not changed.

Before discussing and evaluating the changes in more detail, the major changes in the amended Copyright Law compared to the Copyright Law of 2010 are summarized and it is shown which of the amendments contained in the 2014 draft were considered:

Article (2010)[1007]	**Article (2020)**[1008]	**Changes**	**Origin of provision**[1009]	**Comments / Reference to 2014 Draft**
2, 9, 11, 16, 19, 21, 22	**2, 9, 11, 12, 18, 21, 23, 24**	- The term "other organizations" is changed to "unincorporated organizations"	New	*This change was also included in the 2014 draft, e.g. in Article 2*
9, 11, 16, 19, 21	**9, 11, 12, 18, 21, 23**	- The term "Chinese citizens" is changed to "natural persons"	New	*This change was also included in the 2014 draft, e.g. in Article 2*
3, 10, 15, 46, 47, 53	**3, 10, 17, 48, 52, 59**	- The term to describe cinematographic works is generally changed to "audiovisual works"	Beijing Treaty	*This change was also included in the 2014 draft, e.g. in Article 5*

1006 *Copyright Law of the People's Republic of China* (1990/2020 version) (provided by npc.gov.cn).
1007 This column refers to the articles of the current Copyright Law (2010 version).
1008 This column refers to the articles of the newly amended Copyright Law (2020 version).
1009 This column indicates the origin of the respective provision if it has been taken from another source, e.g. from a regulation.

3	**3**	- The general descriptions for copyrightable works now directly refers to "intellectual achievements" that "can be fixed in a certain form" (reference to "tangible form" is deleted) - The list of works is open-ended referring to "other intellectual achievements that meet the characteristics of the work"	Article 2 IR New	*This change was also included in Article 5 of the 2014 draft*
4		- Copyright related works are directly referred to in Article 4	New	*This was also proposed in Article 7 of the 2014 draft*
5		- The term "current news" is changed to "pure factual information"	New	*This was also proposed in Article 9 of the 2014 draft*
7, 28	**7, 8, 30**	- The term "copyright administration department under the State Council" is changed to	New	

		"national department for copyright"		
8	**8**	- The section on collective copyright management is updated including the collection of royalties and establishment of rights information inquiry system - Royalties are to be determined by negotiation between the CMO and the user representatives - Possibility for user representatives is added to appeal to the national copyright department and/or people's courts - In addition to litigation and arbitration CMOs can also act as a part in mediation activities - The national department for	Partially Articles 2, 3, 4, 24 RCCM New New New Article 5 RCCM	*The 2014 draft provided for a whole section on copyright collective management Articles 61 to 67 which is now only partially reflected*

		copyright shall conduct oversight and management		
10	**10**	- In item (5) "digitisation" is added to the possible ways of reproduction - In item (11) broadcasting rights include rebroadcasting by "wired or wireless means"	New New	*These changes were also included in Article 13 paragraph 2 of the 2014 draft*
11 partially	**12**	- Possibility for copyright holder to register the work	New	*This was also proposed in Article 8 of the 2014 draft*
13	**14**	- It is now stipulated that an owner of a joint work may not be prevented from exercising his/her rights (except for the transfer, exclusive use or pledge) but profits must be shared	Partially Article 9 IR	*This was also proposed in Article 17 of the 2014 draft*
35, 37, 40 partially	**16**	- A new article is added integrating the use of adaptations etc.	New	*This was also included in Article 16 of*

		and the need to obtain permission from the copyright owner and owner of the original work		*the 2014 draft*
15	**17**	- Copyrights in film and television program works are enjoyed by the author - It is now stipulated that the ownership of audiovisual works is to be determined by agreement and, if there is no agreement, the producer is the owner but the creators have the right of authorship and remuneration	New New	*This change was partially included in Article 19 of the 2014 draft*
16	**18**	- In item (1) schematic diagram is added - In item (2) works created by staff of newspapers, agencies and radio stations are added	New New	*These changes were also proposed in Article 20 of the 2014 draft in slightly different wording*

18	**20**	-	Inclusion of the provision that right of publication is not infringed if owner transfers original unpublished work and transferee exhibits the work	New	*This was also proposed in Article 22 of the 2014 draft*
19	**21**	-	Reference to Inheritance Law is deleted and now stated "transfer according to law"	New	
21	**23**	- -	Photographic works are deleted from the protection period of fifty years and by that now fall within the general protection period of lifetime plus fifty years stipulated in paragraph 1 of this Article The term of fifty years for the publication right of legal entities and unincorporated organisations and in relation to	New New	*These changes were also proposed in Article 29 of the 2014 draft*

		audiovisual works starts with the creation of the work; the protection of the further rights with the publication		
22	**24**	- Wording of Article 22 is slightly amended to clarify that use of a work must not impact normal use and unreasonably harm the right holder's lawful rights and interests - In item (6) "adapting, compiling and playing" has been added for classroom use and commercial publication and distribution is prohibited - In item (8) "cultural halls" are added - Item (9) now included the requirement that	New New New New	*These changes were partially included Article 43 of the 2014 draft*

		there must be no aim of profit for free performances		
		- Item (10) specifies that installation or display of the work must be "outdoor"	New	
		- In item (13) the reference to braille is extended to include ways that people with print disabilities can perceive	New	
		- Item (13) now includes an open clause naming "other circumstances provided for by laws and administrative regulations"	New	
23	**25**	- Reference to "9-year compulsory education" is changed to "compulsory education"	New	*This was also proposed in Article 47 the 2014 draft*
26	**28**	- Pledge of copyrights is to be registered in accordance with law; reference	New	

		to State Council is removed		
Ch. 4	**Ch. 4**	- The Chapter is renamed to "Rights related to Copyright"	New	*In the 2014 draft Chapter III was named "Related Rights"*
37	**38**	- "Actors and performing units" are deleted - The last paragraph is deleted as it is now included in Article 16	New	*This was also included in Article 33 of the 2014 draft*
38	**39**	- Rental is added to the rights of the performer	New	*This was also included in Article 34 of the 2014 draft*
n/a	**40**	- A new article is added which further clarifies the rights regarding performances for hire	New	*This was partially also included in Article 36 of the 2014 draft*
42	**44**	- Those permitted by the producers of audio and video recordings to lease shall also obtain the performers' permission	New	*This was also included in Article 39 of the 2014 draft*

n/a	**45**	- The rights of broadcasting stations now also include the right to allow others to spread the work through the information network	New	*This was also included in Article 40 of the 2014 draft*
43	**46**	- In relation to the broadcasting of published works it is further clarified that remuneration needs to be paid to the copyright holder as provided for by law	New	
45	**47**	- The broadcastting right of radio and television stations is further clarified in item (1) stating that rebroadcasting includes wired and wireless means - Dissemination of radio/ television to the public through in-	New New	*This was partially included in Article 42 of the 2014 draft*

		formation networks is added as item (3) - A paragraph is added emphasizing that the exercise by radio/ television stations must not affect, restrict or infringe upon others' exercise of copyright and related rights	 New	
Chapter 5	**Chapter 5**	- The Chapter is renamed to "Protection of Copyright and Rights Related to Copyright"	New	*In the 2014 draft Chapter VII was entitled "The Protection of Rights"*
n/a	**49, 50, 51**	Three articles are added to include regulations regarding technical measures: - right holders may take technical measures which may not be circumvented or damaged without authorization and no services	 Articles 4, 26 RIN	*Articles 68 to 70 in the 2014 draft dealt with technological protection measures integrating RIN*[1010]

[1010] "Regulation on the Protection of Right of Dissemination via Information Network".

		for such activities can be provided - list of limitations: (1) provision of small number of works to teachers or researchers for classroom teaching or scientific research, (2) provision to blind people to perceive work with no aim of profit, (3) if state organs use it to implement their duties, (4) if bodies with security monitoring qualifications are testing the security of computers/systems/ networks, - (5) if research is done on encryption or reverse engineering - prohibition to deliberately delete rights management information or	Partially Article 12 RIN New Article 5 RIN	

		knowingly provide such damages works to the public		
48	**53**	- Inclusion of concrete administrative fines for infringement in case of revenue over 50,000 Yuan of one to five times the amount of illegal business volume and in case of absence of illegal business volume/difficulties in calculations up to 250,000 Yuan can be fined - Item (6) now includes the provision of technical circumvention devices/services to others - Item (7) now includes the spreading of works with deleted/changed rights management information if the	Article 18, 19, 36 IR New New	*This was also proposed in Articles 77, 78 of the 2014 draft* *These additions were also proposed in Article 78 (2), (3) and (4) of the 2014 draft*

			deletion/change is known or should have been known		
49	**54**	-	The regulations on damages are updated to include three ways of compensation, namely actual loss, illegal income or multiple of the license fee	New	*This was also included in Article 76 of the 2014 draft*
		-	In serious cases, the compensation determined using one of the methods can be increased to up to five times ("punitive damages")	New	*This was partially included in Article 76 of the 2014 draft with the maximum of three times the amount*
		-	If the compensation using one of the methods is difficult to calculate a minimum of 500 Yuan and maximum compensation of 5 Million Yuan (previously 500,000 Yuan) can be awarded based on the circum-	New	*See Article 76 of the 2014 draft but amount has been increased from 1 Million to 5 Million Yuan*

		stances of the infringement - The court is granted the right to order disclosure of books and materials to determine the compensation amount; if not provided court may determine the amount on the basis of the right holder's position - Right holders can apply for destruction of the infringing copies	New New	*See Article 76 of the 2014 draft*
n/a	**55**	- The new article stipulates the investigating rights of the authorities and the obligation of assistance of the respective parties	New	*This was also proposed in Article 79 of the 2014 draft*
50	**56**	- In relation to interim measures reference to the Civil Procedure Law is deleted	New	

51	**57**	-	In relation to evidence preservation the further rules regarding the timing are deleted	New	
53	**59**	-	A second paragraph is added clarifying that in litigation, the defendant infringer has to provide evidence proving that he had permission from the right holder	New	
54 partially	**61**	-	In relation to the civil liability of the parties for non-performance or non-compliance of contractual obligations, reference is made to the applicability of relevant provision and direct reference to the General Principles of Civil Law, the Contract Law is deleted	New	

n/a	**65**	-	A new article is added which clarifies that "older" photographic works that would still be valid under the new regime are no longer protected	New	*This was included Article 29 of the 2014 draft*
60	**66**	-	The reference to "policies" is deleted	New	
35, 44, 54, 56		-	These articles are deleted (but partially included in other articles as indicated)		

As it can be seen in the above table, many of the changes undertaken in the draft published by the NPC Standing Committee in April 2020 were already included in the 2014 draft. Reference is also made to the assessment of the major changes of the 2014 draft in *Chapter 4 II. 4. e).*

What is very promising to see is the increase of maximum damage compensation to 5 Million Yuan whereas the 2014 draft only proposed for a raise to 1 Million Yuan from the currently stipulated 500,000 Yuan. Furthermore, the provision now includes a minimum amount of 500 Yuan. By that, China is enhancing the deterrent effect of the copyright law toward infringers. Furthermore, the amended Article 54 (former 49) of the new draft clarifies that there are three methods for damage calculation, namely actual loss, illegal income and hypothetical license fee. According to the new provision, damages can be calculated based on illegal income or hypothetical license/royalties when the actual loss is difficult to calculate. Only in the case of non-determinability of the court by one of the above methods, a damage up to 5 Million Yuan can be awarded. Thus, the newly drafted Article 54 better stipulates the process for damage calculation. In comparison to the 2014 draft the choice of the right holder has been slightly weakened. In addition, the last paragraph of Article 54 now includes the right to request destruction of the infringing copies and machinery used.

Another positive change is the compared to the 2014 draft is the fact that the "private use" limitation is not limited to reproduction but simply states "use of the work" which is much broader and better reflects the public interest.

However, important further integrations of the existing regulations such as

- the inclusion of definitions, further provisions on collective right management,
- rules on the responsibilities/possible exemptions of network service providers as well as
- the inclusion of provisions regarding the protection of computer software

have been omitted in the promulgated amendment. The amendment also does not address the criticized parts of the 2014 draft such as the clarification of limitations to the circumvention of technological measures (e.g. in relation to private use).

Additionally, it is very unfortunate to see that the amendment does not provide for a change of the structure of the law as it was proposed in the 2014 draft. A clearer structure would have significantly enhanced the understanding of the law.

Thus, in some ways, the new draft seems like a weaker version of the 2014 draft. One possible explanation for this could be that a "smaller" amendment to the current legislation is probably processed much faster than the previously proposed substantial revision and that China wanted to speed up the promulgation the new copyright law to

- on the one side, fulfil its own set goals and
- on the other side to adhere to the agreements in the U.S.-China Trade Deal.

It remains to be seen whether further amendments – in particular to enhance the coherency and transparency of the copyright systems – will be made to the legislation after it comes into force on 1 June 2021.

5. Important Developments Following the Promulgation of the Law

In addition to the passed 2020 Amendment of the Copyright Law, the NCAC and the SPC have issued promising notifications which will hopefully further improve the enforcement of copyrights and related rights in China.

a) Notice by the NCAC on Administrative Enforcement

On 15 November 2020, the NCAC issued a "*Notice on Further Improving the Examination and Determination of Evidence for Copyright Administrative Enforcement*"[1011] after extensive public consultation taking place throughout the year. By that Notice, the NCAC aims at strengthening the supervision of administrative enforcement by providing guidance on the evidence to be submitted by the copyright holder/licensee and clarifying that the enforcing agency shall presume that the complaint is justified if there is no evidence to the contrary; meaning that if an infringement can be shown by the complainant and evidence to the contrary provided by the respondent is insufficient, the enforcement agency shall determine that the complained act constitutes a copyright infringement.[1012] Furthermore, it is clarified that no appraisal agency needs to be engaged if the documentation provided by the right holder is sufficient to determine an infringement.[1013]

The NCAC's Notice reads very promisingly. It is to be hoped that this will actually lead to a lightening of the burden of proof on the part of the applicants and so that they will be better able to enforce their rights as a result.

b) SPC's Opinion on Strengthening the Protection of Copyright

In November 2020, the SPC also issued various interpretations including updates to already existing interpretations relating to the protection of copyrights[1014], in particular

---

[1011] NCAC "Notice on Further Improving the Examination and Determination of Evidence for Copyright Administrative Enforcement" (15 November 2020).

[1012] See Section 1. "Proof of Rights" and Section 2. "Evidence of Infringement".

[1013] See Section 3. "Determination of Infringement".

[1014] *"The Supreme People's Court's Interpretation on Several Issues Concerning the Application of Law in the Trial of Patent Infringement Disputes (2)" and other eighteen intellectual property judicial interpretations* (2020 - adopted 23 December 2020, effective 1 January 2021), Supreme People's Court of the People's Republic of China (provided by court.gov.cn).

- the "*Interpretation on Several Issues Concerning the Application of Law in the Trial of Copyright Civil Dispute Cases*" [1015] and
- the "*Provisions on Several Issues Concerning the Application of Law in the Trial of Civil Dispute Cases Infringing the Right of Information Network Communication*"[1016].

These further interpretations/provisions provide, inter alia, further guidance for courts relating to the evidence to be provided by the claimants and clarifying that if there is no proof to the contrary, the defendant has to bear civil liability. They also include further clarifications on the respective, jurisdictions, the damage calculations and the statute of limitations. In relation to the right of information network communication the SPC provides clarification that right holders can submit notifications via written letter, fax, e-mail, etc. and if the provider fails to take action in a timely manner, the courts shall affirm that the provider knows of the infringement.

The SPC's recent efforts to improve the application of copyright legislation in the courts and thereby strengthen the rights of right holders is a promising step in the right direction. It remains to be seen whether this will actually be implemented by the courts.

c) SPC's Interpretation on Punitive Damages

On 3 March 2021, the SPC implemented the "*Interpretation on the Application of Punitive Damages in Civil Cases of Infringement of Intellectual Property Rights*"[1017] which aims at providing guidance to courts to accurately apply punitive damages. In particular, the interpretations clarify at

---

[1015] Section 10. [Original title: 十、修改《最高人民法院关于审理著作权民事纠纷案件适用法律若干问题的解释》Shí, xiūgǎi "zuìgāo rénmín fǎyuàn guā nyú shěnlǐ zhùzuòquán mínshì jiūfēn ànjiàn shìyòng fǎlǜ ruògān wèntí de jiěshì "] ibid.

[1016] Section 11. [Original title: 十一、修改《最高人民法院关于审理侵害信息网络传播权民事纠纷案件适用法律若干问题的规定》Shíyī, xiūgǎi "zuìgāo ré nmín fǎyuàn guānyú shěnlǐ qīnhài xìnxī wǎngluò chuánbò quán mínshì jiūfēn à njiàn shìyòng fǎlǜ ruògān wèntí de guīdìng"] ibid.

[1017] *Interpretation on the Application of Punitive Damages in Civil Cases of Infringement of Intellectual Property Rights* (2021 - adopted 7 February 2021, effective 3 March 2021), Supreme People's Court of the People's Republic of China (provided by court.gov.cn).

what time punitive damages can be claimed, how "serious intentional infringement" is determined and how the damages shall be calculated. Article 3 of the Interpretation contains a non-exclusive list of regulatory examples in which "intentional infringement" is presumed (e.g. continuance of infringement after notification/warning, pre-existing business relationship between complainant and respondent). Article 4 of the Interpretation contains an open-ended list of circumstances which lead to the determination of "serious infringement" (e.g. repeated violations, destroying evidence, endangerment of national security).

In addition, the SPC has also announced to summarize the trial experience for further guidance.

It is hoped that the SPC's Interpretation will result in courts applying the rules on punitive damages correctly, further strengthening the options available to right holders and the "deterrent" function of the reformed Copyright Law.

6. Summary

It can be summarized that 2020 was a relevant and very important year for the further development of copyright protection in China. In addition to the amendment of the Copyright Law, the NCAC and SPC also made important changes that will significantly strengthen the ability of right holders and hopefully provide better enforcement in the area of copyright infringement. It remains to be seen how the situation will further develop once the 2020 Amendment comes into force in June 2021.

CHAPTER 5 – CONCLUSION AND OUTLOOK

The Chinese Copyright Law has a long history of development.

It has been shown that the protection of intellectual property rights is not indigenous to the legal concept in the People's Republic of China and hence, not a result of the long Chinese culture because the concept of protecting individual rights is contrary to the understanding of society, which evolved in China from Confucianism and Buddhism.[1018] Intellectual property legislation in China can be best described as a legal transplant.[1019] In general, it can be said that the Chinese conception of law is very different to the conception of the Western countries.

In China, social advancement was seen as learning the width of classical literature and becoming familiar with the Chinese history rather than studying new subjects (technical training)[1020]; as Confucius' said

> *'I transmit rather than create; I believe in and love the Ancients'.*[1021]

Copying was seen as a form of 'flattery' because an imitation confirmed the worthiness of a creation and did not constitute an offence to the creator nor was the creation of something new seen to be worthy of receiving monetary credit for it.[1022] The first emergence of copyright or at least a right similar to copyright was during the Sui- and Tan-Dynasty, a time in which

---

[1018] Alford, *To Steal a Book Is an Elegant Offense: Intellectual Property Law in Chinese Civilization* (1995), 2; and Li, "The Sky is High and the Emperor is Far Way" *Bol Mex Derecho Comp* 36, 108 (2003), 954; also see Ocko, "Copying, Culture, and Control" *Yale J.L.& Human.* 8, 2 - Article 10 (1996), 560; Mark A. Groombridge in Long, *Intellectual Property Law in Emerging Markets* (2000), 13; Wei, *Der Urheberrechtsschutz in China mit Hinweisen auf das Deutsche Recht* (1994), 3.

[1019] Li, "The Sky is High and the Emperor is Far Way" *Bol Mex Derecho Comp* 36, 108 (2003), 954; also see Ocko, "Copying, Culture, and Control" *Yale J.L.& Human.* 8, 2 - Article 10 (1996), 560.

[1020] Alford, *To Steal a Book Is an Elegant Offense: Intellectual Property Law in Chinese Civilization* (1995), 22, 25.

[1021] The Analects of Confucius, bk.7 ch.1 as qoted in ibid., 9.

[1022] Mark A. Groombridge in Long, *Intellectual Property Law in Emerging Markets* (2000), 13.

handwritten books could not satisfy the demand anymore.[1023] At that time, the printing companies were granted the 'privilege of printing' that had the aim to control publication of the works and by that, retaining harmony in the Chinese feudal state.[1024] However, no right was granted to the author/creator of the literary work.[1025] In the late Qing-Dynasty, strengthening of the foreign policy made it inevitable for China to introduce some kind of copyright protection and eventually, the Great Qing Copyright was formulated in 1910.[1026] Unfortunately, the law that can be described as a milestone in the development of Copyright Law in China was only effective for one year before all regulations were abolished once the Qing were overthrown.[1027]

Except for some copyright legislation during the reign of the KMT, no major developments were recorded during the reign of the KMT and the era of Mao Zedong in which no emphasis was put on the protection of the individual including intellectual property protection.[1028] The importance of copyright protection had almost completely vanished during that time.

This way of thinking was challenged heavily when China opened its economy to the world during the Open Door Policy. The CCP wanted to reconstruct the whole economy and although intellectual property rights were contrary to socialist understanding[1029], they were thought to be essential for the 'four modernizations program' to be fulfilled.[1030] Intellectual property protection was supposed to bring foreign investment, encourage foreign trade, improve the market as a whole and hence, the CCP recognized

[1023] Wei, *Der Urheberrechtsschutz in China mit Hinweisen auf das Deutsche Recht* (1994), 1.

[1024] Qu, *Copyright in China* (2002), 3; Wei, *Der Urheberrechtsschutz in China mit Hinweisen auf das Deutsche Recht* (1994), 2.

[1025] Wei, *Der Urheberrechtsschutz in China mit Hinweisen auf das Deutsche Recht* (1994), 2.

[1026] Yufeng and Ng, "Understanding the Great Qing Copright Law" *J. Copyright Soc'y U.S.A.* 56 (2008-2009), 768, 771.

[1027] Kong, *WTO, Internationalization and the Intellectual Property Rights Regime in China* (2005), 6; Yufeng and Ng, "Understanding the Great Qing Copright Law" *J. Copyright Soc'y U.S.A.* 56 (2008-2009), 772.

[1028] Levi, *Modern China's Foreign Policy* (1953), 190; Qu, *Copyright in China* (2002), 27, 39.

[1029] Yu, "Piracy, Prejudice, and Perspectives" *B.U. Int'l L.J.* 19, 1 (2001), 21.

[1030] Nie, *The Enforcement of Intellectual Property Rights in China* (2006), 181.

that those were necessary in order to establish a strong Socialist country.[1031] Also, it was understood by China that foreign investors feared to invest in China unless their intellectual property rights were secured in some way.[1032]

Finally, the first real Copyright Law of the People's Republic of China was enacted in 1990 and it can be said that it was one of the most important laws that shaped the modern protection of intellectual property rights in China.[1033]

Since 1992, China has acceded to many international as well as bilateral agreements and has amended its copyright legislation extensively. The most important step for China in this regard was becoming a member of the World Trade Organization in 2001.[1034] In 2012, China was even the host for a Diplomatic Conference that led to the adoption of the Beijing Treaty – the first international intellectual property treaty that was established in China.[1035] China has come from a country with no acceptance of intellectual property rights to a country with much intellectual property legislation in quite a short period (1979 up until now). Since then, the legislation is constantly changing in order to adjust to international standards.

In the course of time, China has amended its Copyright Law (in 2001 and 2010) and has brought forward some major reforms in form of regulations (especially in 2013). By amending the law to suit international demands, China has – in some parts accepted – that its ideologies and hence, its economy had to be amended in order to play a role in the world; it can be said that this transformation happened due to the advancement of technology and the 'liberalization of thoughts' (解放 思想 Jiěfàng sīxiǎng).[1036]

[1031] Ibid.
[1032] Qu, *Copyright in China* (2002), 39.
[1033] Kong, *WTO, Internationalization and the Intellectual Property Rights Regime in China* (2005), 17.
[1034] WTO "Accession of the People's Republic of China" Protocol WT/L/432.
[1035] Liu and Huang, "On the Beijing Treaty on Audivisual Performances and the Upgrading of China's Copyright Law (English Title)" *Journal of Shaoyang University - Social Science Edition* 3, 4 (2014), 19.
[1036] Feng and Huang, "International Standards and Local Elements" *J. Copyright Soc'y U.S.A.* 49 (2001-2002), 921.

The current Chinese Copyright Law is a mixture of various legislations from other countries and can be best described as a hybrid between the Anglo-American copyright and the European droit d'auteur with an own socialist touch.[1037] However, as it has been shown, due to the fact that the Chinese copyright framework is a mixture of different systems, it becomes clear once again that that the copyright legislation is a transplant and not a law that has grown and flourished historically in China.

When looking at the statistics of the last years it becomes apparent that the registration of copyright works is constantly increasing[1038], which shows that the creative scene in China is constantly rising and that copyrights gain more and more importance. Furthermore, it can be seen that copyright litigation is constantly increasing and also, higher fines are imposed by the administrative authorities.[1039] It is hoped that the stronger enforcement will deter potential infringers and will eventually lead to a reduction of infringement activities taking place in China.

Another important step and a sign towards intellectual property protection including copyright protection is the introduction of the specialized intellectual property courts in Beijing, Shanghai and Guangzhou by the Standing Committee of the National People's Congress in 2014 and the constant increase of IP tribunals all over China as well as centralized training events.[1040]

However, although the Chinese Copyright Law looks quite advanced in the books it is still lacking transparency and sufficient enforcement. One of the major problems is the vast amount of regulations that make it difficult for the Chinese citizens to fully understand the law and thus, to fight for their

---

[1037] See also Enders and Steiner, "Urheberrechtsreform und Urheberrechtsdurchsetzung" *ZChinR* 17, 2 (2010), 95.
[1038] See *Chapter 3 I. 2. c)* of this dissertation.
[1039] See *Chapter 3 III. 2. g)* of this dissertation.
[1040] *Decision of the Standing Committee of the National People's Congress on Establishing Intellectual Property Right Courts in Beijing, Shanghai and Guangzhou* (31 August 2014), Standing Committee of the National People's Congress; also see Li, "Special intellectual property courts in China" (2016), 303; for more detailed information, see Lee and Zhang, "Specialised IP courts in China - judicial governance of intellectual property rights" *IIC* 48, 8 (2017), 900-924.

rights. Further, China is still experiencing corruption and lack of judicial independence as well as obstructive local protectionism.

As shown, the enforcement system in China consists of two channels, namely the administrative track and the judicial track. This means that right holders can chose whether they want to pursue their rights by filing a complaint and let the administrative authorities take the necessary actions or file a lawsuit and inter alia, also claim damage compensation for the loss suffered from the infringing activity.[1041] For China, this system has been proven to be a good solution.[1042] Especially at the time of the introduction of the Copyright Law the administrative track was used a lot by Chinese citizens[1043], probably due to the fact that the administrative track is less costly and the requirements to file an administrative complaint are lower than in the judicial track. In other words, the hurdles for a right holder to enforce his/her rights and oppose to the infringement of the copyright(s) are not quite as high in the administrative track. However, when looking at the statistics, a shift from administrative cases to court cases can be seen during the last years. A reason for this might be that the administrative proceedings do not allow for damage compensation by the infringer whereas such can be claimed in court and is often awarded to the right holders.

Currently, there are no indications that the administrative track will be abolished in the near future. The NCAC is an important authority in China and strongly impacts the development of copyright protection. In fact, during the last years more extensive powers such as the possibility of taking more stringent measures and imposing higher fines upon the infringer have been given to the administrative authorities. Although the judicial track might be more attractive to many right holders due to the possibility to claim damage compensation, the administrative track is still a good tool to take fast action against infringers, in particular in smaller cases. Furthermore, the evidence collected during an administrative procedure can then

1041 Ross, "Enforcing Intellectual Property Rights in China" *China Bus. Rev.* (2012), 25.

1042 Feng and Huang, "International Standards and Local Elements" *J. Copyright Soc'y U.S.A.* 49 (2001-2002), 940.

1043 Ross, "Enforcing Intellectual Property Rights in China" *China Bus. Rev.* (2012), 25.

be used in a civil proceeding. Hopefully, the maintenance of the dual system will contribute to the further improvement of copyright enforcement in China.

The 2014 draft of the Copyright Law for China was trying to minimize the transparency and enforcement problems by updating the law and integrating the major regulations into one legislation piece to create a unified law. By that, the law would become much more transparent and easier for the Chinese population to understand and would open less burdensome possibilities for the authors/creators to actually fight for their rights. Also, the 2014 draft aimed at strengthening the protection of related rights which only played a secondary role in the Chinese protection of copyright. With regard to the enforcement of the law, it was very encouraging to see that the 2014 draft of the copyright law enhanced the scope of civil remedies as well as possibilities for administrative punishment.[1044] However, the draft still showed some weaknesses that would hopefully be solved in the further development of the legislation. Due to the passage of time since the 2014 draft, it was of utmost importance that technological advancement is sufficiently taken into account and integrated in the further elaboration of the new legislation.

Unfortunately, the reform of the Copyright Law came to a standstill after the publication of the third draft in 2014. The very promising beginning of the reform in 2012 with the collection of opinions and the publication of two drafts was unfortunately not continued. Until 2019, not much had happened in the legislative process. Here and there, high-ranking officials from the SPC and the NCAC have commented on the importance of the further development of intellectual property legislation including the Copyright Law and have positively highlighted the reform, but unfortunately no further progress was made. It was hoped that the copyright law would once again receive more attention in 2020 and that the legislative process will continue.

In this regard, also the negotiations with the U.S. and finally, the stipulation of the Trade Agreement in January 2020 can be considered as important steps forward.

Finally, on 26 April 2020 the NPC Standing Committee published the long-awaited new draft and after a second deliberation in August 2020,

[1044] Xue, "A User-Unfriendly Draft: 3rd Revision" *JICTL* 7, 4 (2012), 353.

promulgated the amendment on 11 November 2020. Contrary to expectations, the 2020 Amendment does not build up on the previous drafts from 2012 and 2014 but rather on the 2010 Copyright Law. Many of the proposed changes in the 2020 Amendment were already included in the 2014 draft. Very promising to see is the increase of maximum damage compensation to 5 Million Yuan whereas the 2014 draft only provided for a raise to 1 Million Yuan from the currently stipulated 500,000 Yuan. By that, China is enhancing the deterrent effect of the copyright law toward infringers.

However, important further integrations of the existing regulations such as the inclusion of definitions, further provisions on collective right management, rules on the responsibilities/possible exemptions of network service providers as well as the inclusion of provisions regarding the protection of computer software have been omitted in the 2020 Amendment. Unfortunately, also the structure of the law has not been changed as it was provided for in the 2014 draft and which would have enhanced the understanding of the law.

Thus, in some ways, the 2020 Amendment seems like a weaker version of the 2014 draft. One possible explanation could be that a less substantial amendment to the legislation is promulgated much faster and by that China could fulfil its own set goals and timely adhere to the agreements in the U.S.-China Trade Deal. It remains to be seen whether further amendments – in particular to enhance the coherency and transparency of the copyright system – will be made to the legislation after it comes into force on 1 June 2021.

In addition to the 2020 Amendment of the Copyright Law, the NCAC and the SPC issued promising notices/interpretations that strengthen the possibilities of right holders and will hopefully lead to a better enforcement of the legislations.

Summarizing, it can be said that the reform of the Chinese copyright legislation over the last years has brought forward many good and promising developments. It can be seen that China has woken up and understood the importance of intellectual property protection and that more emphasis needs to be placed on adequate legislation and enforcement in order to remain one of the fastest emerging markets in the world.

However, it needs to be emphasized that a better legislation does not necessarily mean that the enforcement of such will also be improved. As already stated, China is still experiencing great problems with corruption, unequal treatment, independence of the judiciary and local protectionism. It is hoped that the growing importance of intellectual property protection and the recognition of the advantages of a strong protection system will reduce these hurdles and eventually overcome these.

For now, it can be said:

> *"Yes, copying still exists in China but the protection against it is constantly improving."*

ANNEX – GERMAN SUMMARY

Diese Dissertation konzentriert sich auf die rechtshistorische Entwicklung des Urheberrechts in der Volksrepublik China mit dem Ziel, die derzeitige Reform des Urheberrechts und die Probleme, mit denen China konfrontiert war und ist, zu verstehen.

Mit der Arbeit soll gezeigt werden, dass China das Kopieren nicht einfach toleriert (wie von vielen angenommen wird), sondern dass intensive Anstrengungen unternommen wurden und werden, um den Schutz urheberrechtlich geschützter Werke zu verbessern. Hierbei wird sich kritisch mit der derzeitigen Gesetzeslage sowie insbesondere der Durchsetzung auseinandergesetzt und aufgezeigt, welche Schwächen derzeit existieren.

I. Struktur

Kapitel 1 stellt das Urheberrecht und seine Herausforderungen in China vor und skizziert die Struktur dieser Dissertation.

In **Kapitel 2** werden zunächst die Rechtswahrnehmung und die Rechtsquellen in China aufgezeigt, um die Entwicklung und Funktionsweise des Urheberrechts in China zu verstehen. Sodann wird der gesamte historische Hintergrund und die Entwicklung des Rechts des geistigen Eigentums, insbesondere des Urheberrechts, in China analysiert. Ein weiterer Schwerpunkt liegt auf den internationalen Beziehungen Chinas sowie auf den Abkommen und Konventionen, denen China beigetreten ist. Der Beitritt Chinas zu verschiedenen internationalen Abkommen ist wichtig, um die rasche Entwicklung der chinesischen Gesetzgebung im Bereich des geistigen Eigentums und die daraus resultierenden Herausforderungen bei der Anpassung an internationale Standards zu verstehen.

Anschließend wird in **Kapitel 3** das aktuelle Urheberrechtsgesetz der Volksrepublik China diskutiert und anhand der Hauptregelungen analysiert. Um die Struktur des chinesischen Urheberrechtsgesetzes besser zu verstehen, widmet sich ein Unterabschnitt dieses Kapitels mit einer vergleichenden Analyse des chinesischen Urheberrechtsgesetzes zu den Urheberrechtssystemen der Vereinigten Staaten von Amerika (anglo-amerikanisches System) und der Bundesrepublik Deutschland (europäisches Droit d'Auteur-System). Sodann setzt sich die Dissertation kritisch mit dem zweigleisigen Durchsetzungssystem bei Urheberrechtsverletzungen auseinander und es werden die Stärken und Schwächen des Systems diskutiert. Das Kapitel endet mit einer Statistik der Urheberrechtsfälle in China, die die Entwicklungen der letzten Jahre aufzeigt.

Kapitel 4 beginnt mit einem Überblick über den Gesetzgebungsprozess in China und geht dann auf den Reformprozess des chinesischen Urheberrechtsgesetzes ein. In einem ersten Schritt wird die Entwicklung der Entwürfe des zu reformierenden Urheberrechtsgesetzes diskutiert. In einem zweiten Schritt wird der umfassende dritte Entwurf aus 2014 genauer analysiert, ein Überblick über die vorgesehenen Änderungen im Vergleich zu dem derzeitigen Urheberrechtsgesetz gegeben und die wichtigsten Änderungen des im ersten Teil der Reform zwischen 2012 und 2014 entworfenen Gesetzes kritisch diskutiert. Sodann wird ein Überblick zu den aktuellen in Entwicklungen in China – insbesondere den Verhandlungen zwischen den USA und China – gegeben. Im Anschluss daran wird der zweite Teil der Reform, die in 2020 wiederaufgenommen wurde, vorgestellt und das endgültig verkündete Gesetz, das im Juni 2021 in Kraft treten wird, kritisch analysiert und bewertet.

Kapitel 5 fasst die Ergebnisse der Dissertation zusammen und zeigt sowohl die Verbesserungen als auch die noch bestehenden Schwächen des verkündeten geänderten Urheberrechtsgesetzes in China auf. Ferner wird ein Ausblick auf die weitere Entwicklung des Urheberrechts aus Sicht der Autorin gegeben.

II. Zusammenfassung

Das chinesische Urheberrechtsgesetz hat eine lange Entstehungsgeschichte.

Bei der rechtshistorischen Analyse ist deutlich geworden, dass der Schutz der Rechte an geistigem Eigentum in der Volksrepublik China kein einheimisches Rechtskonzept und damit kein Ergebnis der langen chinesischen Kultur ist. Das Konzept des Schutzes der Rechte des Einzelnen widerspricht dem Verständnis der Gesellschaft, das sich in China aus dem Konfuzianismus und dem Buddhismus entwickelt hat.[i]

[i] Alford, *To Steal a Book Is an Elegant Offense: Intellectual Property Law in Chinese Civilization* (1995), 2; und Li, "The Sky is High and the Emperor is Far

Die Gesetzgebung im Bereich des geistigen Eigentums in China lässt sich am besten als eine rechtliche Transplantation beschreiben.[ii] Generell lässt sich sagen, dass sich die chinesische Rechtsauffassung stark von der Auffassung der westlichen Länder unterscheidet.

Das Kopieren wurde schon zu Zeiten von Konfuzius als eine Form der „Schmeichelei“ angesehen, weil eine Nachahmung die Würdigkeit einer Schöpfung bestätigte und keine Beleidigung für den Schöpfer darstellte und dagegen die Schöpfung von etwas Neuem nicht als würdig erachtet wurde, um dafür eine geldwerte Anerkennung zu erhalten.[iii] Bereits in der Sui- und Tan-Dynastie gab es erste Bestrebungen, Regelungen für die Vervielfältigung zu erschaffen, da die Nachfrage durch handgeschriebene Bücher nicht mehr befriedigt werden konnte.[iv] Das sogenannte „Druckprivileg“ hatte das Ziel, die Veröffentlichung der Werke zu kontrollieren, um so die Harmonie im chinesischen Feudalstaat zu erhalten.[v] Dem Autor/Schöpfer des literarischen Werkes wurde jedoch kein Recht gewährt.[vi]

In der späten Qing-Dynastie machte die Stärkung der Außenpolitik es für China unumgänglich, eine Art Urheberrechtsschutz einzuführen; schließlich wurde 1910 das Große Qing-Urheberrecht erlassen.[vii] Leider war das Gesetz, das als ein Meilenstein in der Entwicklung des Urheberrechts in

Way" *Bol Mex Derecho Comp* 36, 108 (2003), 954; siehe auch Ocko, "Copying, Culture, and Control" *Yale J.L.& Human.* 8, 2 - Article 10 (1996), 560; Mark A. Groombridge in Long, *Intellectual Property Law in Emerging Markets* (2000), 13; Wei, *Der Urheberrechtsschutz in China mit Hinweisen auf das Deutsche Recht* (1994), 3.

[ii] Li, "The Sky is High and the Emperor is Far Way" *Bol Mex Derecho Comp* 36, 108 (2003), 954; siehe auch Ocko, "Copying, Culture, and Control" *Yale J.L.& Human.* 8, 2 - Article 10 (1996), 560.

[iii] Mark A. Groombridge in Long, *Intellectual Property Law in Emerging Markets* (2000), 13.

[iv] Wei, *Der Urheberrechtsschutz in China mit Hinweisen auf das Deutsche Recht* (1994), 1.

[v] Qu, *Copyright in China* (2002), 3; Wei, *Der Urheberrechtsschutz in China mit Hinweisen auf das Deutsche Recht* (1994), 2.

[vi] Wei, *Der Urheberrechtsschutz in China mit Hinweisen auf das Deutsche Recht* (1994), 2.

[vii] Yufeng and Ng, "Understanding the Great Qing Copright Law" *J. Copyright Soc'y U.S.A.* 56 (2008-2009), 768,771.

China bezeichnet werden kann, nur ein Jahr lang in Kraft, bevor alle Regelungen nach dem Sturz der Qing abgeschafft wurden.[viii]

In der darauffolgenden Zeit war die Bedeutung des Urheberrechtsschutzes fast vollständig verschwunden.

Diese Denkweise wurde stark in Frage gestellt, als China im Rahmen der Reform- und Öffnungspolitik seine Wirtschaft für die Welt öffnete. Die Kommunistische Partei wollte die gesamte Wirtschaft erneuern, und obwohl geistige Eigentumsrechte dem sozialistischen Verständnis widersprachen[ix], hielt man sie für wesentlich, damit das Reformprogramm „Vier Modernisierungen" erfüllt werden konnte.[x] Der Schutz des geistigen Eigentums sollte ausländische Investitionen bringen, den Außenhandel fördern, den Markt insgesamt verbessern; daher erkannte die Kommunistische Partei, dass dieser Schutz notwendig war, um ein starkes sozialistisches Land zu errichten.[xi] Man verstand auch, dass ausländische Investoren sich davor fürchteten, in China zu investieren, wenn ihre geistigen Eigentumsrechte nicht in irgendeiner Weise gesichert würden.[xii] Schließlich wurde 1990 das erste bedeutende Urheberrechtsgesetz der Volksrepublik China erlassen – eines der wichtigsten Gesetze, das den modernen Schutz der geistigen Eigentumsrechte in China geprägt hat.[xiii]

Seit 1992 ist China vielen internationalen und bilateralen Abkommen beigetreten und hat seine Urheberrechtsgesetzgebung umfassend geändert. Von größter Bedeutung war hierbei der Beitritt zur Welthandelsorganisation im Jahr 2001.[xiv] Im Jahr 2012 war China sogar Gastgeber einer diplomatischen Konferenz, die zur Verabschiedung des Vertrags von Peking („Beijing Treaty on Audiovisual Performances") führte – dem ersten internationalen Vertrag über geistiges Eigentum, der in China geschlossen

[viii] Kong, *WTO, Internationalization and the Intellectual Property Rights Regime in China* (2005), 6; Yufeng and Ng, "Understanding the Great Qing Copright Law" *J. Copyright Soc'y U.S.A.* 56 (2008-2009), 772.
[ix] Yu, "Piracy, Prejudice, and Perspectives" *B.U. Int'l L.J.* 19, 1 (2001), 21.
[x] Nie, *The Enforcement of Intellectual Property Rights in China* (2006), 181.
[xi] Ibid.
[xii] Qu, *Copyright in China* (2002), 39.
[xiii] Kong, *WTO, Internationalization and the Intellectual Property Rights Regime in China* (2005), 17.
[xiv] WTO "Accession of the People's Republic of China" Protocol WT/L/432.

wurde.[xv] China ist in recht kurzer Zeit (1979 bis heute) von einem Land ohne Akzeptanz der Rechte an geistigem Eigentum zu einem Land mit zahlreichen Gesetzen im Bereich des geistigen Eigentums geworden. Die Gesetze und dazugehörigen Richtlinien, Verordnungen et cetera ändern sich ständig, um sich an die internationalen Standards anzupassen.

Im Laufe der Zeit hat China das Urheberrechtsgesetz von 1990 zweimal geändert (2001 und 2010) und einige wichtige Reformen in Form von Verordnungen vorangebracht (insbesondere in 2013). Durch die Anpassung des Gesetzes an internationale Anforderungen/Standards hat China – in Teilen – akzeptiert, dass sein Wertesystem und damit auch seine Wirtschaft geändert werden mussten, um in der Welt eine Rolle spielen zu können; man kann sagen, dass dieser Wandel durch den Fortschritt der Technologie und die „Liberalisierung der Gedanken" erfolgte.[xvi]

Das geltende chinesische Urheberrecht ist eine Mischung aus Gesetzgebungen verschiedener Länder und kann am besten als eine Mischform zwischen dem anglo-amerikanischen Urheberrecht und dem europäischen Urheberrecht mit sozialistischen Einflüssen beschrieben werden.[xvii] Wie sich jedoch gezeigt hat, wird aufgrund der Tatsache, dass das chinesische Urheberrechtssystem eine Mischung aus verschiedenen Systemen ist, einmal mehr deutlich, dass die Urheberrechtsgesetzgebung eine Transplantation und kein Gesetz ist, das in China historisch gewachsen ist.

Ein Blick auf die Statistiken der letzten Jahre zeigt, dass die Registrierung von urheberrechtlich geschützten Werken ständig zunimmt[xviii], – ein Hinweis auf die Innovationskraft und den Bedeutungszuwachs der Urheberrechte in China. Darüber hinaus zeigt sich eine deutliche und ständige Zunahme der Anzahl an Urheberrechtsstreitigkeiten und der Höhe der von den Verwaltungsbehörden verhängten Bußgelder.[xix] Es ist zu hoffen, dass die stärkere Durchsetzung potenzielle Rechtsverletzer abschreckt und

---

[xv] Liu and Huang, "On the Beijing Treaty on Audivisual Performances and the Upgrading of China's Copyright Law (English Title)" *Journal of Shaoyang University - Social Science Edition* 3, 4 (2014), 19.

[xvi] Feng and Huang, "International Standards and Local Elements" *J. Copyright Soc'y U.S.A.* 49 (2001-2002), 921.

[xvii] Siehe auch Enders and Steiner, "Urheberrechtsreform und Urheberrechtsdurchsetzung" *ZChinR* 17, 2 (2010), 95.

[xviii] Siehe *Chapter 3 I. 2. c)* dieser Dissertation.

[xix] Siehe *Chapter 3 III. 2. g)* dieser Dissertation.

schließlich zu einer Verringerung der in China stattfindenden Verletzungsaktivitäten führt. Ein weiterer wichtiger Schritt und ein Zeichen auf dem Weg zum Schutz des geistigen Eigentums einschließlich des Urheberrechtsschutzes ist die Einführung der spezialisierten Gerichte für Geistiges Eigentum in Peking, Shanghai und Guangzhou im Jahr 2014 und die ständige Zunahme der Tribunale für Geistiges Eigentum in ganz China sowie zentralisierte Schulungsveranstaltungen.[xx]

Obwohl das chinesische Urheberrechtsgesetz in den Büchern recht fortschrittlich aussieht, mangelt es ihm jedoch immer noch an Transparenz und ausreichender Durchsetzung. Eines der Hauptprobleme sind die zahlreichen verschiedenen Vorschriften (Richtlinien, Verordnungen et cetera), die es den chinesischen Bürgern erschweren, das Gesetz vollständig zu verstehen und somit für ihre Rechte zu kämpfen. Darüber hinaus leidet China noch immer unter Korruption und mangelnder richterlicher Unabhängigkeit sowie obstruktivem lokalen Protektionismus.

Das Durchsetzungssystem in China ist ein zweigleisiges System mit einem administrativen und einem gerichtlichen Weg. Das bedeutet, dass die Rechteinhaber wählen können, ob sie ihre Rechte durch Einreichen einer Beschwerde geltend machen wollen und die Verwaltungsbehörden die erforderlichen Maßnahmen ergreifen lassen, oder ob sie Klage erheben und u.a. Schadensersatz für den durch die verletzende Tätigkeit erlittenen Verlust fordern wollen.[xxi] Für China hat sich dies als eine gute Lösung erwiesen.[xxii] Vor allem zur Zeit der Einführung des Urheberrechtsgesetzes wurde der Verwaltungsweg von chinesischen Staatsbürgern viel genutzt[xxiii], wahrscheinlich aufgrund der Tatsache, dass dieser weniger kostspielig ist

---

[xx] *Decision of the Standing Committee of the National People's Congress on Establishing Intellectual Property Right Courts in Beijing, Shanghai and Guangzhou* (31 August 2014), Standing Committee of the National People's Congress; siehe auch Li, "Special intellectual property courts in China" (2016), 303; für weitere Informationen siehe auch Lee and Zhang, "Specialised IP courts in China - judicial governance of intellectual property rights" *IIC* 48, 8 (2017), 900-924.

[xxi] Ross, "Enforcing Intellectual Property Rights in China" *China Bus. Rev.* (2012), 25.

[xxii] Feng and Huang, "International Standards and Local Elements" *J. Copyright Soc'y U.S.A.* 49 (2001-2002), 940.

[xxiii] Ross, "Enforcing Intellectual Property Rights in China" *China Bus. Rev.* (2012), 25.

und die Anforderungen zur Einreichung einer Verwaltungsbeschwerde niedriger sind als bei der gerichtlichen Verfolgung. Mit anderen Worten, die Hürden für die Rechteinhaber, ihre Rechte durchzusetzen und sich der Verletzung ihrer Urheberrechte zu widersetzen, sind in der administrativen Schiene nicht ganz so hoch. In den letzten Jahren ist jedoch eine Verlagerung von Verwaltungsverfahren zu Gerichtsverfahren zu beobachten. Ein Grund dafür könnte darin liegen, dass die Verwaltungsverfahren keinen Schadensersatz durch den Verletzer zulassen, während dieser vor Gericht eingeklagt werden kann und den Rechteinhabern auch oft zugesprochen wird.

Derzeit gibt es keine Anzeichen dafür, dass die administrative Schiene in naher Zukunft abgeschafft wird. Der NCAC ist eine wichtige Behörde in China und hat einen starken Einfluss auf die Entwicklung des Urheberrechtsschutzes.

Tatsächlich wurden den Verwaltungsbehörden in den letzten Jahren weitergehende Befugnisse eingeräumt, wie die Möglichkeit, strengere Maßnahmen zu ergreifen und höhere Geldstrafen gegen die Rechtsverletzer zu verhängen. Obwohl der Rechtsweg für viele Rechteinhaber aufgrund der Möglichkeit, Schadensersatz zu fordern, attraktiver sein mag, ist der Verwaltungsweg immer noch ein gutes Instrument, um schnell gegen Rechtsverletzer vorzugehen, insbesondere in kleineren Fällen. Darüber hinaus können die während eines Verwaltungsverfahrens gesammelten Beweise dann in einem Zivilverfahren vor Gericht verwendet werden. Es ist zu hoffen, dass die Beibehaltung des dualen Systems zur weiteren Verbesserung der Urheberrechtsdurchsetzung in China beitragen wird.

Der Entwurf des neuen Urheberrechtsgesetzes für China aus 2014 hat versucht, die Transparenz- und Durchsetzungsprobleme zu minimieren, indem einige Vorschriften aktualisiert und die wichtigsten Bestimmungen in einem einzigen Gesetzestext zusammengefasst wurden, um ein einheitliches Gesetz zu schaffen. Dadurch würde das Gesetz sehr viel transparenter und leichter verständlich werden und den Urhebern/Schöpfern die Möglichkeit eröffnen, tatsächlich für ihre Rechte zu kämpfen. Darüber hinaus zielte der Entwurf aus 2014 darauf ab, den Schutz verwandter Schutzrechte zu stärken, die bisher im chinesischen Urheberrechtsschutz nur eine untergeordnete Rolle spielten.

Im Hinblick auf die Durchsetzung des Gesetzes war es sehr ermutigend zu sehen, dass die vorgeschlagene Revision des Urheberrechtsgesetzes den

Umfang der zivilrechtlichen Rechtsbehelfe wie auch der administrativen Sanktionsmöglichkeiten erweitert hat.[xxiv] Der Entwurf zeigte jedoch auch einige Schwächen auf, die hoffentlich bei der Weiterentwicklung des Gesetzentwurfs behoben werden würden. Aufgrund der seit dem Entwurf von 2014 verstrichenen Zeit war es von größter Bedeutung, dass der technologische Fortschritt ausreichend berücksichtigt und in die weitere Ausarbeitung des neuen Gesetzestextes integriert würde.

Leider ist die Reform des Urheberrechtsgesetzes nach der Veröffentlichung des dritten Entwurfs im Jahr 2014 zunächst zum Stillstand gekommen. Der vielversprechende Beginn der Reform im Jahr 2012 mit der Sammlung von Stellungnahmen und der Veröffentlichung von zwei Entwürfen hat sich leider nicht fortgesetzt. Seit der Veröffentlichung des dritten Entwurfs im Jahr 2014 hatte sich im Gesetzgebungsverfahren nicht viel getan. Hier und da haben hochrangige Beamte des Verfassungsgerichts Chinas und der Nationalen Urheberrechtsbehörde Chinas die Bedeutung der Weiterentwicklung der Gesetzgebung zum geistigen Eigentum einschließlich des Urheberrechtsgesetzes kommentiert und die Reform positiv hervorgehoben, – leider sind bis 2019 keine weiteren Fortschritte erzielt worden. Es war zu hoffen, dass dem Urheberrecht im Jahr 2020 wieder mehr Aufmerksamkeit geschenkt und der Gesetzgebungsprozess weiter vorangebracht wird. In diesem Zusammenhang können auch die Verhandlungen mit den USA und schließlich das Handelsabkommens im Januar 2020 als wichtige Schritte nach vorne betrachtet werden.

Am 26. April 2020 veröffentlichte der Ständige Ausschuss des Nationalen Volkskongresses endlich den lang erwarteten neuen Entwurf und nach einer zweiten Beratung im August 2020 wurde die Änderung am 11. November 2020 verkündet. Entgegen den Erwartungen baut die Gesetzesänderung von 2020 nicht auf den vorherigen Entwürfen aus 2012 und 2014 auf, sondern auf dem Urheberrechtsgesetz von 2010. Viele der nunmehr vorgenommenen Änderungen waren bereits im Entwurf von 2014 enthalten. Sehr vielversprechend ist die Anhebung des maximalen Schadensersatzes auf 5 Millionen Yuan, während der Entwurf von 2014 lediglich eine Anhebung von den derzeit vorgesehenen 500.000 Yuan auf 1 Million Yuan vorsah. Damit verstärkt China die abschreckende Wirkung des Urheberrechtsgesetzes gegenüber Rechtsverletzern.

[xxiv] Xue, "A User-Unfriendly Draft: 3rd Revision" *JICTL* 7, 4 (2012), 353.

Leider sind jedoch wichtige weitere Einbeziehungen der zahlreichen Verordnungen und Richtlinien wie unter anderem, die Aufnahme von Definitionen, weiteren Bestimmungen über die kollektive Rechtewahrnehmung, Regelungen zu den Verantwortlichkeiten/möglichen Ausnahmen von Netzwerkdienstleistern sowie die Aufnahme von Bestimmungen zum Schutz von Computersoftware ausgelassen worden. Auch die Struktur des Gesetzes wurde nicht geändert, wie es im Entwurf von 2014 vorgesehen war und welches zum Verständnis des Gesetzes beigetragen hätte. Somit erscheint die Gesetzesänderung von 2020 in gewisser Weise wie eine schwächere Version des Entwurfs von 2014. Eine mögliche Erklärung dafür könnte sein, dass China die Revision des Urheberrechtsgesetzes beschleunigen wollte, um einerseits die eigenen gesteckten Ziele zu erfüllen und andererseits die Vereinbarungen des Handelsabkommens zwischen den USA und China einzuhalten. Es bleibt abzuwarten, ob nach dem Inkrafttreten am 1. Juni 2021 weitere Änderungen – insbesondere zur Verbesserung der Kohärenz und Transparenz des Urheberrechtssystems - an dem Gesetz vorgenommen werden.

Neben der Urheberrechtsänderung von 2020 haben die Nationale Urheberrechtsbehörde Chinas und das Verfassungsgericht Chinas vielversprechende Hinweise/Interpretationen herausgegeben, die die Möglichkeiten der Rechteinhaber stärken und hoffentlich zu einer besseren Durchsetzung der Gesetzgebung führen werden.

Zusammenfassend lässt sich sagen, dass die Reform der chinesischen Urheberrechtsgesetzgebung über die letzten Jahre viele gute und vielversprechende Entwicklungen vorangebracht hat. Es lässt sich feststellen, dass in China die Bedeutung des Schutzes des geistigen Eigentums deutlich an Zuwachs gewonnen hat. Es wurde erkannt, dass mehr Gewicht auf eine angemessene Gesetzgebung und Durchsetzung gelegt werden muss, um einer der am schnellsten aufstrebenden Märkte der Welt zu bleiben.

Es muss jedoch betont werden, dass eine bessere Gesetzgebung nicht notwendigerweise bedeutet, dass auch die Durchsetzung solcher Gesetze verbessert wird. Wie bereits erwähnt, hat China nach wie vor große Probleme mit Korruption, Ungleichbehandlung, Unabhängigkeit der Justiz und lokalem Protektionismus. Es ist zu hoffen, dass die wachsende Bedeutung des Schutzes des geistigen Eigentums und die Anerkennung der Vorteile eines starken Schutzsystems diese Hürden verringern und schließlich überwinden wird.

REFERENCE LIST

"A Brief Explanation concerning the 'Copyright Law of the People's Republic of China' (Revision Draft)", [Original title: 关于《中华人民共和国著作权法》（修改草案）的简要说明 Guānyú "Zhōnghuá Rénmín Gònghéguó Zhùzuòquán Fǎ" (Xiūgǎi Cǎo'àn) De Jiǎnyào Shuōmíng], March 2012 - posted on 31 March 2012, updated on 4 October 2012, National Copyright Administration of China (provided by China Copyright and Media - Rogier Creemers: https://chinacopyrightandmedia.wordpress.com/2012/04/06/a-brief-explanation-concerning-the-copyright-law-of-the-peoples-republic-of-china-revision-draft/, accessed: 6 March 2021) [in English/Chinese].

"A Brief Explanation concerning the Revision and Perfection of the 'Copyright Law of the People's Republic of China' (Second Revision Draft)", [Original title: 关于《中华人民共和国著作权法》（修改草案第二稿）修改和完善的简要说明Guānyú "Zhōnghuá Rénmín Gònghéguó Zhùzuòquán Fǎ" (Xiūgǎi Cǎo'àn Dì Èr Gǎo) Xiūgǎi Hé Wánshàn De Jiǎnyào Shuō míng], July 2012 - posted on 7 July 2012, updated on 5 October 2012, National Copyright Administration of China (provided by China Copyright and Media - Rogier Creemers: https://chinacopyrightandmedia.wordpress.com/2012/07/07/a-brief-explanation-concerning-the-revision-and-perfection-of-the-copyright-law-of-the-peoples-republic-of-china-second-revision-draft/, accessed: 6 March 2021) [in English/Chinese].

"Explanation of the 'Copyright Law of the People's Republic of China' (Submission Version of the Revision Draft)", [Original title: 关于《中华人民共和国著作权法》（修订草案送审稿）的说明 Guānyú "Zhōnghuá Rénmín Gònghéguó Zhùzuòquán Fǎ" (Xiūdìng Cǎo'àn Sòng Shěn Gǎo) De Shuōmíng], June 2014 - posted on 18 June 2014, State Council Legal Affairs Office (provided by China Copyright and Media - Rogier Creemers: https://chinacopyrightandmedia.wordpress.com/2014/06/18/state-council-publishes-new-copyright-law-revision-draft/, accessed: 6 March 2021) [in English/Chinese].

"The Supreme People's Court's Interpretation on Several Issues Concerning the Application of Law in the Trial of Patent Infringement Disputes (2)" and other eighteen intellectual property judicial interpretations, [Original title: 《最高人民法院关于审理侵犯专利权纠纷案件应用法律若干问题的解释（二）》等十八件知识产权类司法解释的决定 zuìgāo rénmín fǎyuàn guānyú shěnlǐ qīnfàn zhuānlì quán jiūfēn ànjiàn yìngyòng fǎlǜ ruògān wèntí de jiěshì (èr)" děng shíbā jiàn zhīshì chǎn quán lèi sīfǎ jiěshì de juédìng], 2020 - adopted 23 December 2020, effective 1 January 2021, Supreme People's Court of the People's Republic of China (provided by court.gov.cn: http://www.court.gov.cn/fabu-xiangqing-282671.html, accessed: 6 March 2021) [in Chinese].

AFD China Intellectual Property Law Office, "China NAC and WIPO sign MOU to Cooperate in All Respects of

Copyright", 24 December 2015 (Lexology: https://www.lexology.com/library/detail.aspx?g=ca968235-ea70-4743-a2f8-d34752faf7a1, accessed: 6 March 2021) [in English].

Agreed Statements concerning the WIPO Copyright Treaty, 1996 - adopted by the Diplomatic Conference on 20 December 1996, WIPO (provided by WIPO: http://www.wipo.int/treaties/en/text.jsp?file_id=295456, accessed: 5 March 2021) [in English].

Agreement on Trade-Related Aspects of Intellectual Property Rights (TRIPS Agreement), 1994 - 15 Apr 1994, 1869 UNTS 299; 33 ILM 1197 (Annex 1C of the Marrakesh Agreement establishing the World Trade Organization, signed in Marrakesh, Morocco on 15 April 1994, 33 I.L.M. 1125) (provided by WTO: https://www.wto.org/english/docs_e/legal_e/27-trips.pdf, accessed: 5 March 2021) [in English].

Ahl, Björn, "Chinese Law and International Treaties", *Hong Kong Law Journal* 39, 3 (2009): 737-752 [in English].

Alford, William P., *To Steal a Book Is an Elegant Offense: Intellectual Property Law in Chinese Civilization*, Stanford: Stanford University Press, 1995 [in English].

Amendment to the Copyright Law of the People's Republic of China (Draft), [Original title: 中华人民共和国著作权法修正案(草案) Zhōnghuá Rénmín Gònghéguó Zhùzuòquán Fǎ Xiūzhèng Àn (Cǎo'àn)], 26 April 2020, NPC Standing Committee (provided by NPC Observer: https://npcobserver.files.wordpress.com/2020/04/copyright-law-draft-amendment.pdf, accessed: 5 March 2021) [in Chinese].

Amendment to the Copyright Law of the People's Republic of China (Draft) (Second Review Draft), [Original title: 中华人民共和国著作权法修正案(草案) (二次审议稿) Zhōnghuá rénmín gònghéguó zhùzuòquán fǎ xiūzhèng àn (cǎo'àn) (èr cì shěnyì gǎo)], 8 August 2020, NPC Standing Committee (provided by NPC Observer: https://npcobserver.com/wp-content/uploads/2020/08/copyright-law-2nd-draft-amendment.pdf, accessed: 5 March 2021) [in Chinese].

American Bar Association "Joint Comments of the American Bar Association Section of Intellectual Property Law and Section of International Law on the Draft Amendments to China's Copyright Law ", 8 June 2012, (https://www.americanbar.org/content/dam/aba/administrative/intellectual_property_law/advocacy/abaipl_comments_china_cr_revisions.authcheckdam.pdf, accessed: 6 March 2021) [in English].

American Chamber of Commerce in China (in cooperation with Deloitte) "2019 China Business Climate Survey Report", 2019, (https://www2.deloitte.com/content/dam/Deloitte/au/Documents/international-specialist/deloitte-amcham-2019-china-business-climate-survey-report-bilingual-190301.pdf, accessed: 3 March 2021) [in English].

Angle, Stephen C., *Human Rights and Chinese Thought - A Cross-Cultural Inquiry*, Cambridge, UK: Cambridge University Press, 2002 [in English].

Barsherfsky, Charlene (U.S. Trade Representative) "U.S.-China Relationship - Statement in front of the Subcommittee on Trade of the House Ways and Means Committee" U.S. Department of State Dispatch Vol 7 Iss 25, Washington D.C., 17 June 1996, Document No. 9609133739 324-325 [in English].

Beijing Treaty on Audiovisual Performances (WIPO) (Beijing Treaty), 2012 - adopted in Beijing on 24 June 2012, effective 28 April 2020, TRT/BEIJING/001 (provided by WIPO: http://www.wipo.int/wipolex/en/treaties/text.jsp?file_id=295838, accessed: 5 March 2021) [in English].

Berkman, Jeffrey W., "Intellectual Property Rights in the P.R.C.: Impediments to Protection and the Need fo the Rule of Law", *Pacific Basin Law Journal* 15, 1 (1996): 1-44 [in English].

Berne Convention for the Protection of Literary and Artistic Works (Berne Convention), 1979 - adopted 1886, last amended 1979, TRT/BERNE/001 (provided by WIPO: https://wipolex.wipo.int/en/text/283693, accessed: 5 March 2021) [in English].

Berne Convention Implementation Act of the United States of America (U.S. Berne Convention Implementation Act), 1988 - 31 Oct 1988, PL 100-568, 102 STAT. 2853 [in English].

Birden, Paul B., "Technology Transfers to China: An Outline of Chinese Law", *Loyola of Los Angeles International and Comparative Law Review* 16 (1994): 413-453 [in English].

Blazey, Patricia, and Tian, YiJun, *Intellectual Property Law in China*, The Chinese Commercial Legal System, edited by Patricia Blazey and Kay-Wah Chan, Sydney, Australia: Thomson Lawbook Co., 2008 [in English].

Blomqvist, Jørgen, *Primer on International Copyright and Related Rights*, Cheltenham, UK and Northhampton, USA: Edward Elgar Publishing, 2014 [in English].

Blume, Andreas, "Produkt- und Markenpiraterie in der Volksrepublik China ", [Translated title: Counterfeiting and piracy in the People's Republic of China], *China Analysis* 33 (2004): 1-57 [in German].

Blustein, Paul, "Hopes Raised For Ending China Copyright Dispute" *The Washington Post, Washington, D.C., at D10 (Volume 119, Issue 191)*, 13 June 1996 [in English].

Bodde, Derk, "Basic Concepts of Chinese Law: The Genesis and Evolution of Legal Thought in Traditional China", *Proceedings of the American Philosophical Society* 107, 5 (1963): 374-398 [in English].

Boyarski, Jason R., Fishman, Renee M., Josephberg, Kara, Linn, Jane, Pollack, Jane, and Victoriano, Jenna,

"International Developments - WIPO Copyright Treaty Enters into Force", *Intellectual Property & Technology Law Journal* 14, 3 (March 2002) [in English].

Bu, Yuanshi, *Einführung in das Recht Chinas* [Translated title: Introduction to Chinese Law], Schriftenreihe der Juristischen Schulung / Ausländisches Recht, Band 191 ed. München: Verlag C.H. Beck, 2009 [in German].

Butterton, Glenn R., "Pirates, Dragons and U.S. Intellectual Property Rights in China: Problems and Prospects of Chinese Enforcement", *Arizona Law Review* 38 (1996): 1081-1123 [in English].

CGTN, "China intensifies IP protection with 25 centers set up nationwide", 23 December 2019 (gov.cn: http://english.www.gov.cn/news/videos/201912/23/content_WS5dfff70dc6d0bcf8c4c19417.html, accessed: 6 March 2021) [in English].

China IPR, "State Council Legislative Affairs Office Releases NCA Draft of Copyright Law for Public Comment", 9 June 2014 (China IPR: https://chinaipr.com/2014/06/09/state-council-legislative-affairs-office-releases-nca-draft-of-copyright-law-for-public-comment/, accessed: 6 March 2021) [in English].

China-United States: Agreement Regarding Intellectual Property Rights (MoU U.S.-China IP Enforcement 1995), 1995 - July 1995, 34 I.L.M. 881, 34 I.L.M. 881 (1995), 1995 WL 528321 (I.L.M.) [in English].

China: Inspector General of Customs, *Treaties, Conventions, Etc., Between China and Foreign States*, 2 ed. 1 - Russia, International Protocol, Great Britain, United States of America, France, Import Tariff Agreement, China. Imperial Maritime Customs. III.- Miscellaneous Series No. 30, Shanghai, China: Statistical Department of the Inspectorate General of Customs, 1908 [in English].

Civil Procedure Law of the People's Republic of China (Civil Procedure Law PRC), [Original title: 中华人民共和国民事诉讼法 Zhōnghuá Rénmín Gònghéguó Mínshì Sùsòng Fǎ], 1991/2017 version - adopted 9 April 1991, amended 28 October 2007, 31 August 2012, 27 June 2017, effective 1 July 2017, (provided by cicc.court.gov.cn: http://cicc.court.gov.cn/html/1/219/199/200/644.html, accessed: 18 March 2021) [in English].

CNIPA "2020-2021 Implementation of the 'Opinions on Strengthening the Protection of Intellectual Property' Promotion Plan" [Original title: 2020—2021年贯彻落《关于强化知识产权保护的意见》推进计划 2020—2021 Nián guànchè luòshí "guānyú qiánghuà zhīshì chǎnquán bǎohù de yìjiàn" tuījìn jìhuà], 20 April 2020, (https://www.163.com/dy/article/FAO4U06B05149FJG.html, accessed: 3 March 2021) [in Chinese].

Cohen, Julie E., Loren, Lydia Pallas, Okediji, Ruth L., and O'Rourke, Maureen A., *Copyright in a Global Information Economy*, Aspen Casebook Series, 4 ed.

New York, USA: Wolters Kluwer, 2015 [in English].

Confucius, *The Analects of Confucius (English translation by James Legge)*, Auckland, NZ: The Floating Press, 2010 [in English].

Constitution of the People's Republic of China (Constitution PRC), [Original title: 中华人民共和国宪法 Zhōnghuá Rénmín Gònghéguó Xiànfǎ], 1982/2018 version - adopted 4 December 1982, amended 12 April 1988, 29 March 1993, 15 March 1999, 14 March 2004, 11 March 2018, (provided by NPC Observer: https://npcobserver.files.wordpress.com/2018/12/PRC-Constitution-2018.pdf, accessed: 5 March 2021) [in English].

Copyright Law of the People's Republic of China (Copyright Law PRC), [Original title: 中华人民共和国著作权法 Zhōnghuá Rénmín Gònghéguó Zhùzuòquán Fǎ], 1990/2020 version - adopted 7 September 1990, effective 1 June 1991, amended 27 October 2001, 26 February 2010, 11 November 2020, effective 1 June 2021, (provided by npc.gov.cn: http://www.npc.gov.cn/npc/c30834/202011/848e73f58d4e4c5b82f69d25d46048c6.shtml, accessed: 5 March 2021) [in Chinese].

Copyright Law of the People's Republic of China (Copyright Law PRC), [Original title: 中华人民共和 国著作权法 Zhōnghuá Rénmín Gònghéguó Zhùzuòquán Fǎ], 1990 - adopted 7 September 1990, effective 1 June 1991, (provided by WIPO:

http://www.wipo.int/wipolex/en/text.jsp?file_id=336460, accessed: 5 March 2021) [in English].

Copyright Law of the People's Republic of China (Copyright Law PRC), [Original title: 中华人民共和 国著作权法 Zhōnghuá Rénmín Gònghéguó Zhùzuòquán Fǎ], 1990/2001 version - adopted 7 September 1990, effective 1 June 1991, amended 27 October 2001, (provided by WIPO: http://www.wipo.int/wipolex/en/text.jsp?file_id=125980, accessed: 5 March 2021) [in English].

Copyright Law of the People's Republic of China (Copyright Law PRC), [Original title: 中华人民共和 国著作权法 Zhōnghuá Rénmín Gònghéguó Zhùzuòquán Fǎ], 1990/2010 version - adopted 7 September 1990, effective 1 June 1991, amended 27 October 2001, 26 February 2010, effective 1 April 2010, (provided by WIPO: http://www.wipo.int/wipolex/en/text.jsp?file_id=186569, accessed: 5 March 2021) [in English].

Copyright Law of the People's Republic of China "First Revision Draft", [Original title: 中华人民共和国著作权法（修改草案）Zhōnghuá Rénmín Gònghéguó Zhùzuòquán Fǎ (Xiūgǎi Cǎo'àn)], March 2012 - posted on 31 March 2012, updated on 8 April 2012, National Copyright Administration of China (provided by China Copyright and Media - Rogier Creemers: https://chinacopyrightandmedia.wordpress.com/2012/03/31/copyright-law-of-the-peoples-republic-of-china-revision-draft/, accessed: 6 March 2021) [in English/Chinese].

Copyright Law of the People's Republic of China "Second Revision Draft", [Original title: 中华人民共和国著作权法（修改草案第二稿）Zhōnghuá Rénmín Gònghéguó Zhùzuòquán Fǎ (Xiūgǎi Cǎo'àn Dì Èr Gǎo)], July 2012 - posted on 7 July 2012, updated on 18 June 2014, National Copyright Administration of China (provided by China Copyright and Media - Rogier Creemers: https://chinacopyrightandmedia.wordpress.com/2012/07/07/copyright-law-of-the-peoples-republic-of-china-second-revision-draft/, accessed: 6 March 2021) [in English/Chinese].

Copyright Law of the People's Republic of China "Third Revision Draft, Submission Version", [Original title: 中华人民共和国著作权法（修订草案送审稿）Zhōnghuá Rénmín Gònghéguó Zhùzuòquán Fǎ (Xiūdìng Cǎo'àn Sòng Shěn Gǎo)], June 2014 - posted on 6 June 2014, updated on 18 June 2014, National Copyright Administration of China (provided by China Copyright and Media - Rogier Creemers: https://chinacopyrightandmedia.wordpress.com/2014/06/06/copyright-law-of-the-peoples-republic-of-china-revision-draft-submission-version/, accessed: 6 March 2021) [in English/Chinese].

Criminal Law of the People's Republic of China (Criminal Law PRC), [Original title: 中华人民共和国刑法 Zhōnghuá Rénmín Gònghéguó Xíngfǎ], 1979/1997 version - adopted 1 July 1979, amended 14 March

1997, (provided by WIPO: https://wipolex.wipo.int/en/text/181340, accessed: 5 March 2021) [in English].

Criminal Law of the People's Republic of China (Amendment XI) (Criminal Law PRC (Amendment XI)), [Original title: 中华人民共和国刑法修正案（十一） Zhōnghuá rénmín gònghéguó xíngfǎ xiūzhèng àn (shíyī)], 2021 - adopted 26 December 2020, in force 1 March 2021, (provided by npc.gov.cn: http://www.npc.gov.cn/npc/c30834/202012/850abff47854495e9871997bf64803b6.shtml, accessed: 4 March 2021) [in Chinese].

Crothall, Geoffrey, "Beijing slams 'irrational' US policy over piracy" *South China Morning Post (Section: Business News), Beijing, at 4*, 1 July 1994 [in English].

Decision of the Standing Committee of the National People's Congress on Amending the "Copyright Law of the People's Republic of China", [Original title: 全国人民代表大会常务委员会关于修改《中华人民共和国著作权法》的决定 Quánguó rénmín dàibiǎo dà huì chángwù wěiyuánhuì guānyú xiūgǎi "zhōnghuá rénmín gònghéguó zhùzuòquán fǎ" de juédìng], 11 November 2020 - Adopted at the 23rd Meeting of the Standing Committee of the 13th National People's Congress, NPC Standing Committee (provided by npc.gov.cn: http://www.npc.gov.cn/npc/c30834/202011/272b72cdb759458d94c9b875350b1ab5.shtml, accessed: 5 March 2021) [in Chinese].

Decision of the Standing Committee of the National People's Congress on Establishing Intellectual Property Right Courts in Beijing, Shanghai and Guangzhou, [Original title: 全国人大常委会关于在北京、上海、广州设立知识产权法院的决定 Quánguó Réndà Chángwěi Huì Guānyú Zài Běijīng, Shàng hǎi, Guǎngzhōu Shèlì Zhīshì Chǎnquán Fǎyuàn De Juédìng], 31 August 2014, Standing Committee of the National People's Congress (provided by PKU Law: http://en.pkulaw.cn/display.aspx?cgid=af982b2d9d378226bdfb&lib=law, accessed: 5 March 2021) [in English/Chinese].

Decision of the Standing Committee of the National People's Congress on Punishment of the Crimes of Infringing Copyright, [Original title: 全国人大常委会关于惩治侵犯著作权的犯罪的决定 Quánguó Réndà Chángwěi Huì Guānyú Chéngzhì Qīnfàn Zhùzuòquán De Fànzuì De Juédìng], 1994 - promulgated and effective 5 July 1994, invalidated 1 October 1997, Standing Committee of the National People's Congress (provided by AsianLII: http://www.asianlii.org/cn/legis/cen/laws/dotscotnpcopotcoic1087/, accessed: 5 March 2021) [in English].

DEQI Intellectual Property Law Corporation, "Beijing Intellectual Property Court: Foreign-related Intellectual Property Cases Increasing Year by Year", 20 January 2020 (Lexology: https://www.lexology.com/library/detail.aspx?g=62f25070-8679-4b84-bf67-

202b3109e949&utm_source=Lexology+Daily+Newsfeed&utm_medium=HTML+email+-+Body+-+General+section&utm_campaign=Lexology+subscriber+daily+feed&utm_content=Lexology+Daily+Newsfeed+2020-01-22&utm_term=, accessed: 6 March 2021) [in English].

Detailed Regulations for the Enforcement of the Copyright Law (Detailed Regulations for the Enforcement of the Copyright Law), 1928 - *The Chinese Law Review* (1929-1931) 4 (2) 6-7 [in English].

Devonshire-Ellis, Chris, Scott, Andy, and Woollard, Sam, *Intellectual Property Rights in China*, 2 ed. Berlin: Springer, 2011 [in English].

Dietz, Adolf, "Das chinesische Urheberrecht: Copyright oder droit d'auteur?", in *Urheberrecht im Informationszeitalter - Festschrift für Wilhelm Nordemann zum 70. Geburtstag am 8. Januar 2004* [Translated title: Chinese copyright law: Copyright or droit d'auteur?] edited by Ulrich Loewenheim, 527-538, München: Verlag C.H. Beck, 2004 [in German].

Dreyer, Gunda, "Kapitel I, Teil 1, Abschnitt 1 Allgemeines (§1) ", in *Urheberrecht: Urheberrechtsgesetz, Urheberrechtswahrnehmungsgesetz, Kunsturhebergesetz - Heidelberger Kommentar* [Translated title: Copyright: Copyright Law, Copyright Administration Law, Art Copyright Law - Heidelberger Commentary] edited by Gunda Dreyer, Jost Kotthoff and Astrid Meckel, 39-42, Heidelberg, Germany: C.F. Müller, 2009 [in German].

Dubin, Joseph S., "The Universal Copyright Convention", *California Law Review* 42, 1 (1954): 89-119 [in English].

E-Commerce Law of the People's Republic of China (E-Commerce Law PRC), [Original title: 中华人民共和国电子商务法 Zhōnghuá rénmín gònghéguó diànzǐ shāngwù fǎ], 2018 - adopted 31 August 2018, effective 1 January 2019, (provided by IPKey: https://ipkey.eu/sites/default/files/documents/resources/PRC_E-Commerce_Law.pdf, accessed: 5 March 2021) [in English].

Ehrlich, Eugen, and Ziegert, Klaus A., *Fundamental Principles of the Sociology of Law (translated by Walter L. Moll)*, Harvard Studies in Jurisprudence, 4 ed. 5, New Brunswick, USA and London, UK: Transaction Publishers (1936), 2009 [in English].

Enders, Theodor, "Das neue Urheberrecht der Volksrepublik China", [Translated title: The new copyright law of the People's Republic of China], *Humboldt Forum Recht*, 1/2007 (2007): 1-12 [in German].

Enders, Theodor, and Steiner, Alexandra, "Urheberrechtsreform und Urheberrechtsdurchsetzung", [Translated title: Copyright Reform and Copyright Enforcement], *Zeitschrift für Chinesisches Recht* 17, 2 (2010): 91-117 [in German].

European Chamber of Commerce in China (in cooperation with Roland Berger) "European Business in China - Business Confidence Survey 2019", 2019, (https://static.europeanchamber.com.cn/upload/documents/documents/Business_Confidence_Survey_2019_updated[663].pdf, accessed: 6 March 2021) [in English].

Faison, Seth, "U.S. and China Agree on Pact To Fight Piracy" *The New York Times at A1*, 18 June 1996 [in English].

Feng, Xiaoqing, "The Protection of Copyright in Network Environment: A Review of Recent Reform of the Chinese Copyright Law", *Information and Communications Technology Law* 11, 2 (2002): 161-163 [in English].

Feng, Xiaoqing, and Huang, Frank Xianfeng, "International Standards and Local Elements: New Developments of Copyright Law in China", *Journal of the Copyright Society of the U.S.A.* 49 (2001-2002): 917-947 [in English].

Ficsor, Mihály, *The Law of Copyright and the Internet - The 1996 WIPO Treaties, their Interpretation and Implementation*, Oxford: Oxford University Press, 2002 [in English].

Ficsor, Mihály, "The WIPO "Internet Treaties" The United States as the Driver: The United States as the Main Source of Obstruction - As seen by an Anti-Revolutionary Central European", *The John Marshall Review of Intellectual Property Law* 6, 17 (2006): 17-39 [in English].

Ganea, Peter, "Internationales - WTO-Panel veröffentlicht Ergebnisse zum Streit zwischen den USA und China wegen Defiziten im chinesischen Immaterialgüterrechtsschutz", [Translated title: International - WTO panel publishes findings on the dispute between the USA and China over deficits in Chinese intellectual property protection], *Gewerblicher Rechtsschutz und Urheberrecht International* (2009): 274-275 [in German].

Ganea, Peter, "Volksrepublik China - Neue Zollbestimmungen zum Schutz des geistigen Eigentums", [Translated title: People's Republic of China - New customs regulations to protect intellectual property], *Gewerblicher Rechtsschutz und Urheberrecht International* (2004): 532-533 [in German].

Ganea, Peter, Pattloch, Thomas, and Heath, Christopher, *Intellectual Property Law in China*, The Hague, The Netherlands: Kluwer Law International, 2005 [in English].

General Agreement on Tariffs and Trade (GATT), 1947 - 55 U.N.T.S. 194 [in English].

General Principles of the Civil Law of the People's Republic of China (General Principles of the Civil Law PRC), [Original title: 中华人民共和国民法通则 Zhōng huá Rénmín Gònghéguó Mínfǎ Tōngzé], 1986 - adopted 12 April 1986, effective 1 January 1987, (provided by WIPO: http://www.wipo.int/wipolex/en/text.jsp?file_id=182628, accessed: 5 March 2021) [in English].

Grüneis, Barbara, "Produktpiraterie in China - Durchsetzung geistiger Eigentumsrechte vs. wirtschaftliche Entwicklung ", [Translated title: Product piracy in China - enforcement of intellectual property rights vs. economic development], Dissertation submitted to the Technical University of Munich, Germany, 2010.

Guide to the Berne Convention for the Protection of Literary and Artistic Works (Paris Act ,1971), 1978, Geneva, World Intellectual Property Organization (https://www.wipo.int/edocs/pubdocs/en/copyright/615/wipo_pub_615.pdf, accessed: 5 March 2021) [in English].

Guo, Grace, and Meuwissen, Stefaan, "China: looking back at 2019's main IP developments and looking forward at what 2020 may bring", 13 April 2020 (JD Supra: https://www.jdsupra.com/legalnews/china-looking-back-at-2019-s-main-ip-93099/, accessed: 6 March 2021) [in English].

Interpretation of the Supreme People's Court Concerning Several Issues on Application of Law in Hearing Correctly the Civil Copyright, [Original title: 最高人民法院关于审理著作权民事纠纷案件适用法律若干问题的解释 Zuìgāo Rénmín Fǎyuàn Guānyú Shěnlǐ Zhùzuòquán Mínshì Jiūfēn Ànjiàn Shìyòng Fǎlǜ Ruògān Wèntí De Jiěshì], 2002 - adopted 12 October 2002, effective 15 October 2002, Supreme People's Court of the People's Republic of China (provided by WIPO:

http://www.wipo.int/wipolex/en/text.jsp?file_id=181509, accessed: 5 March 2021) [in English].

Interpretation on the Application of Punitive Damages in Civil Cases of Infringement of Intellectual Property Rights, [Original title: 关于审理侵害知识产权民事案件适用惩罚性赔偿的解释 Guānyú shěnlǐ qīnhài zhīshì chǎnquán mínshì ànjiàn shìyòng chéngfá xìng péicháng de jiěshì], 2021 - adopted 7 February 2021, effective 3 March 2021, Supreme People's Court of the People's Republic of China (provided by court.gov.cn: http://www.court.gov.cn/fabu-xiangqing-288861.html, accessed: 6 March 2021) [in Chinese].

Jacobs, Samuel, "The Effect of the 1886 Berne Convention on the U.S. Copyright System's Treatment of Moral Rights and Copyright Term, and Where That Leaves Us Today", *Michigan Telecommunications and Technology Law Review* 23 (2016): 169-190 [in English].

Johnson, Wallace, "Status and Liability for Punishment in the T'ang Code", *Chicago-Kent Law Review* 71, 1 Symposium on Ancient Law, Economics and Society Part II: Ancient Rights and Wrongs / Symposium on Ancient Law, Economics and Society Part II: Ancient Near Eastern Land Laws (1995): 217-229 [in English].

Johnson, Wallace, *The T'ang Code. Volume 1, General Principles - Introduction and Translation*, Princeton, New

Jersey: Princeton University Press, 1979 [in English].

Judge, Joan, *Print and Politics - 'Shibao' and the Culture of Reform in Late Qing China*, Stanford, California: Stanford University Press, 1996 [in English].

Judges Law of the People's Republic of China (Judges Law of the People's Republic of China), [Original title: 中华人民共和国法官法 Zhōnghuá Rénmín Gònghéguó Făguān Fă], 1995/2019 version - adopted 28 February 1995, effective 1 July 1995, amended 30 June 2001, 1 September 2017, 23 April 2019, effective 1 October 2019, (provided by npc.gov.cn: http://www.npc.gov.cn/zgrdw/npc/xinwen/2019-04/23/content_2086082.htm, accessed: 5 March 2021) [in Chinese].

Keith, Ronald C., and Lin, Zhiqiu, "Judicial Interpretation of China's Supreme People's Court as "Secondary Law" with Special Reference to Criminal Law", *China Information* 23 (2009): 223-255 [in English].

Kong, Qingjiang, "Enforcement of WTO Agreements in China - Illusion or Reality?", *Journal of World Trade* 35, 6 (2001): 1181-1214 [in English].

Kong, Qingjiang, *WTO, Internationalization and the Intellectual Property Rights Regime in China*, Singapore: Marshal Cavendish International, 2005 [in English].

Kurtenbach, Elaine, "U.S., China Seek Trade Solution, New Business - Piracy, Auto, Energy Issues at Stake",

17 February 1995 (The Seattle Times, Washington, USA: http://community.seattletimes.nwsource.com/archive/?date=19950217&slug=2105560, accessed: 6 March 2021) [in English].

Lazar, June Cohan, "Protecting Ideas and Ideals: Copyright Law in the People's Republic of China", *Law & Policy in International Business* 27 (1995-1996): 1185-1211 [in English].

Lee, Luke T., and Lai, Whalen W., "The Chinese Conceptions of Law: Confucian, Legalist, and Buddhist", *The Hastings Law Journal* 29 (1977-1978): 1307-1329 [in English].

Lee, Nari, and Zhang, Liguo, "Specialised IP courts in China - judicial governance of intellectual property rights", *International Review of Intellectual Property and Competition Law* 48, 8 (2017): 900-924 [in English].

Legislation Law of the People's Republic of China (Legislation Law PRC), [Original title: 中华人民共和国立法法 Zhōnghuá Rénmín Gònghéguó Lìfǎ Fǎ], 2000/2015 version - adopted 15 March 2000, effective 1 July 2000, amended 15 March 2015, (provided by npc.gov.cn: http://www.npc.gov.cn/zgrdw/npc/dbdhhy/12_3/2015-03/18/content_1930713.htm, accessed: 5 March 2021) [in Chinese].

Levi, Werner, *Modern China's Foreign Policy*, Minnesota Archive Editions, St. Paul, USA: University of Minnesota Press, 1953 [in English].

Li, Lijing, *Die kollektive Urheberrechtswahrnehmung durch Verwertungsgesellschaften in der Bundesrepublik Deutschland und in der Volksrepublik China* [Translated title: The collective administration of copyright by collecting societies in the Federal Republic of Germany and the People's Republic of China], Studienreihe zum Gewerblichen Rechtsschutz und zum Urheberrecht, Band 97, Hamburg: Verlag Dr. Kovač, 2012 [in German].

Li, Ling, "The Sky is High and the Emperor is Far Way: The Enforcement of Intellectual Property Law in China", *Boletín Mexicano de Derecho Comparado* 36, 108 (September- December 2003): 951-1010 [in English].

Li, Mingde, "Special intellectual property courts in China", in *Governance of Intellectual Property Rights in China and Europe* edited by Nari Lee, Niklas Bruun and Mingde Li, 303-317, Cheltenham, UK: Edward Elgar Publishing Limited, 2016 [in English].

Li, Xin, *Urheberrecht in Deutschland und der Volksrepublik China - ein Rechtsvergleich* [Translated title: Copyright law in Germany and the People's Republic of China - a legal comparison], Hamburg: Verlag Dr. Kovač, 2015 [in German].

Li, Yiqiang, "Evaluation of the Sino-American Intellectual Property Agreements: A Judicial Approach to

Solving the Local Protectionism Problem", *Columbia Journal of Asian Law* 10 (1996): 391-424 [in English].

Li, Zhaojie, "Traditional Chinese World Order", *Chinese Journal of International Law* 1, 1 (2002): 20-58 [in English].

Liu, Qiang, and Huang, Liang, "On the Beijing Treaty on Audiovisual Performances and the Upgrading of China's Copyright Law", [Original title: 论《视听表演北京条约》及我国著作权法的完善 Lùn "shìtīng biǎoyǎn běijīng tiáoyuē" jí wǒguó zhù zuòquán fǎ de wánshàn], *Journal of Shaoyang University - Social Science Edition* 3, 4 (2014): 19-23 [in Chinese].

Liu, Wenqi, "Reform of China's Copyright Legislation", *Journal of the Copyright Society of the U.S.A.* 59 (2011-2012): 843-863 [in English].

Long, Cheryl Xiaoning, and Wang, Jun, "Judicial local protectionism in China: An empirical study of IP cases", *International Review of Law and Economics* 42 (2015): 48-59 [in English].

Long, Clarisa, *Intellectual Property Law in Emerging Markets*, Washington D.C.: The AEI Press, 2000 [in English].

Lu, Guoqiang, "15: Recent Developments in Judicial Protection for Intellectual Property in China", in *Volume 25 of IIC Studies in Industrial Property and Copyright Law - New Frontiers of Intellectual Property Law: IP and Cultural Heritage - Geographical Indications -*

Enforcement - Overprotections edited by Christopher Heath and Anselm Kamperman Sanders, Portland, USA and Oxford, Great Britain: Hart Publishing, 2005 [in English].

Lubman, Stanley, "Bird in a Cage: Chinese Law Reform after Twenty Years", *Northwestern Journal of International Law & Business* 20, 3 (1999-2000): 383-423 [in English].

Maskus, Keith E., "Intellectual Property Rights in the WTO Accession: Assessing China's Reforms", in *China and the WTO - Accession, Policy Reform, and Poverty Reduction Strategies* edited by Deepak Bhattasali, Shantong Li and Will Martin, 1-334, Washington D.C., USA: The World Bank and Oxford University Press, 2004 [in English].

Measures for the Registration of Pledge on Copyright, [Original title: 著作权质权登记办法 Zhùzuòquán Zhì Quán Dēngjì Bànfǎ], 2010 - issued 25 November 2010, effective 1 January 2011, National Copyright Administration of the People's Republic of China (provided by WIPO: http://www.wipo.int/edocs/lexdocs/laws/zh/cn/cn281zh.pdf, accessed: 5 March 2021) [in Chinese].

Memorandum of Understanding Between the Government of the United States of America and the Government of the People's Republic of China on the Protection of Intellectual Property (MoU U.S. - China IP Protection 1992), 1992 - 17 January 1992, 34 I.L.M. 676, 34 I.L.M. 676 (1995), 1995 WL 374160 (I.L.M.) [in English].

Murphy, Matthew, "III. Specific Fields and Topics of Law - Chapter 10.4. - Copyright", in *Doing Business in China* edited by Michael J. Moser and Fu Yu, Huntington, NY, U.S.A.: Juris Publishing Inc., 2014 [in English].

Murphy, Matthew A., "Copyright", in *Intellectual Property Law of China* edited by Michael J. Moser, Huntington, NY, U.S.A.: Juris Publishing Inc., 2011 [in English].

Music Copyright Society of China, "General Introduction" (mcsc.com.cn: http://www.mcsc.com.cn/en/situation.html, accessed: 3 March 2021) [in English].

Musungu, Sisule F., and Dutfield, Graham, "Multilateral agreements and a TRIPS-plus world: The World Intellectual Property Organization (WIPO)", *TRIPS Issues Papers (Quaker United Nations Office, Geneva)*, 3 (2003) [in English].

Na, Lu, "New copyright law amendment under fire", 6 April 2012 (china.org: http://www.china.org.cn/arts/2012-04/06/content_25077760.htm, accessed: 6 March 2021) [in English].

NCAC "2016 National Copyright Enforcement Table" [Original title: 2016年全国版权执法情况表 2016 Nián Quá nguó Bǎnquán Zhífǎ Qíngkuàng Biǎo], 11 May 2018, (http://www.ncac.gov.cn/chinacopyright/contents/12566/353173.shtml, accessed: 16 March 2021) [in Chinese].

NCAC, "2018 National Conference on Copyright Protection in Digital Environment Held in Beijing", 11 May 2018 (ncac.gov.cn: http://en.ncac.gov.cn/copyright/contents/10361/375811.shtml, accessed: 16 May 2020) [in English].

NCAC "Announcement of the General Office of the National Copyright Administration on the National Copyright Registration in 2017" [Original title: 国家版权局办公厅关于2017年全国著作权登记情况的通报 Guójiā Bǎnquán Jú Bàngōng Tīng Guānyú 2017 Nián Quánguó Zhùzuòquán Dēngjì Qíngkuàng De Tōngbào], 13 February 2018, (http://www.ncac.gov.cn/chinacopyright/contents/12228/348615.shtml, accessed: 11 March 2021) [in Chinese].

NCAC "Announcement of the National Copyright Administration on the National Copyright Registration in 2019" [Original title: 国家版权局关于2019年全国著作权登记情况的通报 Guójiā Bǎnquán Jú Guānyú 2019 Nián Quánguó Zhùzuòquán Dēngjì Qíngkuàng De Tōngbào], 25 March 2020, (http://www.ncac.gov.cn/chinacopyright/contents/12228/348574.shtml, accessed: 10 March 2021) [in Chinese].

NCAC "Announcement of the National Copyright Administration on the National Copyright Registration in 2020" [Original title: 国家版权局关于2020年全国著作权登记情况的通报 Guójiā Bǎnquán Jú Guānyú 2020 Nián Quánguó Zhùzuòquán Dēngjì Qíngkuàng De

Tōngbào], 16 March 2021, (http://www.ncac.gov.cn/chinacopyright/contents/12228/353816.shtml, accessed: 18 March 2021) [in Chinese].

NCAC, "International Forum on Copyright and Creative Industries in the Digital Economy: New Challenges and Opportunities", 16 December 2019 (ncac.gov.cn: http://en.ncac.gov.cn/copyright/contents/10361/409566.shtml, accessed: 6 March 2021) [in English].

NCAC "National Copyright Enforcement Status in 2015" [Original title: 2015年全国版权执法情况表 2015 Nián Quánguó Bǎnquán Zhífǎ Qíngkuàng Biǎo], 18 January 2017, (http://www.ncac.gov.cn/chinacopyright/contents/12566/353174.shtml, accessed: 16 March 2021) [in Chinese].

NCAC "Notice on Further Improving the Examination and Determination of Evidence for Copyright Administrative Enforcement" [Original title: 国家版权局关于进一步做好著作权行政执法证据审查和认定工作的通知 Guójiā bǎnquán jú guānyú jìnyībù zuò hǎo zhùzuòquán xíngzhèng zhífǎ zhèngjù shěnchá hé rèndìng gōngzuò de tōngzhī], 15 November 2020, (provided by ncac.gov.cn: http://www.ncac.gov.cn/chinacopyright/contents/12228/352404.shtml, accessed: 5 March 2021) [in Chinese].

NCAC "Report on the National Copyright Registration in 2014" [Original title: 关于2014年全国著作权登记情况的

通报 Guānyú 2014 Nián Quánguó Zhùzuòquán Dēngjì Qíngkuàng De Tōngbào], 3 March 2015, (http://www.ncac.gov.cn/chinacopyright/contents/12228/346308.shtml, accessed: 14 March 2021) [in Chinese].

NCAC "Report on the National Copyright Registration in 2015" [Original title: 关于2015年全国著作权登记情况的通报 Guānyú 2015 Nián Quánguó Zhùzuòquán Dēngjì Qíngkuàng De Tōngbào], 4 February 2016, (http://www.ncac.gov.cn/chinacopyright/contents/12228/346332.shtml, accessed: 10 March 2021) [in Chinese].

NCAC "Report on the National Copyright Registration in 2016" [Original title: 关于2016年全国著作权登记情况的通报 Guānyú 2016 Nián Quánguó Zhùzuòquán Dēngjì Qíngkuàng De Tōngbào], 3 Feburary 2017, (http://www.ncac.gov.cn/chinacopyright/contents/12228/346357.shtml, accessed: 10 March 2021) [in Chinese].

NCAC "Report on the National Copyright Registration in 2018" [Original Title: 关于2018年全国著作权登记情况的通报 Guānyú 2018 Nián Quánguó Zhùzuòquán Dēngjì Qíngkuàng De Tōngbào], 1 March 2019, (http://www.ncac.gov.cn/chinacopyright/contents/12228/348594.shtml, accessed: 11 March 2021) [in Chinese].

NCAC "Statistics on National Copyright Enforcement in 2018" [Original title: 2018年全国版权执法情况统计

2018 Nián Quánguó Bǎnquán Zhífǎ Qíngkuàng Tǒ ngjì], 14 January 2020, (http://www.ncac.gov.cn/chinacopyright/contents/12566/353171.shtml, accessed: 16 March 2021) [in Chinese].

NCAC "Statistics on National Copyright Enforcement in 2019" [Original title: 2019年全国版权执法情况统计 Nián Quánguó Bǎnquán Zhífǎ Qíngkuàng Tǒngjì], 29 January 2021, (http://www.ncac.gov.cn/chinacopyright/contents/12566/353599.shtml, accessed: 16 March 2021) [in Chinese].

NCAC "Statistics on National Copyright Law Enforcement in 2014" [Original title: 2014年全国版权执法情况统计 2014 Nián Quánguó Bǎnquán Zhífǎ Qíngkuàng Tǒngjì], 30 October 2015, (http://www.ncac.gov.cn/chinacopyright/contents/12566/353224.shtml, accessed: 16 March 2020) [in Chinese].

NCAC "Statistics Related to Copyright Enforcement in 2017" [Original title: 2017年版权执法相关统计 2017 Nián Bǎnquán Zhífǎ Xiāngguān Tǒngjì], 10 October 2018, (http://www.ncac.gov.cn/chinacopyright/contents/12566/353172.shtml, accessed: 16 March 2021) [in Chinese].

Neigel, Connie, "Piracy in Russia and China: A Different U.S. Reaction", *Law and Contemporary Problems* 63, 4 (2000): 179-199 [in English].

Neuwirth, Rostam J., "Der WTO-Bericht zu China - Measures Affecting the Protection and Enforcement of Intellectual Property Rights: ein Kommentar ", [Translated title: The WTO Report on China - Measures Affecting the Protection and Enforcement of Intellectual Property Rights: a commentary], *Gewerblicher Rechtsschutz und Urheberrecht, Internationaler Teil* 58, 5 (2009): 367-376 [in German].

Newby, Kim, "The Effectiveness of Special 301 in Creating Long Term Copyright Protection for U.S. Companies Overseas", *Syracuse Journal of International Law and Commerce* 21 (1995): 29-63 [in English].

Nie, Jianqiang, *The Enforcement of Intellectual Property Rights in China*, London, UK: Cameron May, 2006 [in English].

Ocko, Jonathan, "Copying, Culture, and Control: Chinese Intellectual Property Law in Historical Context", *Yale Journal of Law & Humanities* 8, 2 - Article 10 (1996): 559-578 [in English].

Omnibus Foreign Trade and Competitiveness Act of the United States of America (U.S. Omnibus Foreign Trade and Competitiveness Act), 1988 - 23 Aug 1988, 19 U.S.C. ch. 17 §§2901 et seq., Pub.L. No. 100-418, 102 Stat. 1107 [in English].

Organic Law of the People's Courts of the People's Republic of China (Organic Law of the People's Courts PRC), [Original title: 中华人民共和国人民法院组织法 Zhōnghuá Rénmín Gònghéguó Rénmín Fǎyuàn Zǔ zhī Fǎ], 1979/2018 version - adopted 1 July 1979, promulgated 5 July 1979, effective 1 January 1980, amended 2 September 1983, 2 December 1986, 31 October 2006, 26 October 2018, effective 1 January 2019, (provided by npc.gov.cn: http://www.npc.gov.cn/zgrdw/npc/xinwen/2018-10/26/content_2064483.htm, accessed: 5 March 2021) [in Chinese].

Organic Law of the People's Procuratorates of the People's Republic of China (Organic Law of the People's Procuratorates PRC), [Original title: 中华人民共和国人民检察院组织法 Zhōnghuá Rénmín Gònghé guó Rénmín Jiǎncháyuàn Zǔzhī Fǎ], 1979/2018 version - adopted 1 July 1979, effective 1 January 1980, amended 2 September 1983, 2 December 1986, 6 October 2018, effective 1 January 2019, (provided by npc.gov.cn: http://www.npc.gov.cn/npc/c12435/201810/b59a94f891794d9980e950c5cd8a0204.shtml, accessed: 5 March 2021) [in Chinese].

Palumbo, Daniele and da Costa, Ana Nicolaci, "Trade war: US-China trade battle in charts", 10 May 2019 (BBC: https://www.bbc.com/news/business-48196495, accessed: 6 March 2021) [in English].

Potter, Pitman B., and Oksenberg, Michel, "A patchwork of IPR protections", *China Business Review* 26, 1 (Jan-Feb 1999): 8-11 [in English].

Prohaska, Frank V., "The 1995 Agreement regarding Intellectual Property Rights between China and the United States: Promises for International Law or Continuing Problems with Chinese Piracy", *Tulsa Journal of Comparative and International Law* 4, 1 (1996): 169-183 [in English].

Provisional Regulations on the Management of Book and Periodical Publishing, Printing and Distribution Sectors, [Original title: 管理书刊出版业印刷业发行业暂行条例 Guǎnlǐ Shūkān Chūbǎn Yè Yìnshuā Yè Fā Hángyè Zhànxíng Tiáolì], 1952 - promulgated 16 August 1952, State Administrative Council (provided by China Copyright and Media - Rogier Creemers: http://chinacopyrightandmedia.wordpress.com/1952/08/16/provisional-regulations-on-the-management-of-book-and-periodical-publishing-businesses-printing-businesses-and-distribution-businesses/, accessed: 5 March 2021) [in English/Chinese].

Provisions of the Supreme People's Court on Certain Issues Related to the Application of Law in the Trial of Civil Cases Involving Disputes over Infringement of the Right of Dissemination through Information Networks, [Original title: 最高人民法院关于审理侵害信息网络传播权民事纠纷案件适用法律若干问题的规定 Zuìgāo Rénmín Fǎyuàn Guānyú Shěnlǐ Qīnhài Xìnxī Wǎngluò Chuánbò Quán Mínshì

Jiūfēn Ànjiàn Shìyòng Fǎlǜ Ruògān Wèntí De Guī dìng], 2012 - issued 17 December 2012, adopted 26 November 2012, effective 1 January 2013, Supreme People's Court of The People's Republic of China (Provided by HFG Law & Intellectual Property: https://www.hfgip.com/sites/default/files/law/provisions_of_the_supreme_people_s_court_on_certain_issues_involving_disputes_over_infringement_2013_english.pdf, accessed: 5 March 2021) [in English].

Provisions of the Supreme People's Court on the Jurisdiction of the Intellectual Property Courts of Beijing, Shanghai and Guangzhou over Cases, [Original title: 最高人民法院关于北京、上海、广州知识产权法院案件管辖的规定 Zuìgāo Rénmín Fǎyuàn Guānyú Běijīng, Shànghǎi, Guǎngzhōu Zhīshì Chǎnquán Fǎyuàn Ànjiàn Guǎnxiá De Guīdìng], 27 October 2014, Supreme People's Court of the People's Republic of China (provided by chinacourt.org: https://www.chinacourt.org/law/detail/2014/10/id/147980.shtml, accessed: 5 March 2021) [in Chinese].

Provisions on the Implementation of the International Copyright Treaties, [Original title: 实施国际著作权条约的规定 Shíshī Guójì Zhùzuòquán Tiáoyuē De Guīdìng], 1992 - promulgated 25 September 1992, effective 30 September 1992, State Council of the People's Republic of China (provided by WIPO: http://www.wipo.int/wipolex/en/text.jsp?file_id=181489, accessed: 5 March 2021) [in English].

Qu, Difan, and Li, Yahong, "The Challenges for the Enforcement against Copyright Violations in China under the TRIPS Agreement", *Frontiers of Law in China* 7, 2 (2012): 245-268 [in English].

Qu, Sanqiang, *Copyright in China*, Beijing: Foreign Languages Press 2002 [in English].

Qu, Sanqiang, *Intellectual Property Law in China*, Alphen aan den Rijn, Netherlands: Kluwer Law International, 2012 [in English].

Quentin, David, and Baggins, Brian, "Quotations from Mao Tse Tung - 1927-1964 - Peking Foreign Language Press - Mao Tse Tung Internet Archive (marxist.org) 2000", 1966 (marxist.org: https://www.marxists.org/reference/archive/mao/works/red-book/ch24.htm, accessed: 6 March 2021) [in English].

Regulations for the Implemenation of the Copyright Law of the People's Republic of China, [Original title: 中华人民共和国著作权法实施条例 Zhōnghuá Rénmín Gònghéguó Zhùzuòquán Fǎ Shíshī Tiáolì], 1991 - 24 May 1991, promulgated 30 May 1991, effective 1 June 1991, National Copyright Administration of the People's Republic of China (provided by WIPO: https://wipolex.wipo.int/en/text/125967, accessed: 5 March 2021) [in English].

Regulations for the Implementation of the Copyright Law of the People's Republic of China, [Original title: 中华人民共和国著作权法实施条例 Zhōnghuá rénmín gònghéguó zhùzuòquán fǎ shíshī tiáolì], 2013 - issued 2 August 2002, effective 15 September 2002, amended 8 January 2011, amended 30 January 2013, effective 1 March 2013, State Council of the People's Republic of China (provided by WIPO: https://wipolex.wipo.int/en/text/456390, accessed: 5 March 2021) [in English].

Regulations for the Protection of Computer Software [Original title: 计算机软件保护条例 Jìsuànjī Ruǎnjiàn Bǎo hù Tiáolì], 1991 - promulgated 4 June 1991, effective 1 October 1991, State Council of the People's Republic of China (provided by AsianLII: http://www.asianlii.org/cn/legis/cen/laws/rftpocs542/, accessed: 5 March 2021) [in English].

Regulations on Computer Software Protection, [Original title: 计算机软件保护条例 Jìsuànjī Ruǎnjiàn Bǎohù Tiáolì], 2013 - issued 20 December 2001, effective 1 January 2002, amended 8 January 2011, amended 30 January 2013, effective 1 March 2013, State Council of the People's Republic of China (provided by WIPO: https://wipolex.wipo.int/en/text/455377, accessed: 5 March 2021) [in English].

Regulations on Copyright Collective Administration, [Original title: 著作权集体管理条例 Zhùzuòquán Jítǐ Guǎnlǐ Tiáolì], 2004 - adopted 22 December 2004, effective 1 March 2005, amended 4 December 2013, State Council of the People's Republic of China (provided by WIPO: https://wipolex.wipo.int/en/text/181505, accessed: 5 March 2021) [in English].

Regulations on Customs Protection of Intellectual Property Rights, [Original title: 中华人民共和国知识产权海关保护条例 Zhōnghuá Rénmín Gònghéguó Zhīshì Chǎn quán Hǎiguān Bǎohù Tiáolì], 2018 - promulgated 2 December 2003, effective 1 March 2004, amended 24 March 2010, amended 19 March 2018, State Council of the People's Republic of China (provided by gov.cn: http://www.gov.cn/gongbao/content/2019/content_5468830.htm, accessed: 6 March 2021) [in Chinese].

Regulations on Customs Protection of Intellectual Property Rights, [Original title: 中华人民共和国知识产权海关保护条例 Zhōnghuá Rénmín Gònghéguó Zhīshì Chǎn quán Hǎiguān Bǎohù Tiáolì], 2003 - promulgated 2 December 2003, effective 1 March 2004, State Council of the People's Republic of China (provided by WIPO: http://www.wipo.int/wipolex/en/text.jsp?file_id=181400, accessed: 5 March 2021) [in English].

Regulations on the Protection of Intellectual Property Rights by Customs, [Original title: 中华人民共和国知识产权海关保护条例 Zhōnghuá Rénmín Gònghéguó Zhī shì Chǎnquán Hǎiguān Bǎohù Tiáolì], 1995 - promulgated 5 July 1993, effective 1 October 1995, State Council of the People's Republic of China (provided by WIPO: http://www.wipo.int/edocs/lexdocs/laws/en/cn/cn013en.pdf, accessed: 5 March 2021) [in English].

Regulations on the Protection of Right of Dissemination via Information Network, [Original title: 信息网络传播

权保护条例 Xìnxī Wǎngluò Chuánbò Quán Bǎohù Tiáolì], 2013 - issued 18 May 2006, effective 1 July 2006, amended 16 January 2013, issued 30 January 2013, effective March 2013, The State Council of the People's Republic of China (provided by HFG Law & Intellectual Property: http://www.hfgip.com/sites/default/files/law/regulations_on_the_protection_of_right_of_dissemination_via_information_network_2013_english.pdf, accessed: 5 March 2021) [in English].

Rights of Certain Authors to Attribution and Integrity (Visual Artists Rights Act of the United States of America) (Rights of Certain Authors to Attribution and Integrity (Visual Artists Rights Act of the United States of America)), 1990 - 1 Dec 1990, 17 U.S.C. § 106a [in English].

Ring, Marcus, *China und das Recht des geistigen Eigentums - Die Vereinbarungen mit der WTO und ihre Umsetzung* [Translated title: China and intellectual property rights - The agreements with the WTO and their implementation], Reihe China Band 17, Hamburg: Diplomica Verlag GmbH, 2008 [in German].

Rosen, Amy, "China vs. United States: A Cosmopolitan Copyright Comparison", *Journal of Technology Law & Policy* 15, Fall 2014 (2014): 1-32 [in English].

Ross, Thomas I., "Enforcing Intellectual Property Rights in China", *China Business Review* (2012): 24-27 [in English].

Sanger, David E., "Chinese Pirate Factories Have Roots Abroad, U.S. Study Says" *The New York Times, Washington*, 3 June 1996 [in English].

Sanger, David E., "Signs Emerge Of China Deal On Sanctions" *The New York Times, Washington*, 13 June 1996 [in English].

Several Provisions on Evidence in Civil Litigation, [Original title: 最高人民法院关于民事诉讼证据的若干规定 Zuì gāo Rénmín Fǎyuàn Guānyú Mínshì Sùsòng Zhèngjù De Ruògān Guīdìng], 2019 - adopted 14 October 2019 amending version of 6 December 2001, effective 1 May 2020, The Supreme People's Court of the People's Republic of China (provided by court.gov.cn: http://www.court.gov.cn/zixun-xiangqing-212721.html, accessed: 6 March 2021) [in Chinese].

Sgambati, Stephanie L., "China's Accession to the Berne Convention: Bandaging the Wounds of Intellectual Property Piracy in China", *Fordham Intellectual Property, Media & Entertainment Law Journal* 3, 1 (1992): 139-174 [in English].

Shi, Jinping, "Copyright registration in China", 20 December 2015 (CCPIT: http://www.ccpit-patent.com.cn/node/2759, accessed: 6 March 2021) [in English].

Sidel, Mark, "Copyright, Trademark and Patent Law in the People's Republic of China", *Texas International Law Journal* 21 (1985-1986): 259-289 [in English].

Sidel, Mark, "The Legal Protection of Copyright and the Rights of Authors in the People's Republic of China, 1949-1984: Prelude to the Chinese Copyright Law", *Columbia Journal of Art and and the Law* 9 (1984-1985): 477-508 [in English].

SIPS (Joseph Simone), "China's new E-commerce Law", 14 March 2019 (WTR: https://www.worldtrademarkreview.com/anti-counterfeiting/chinas-new-e-commerce-law, accessed: 6 March 2021) [in English].

Stevenson, Richard W., "U.S. Cites China for Failing to Curb Piracy in Trade" *The New York Times, Washington*, 1 May 1996 [in English].

Stoianoff, Natalie P., "The Influence of the WTO over China's Intellectual Property Regime", *Sydney Law Review* 34 (2013): 65-89 [in English].

Tao, Zhang, "Protestant Missionary Publishing and the Birth of Chinese Elite Journalism", *Journalism Studies* 8, 6 (2007): 879-897 [in English].

The Copyright Law - trans. N.F. Allman (The Copyright Law - trans. N.F. Allman), 1928 - *The Chinese Law Review* (1929-1931) 4 (2) 1-5 [in English].

The State Council of The People's Republic of China, "White Paper: China and the World Trade Organization", 28 June 2018 (gov.cn: http://english.www.gov.cn/archive/white_paper/201

8/06/28/content_281476201898696.htm, accessed: 6 March 2021) [in English].

The Supreme People's Court of the People's Republic of China, "China first internet court handles over 10,000 cases", 20 August 2018 (court.gov.cn: http://english.court.gov.cn/2018-08/20/content_36798243.htm, accessed: 6 March 2021) [in English].

The Supreme People's Court of the People's Republic of China, "Hainan sets up tribunals for foreign-related civil and commercial, IP cases", 27 September 2019 (court.gov.cn: http://english.court.gov.cn/2019-09/27/content_37514175.htm, accessed: 6 March 2021) [in English].

The Supreme People's Court of The People's Republic of China "Intellectual Property Protection by Chinese Courts in 2019" [Original title: 中国法院知识产权司法保护状况（2019) Zhōngguó fǎyuàn zhīshì chǎnquán sīfǎ bǎohù zhuàngkuàng (2019)], 21 April 2020, (http://www.court.gov.cn/zixun-xiangqing-226501.html, accessed: 6 March 2021) [in Chinese/English].

The Supreme People's Court of The People's Republic of China, "Nation strengthens IPR protections", 13 March 2019 (court.gov.cn: http://english.court.gov.cn/2019-03/13/content_37449349.htm, accessed: 6 March 2021) [in English].

The Supreme People's Court of the People's Republic of China, "Online courts ease access to legal services", 6 December 2019 (court.gov.cn: http://english.court.gov.cn/2019-12/06/content_37528117.htm, accessed: 6 March 2021) [in English].

The Supreme People's Court of The People's Republic of China "The status of judicial protection of intellectual property in Chinese courts (2014)" [Original title: 中国法院知识产权司法保护状况 (2014) Zhōngguó fǎyuàn zhīshì chǎnquán sīfǎ bǎohù zhuàngkuàng (2014)], 20 April 2015, (http://www.court.gov.cn/zixun-xiangqing-14207.html, accessed: 6 March 2021) [in Chinese].

The Supreme People's Court of The People's Republic of China "The status of judicial protection of intellectual property in Chinese courts (2016)" [Original title: 中国法院知识产权司法保护状况（2016年) Zhōngguó Fǎyuàn Zhīshì Chǎnquán Sīfǎ Bǎohù Zhuàngkuàng (2016 Nián)], 27 April 2017, (http://www.court.gov.cn/zixun-xiangqing-42362.html, accessed: 6 March 2021) [in Chinese].

The Supreme People's Court of The People's Republic of China "The status of judicial protection of intellectual property in Chinese courts (2017)" [Original title: 中国法院知识产权司法保护状况 (2017年) Zhōng guó Fǎyuàn Zhīshì Chǎnquán Sīfǎ Bǎohù Zhuàngkuàng (2017 Nián)], 19 December 2018, (http://ipc.court.gov.cn/zh-cn/news/view-75.html, accessed: 6 March 2021) [in Chinese].

The Supreme People's Court of The People's Republic of China "The status of judicial protection of intellectual property in Chinese courts (2018)" [Original title: 中国法院知识产权司法保护状况（2018年）Zhōngguó Fǎyuàn Zhīshì Chǎnquán Sīfǎ Bǎohù Zhuàngkuàng (2018 Nián)], 19 April 2019, (http://www.court.gov.cn/style/system/files/zscqsfbh201811.pdf, accessed: 6 March 2021) [in Chinese/English].

The Supreme People's Court of The People's Republic of China (April 2016) "The status of judicial protection of intellectual property in Chinese courts (2015)" [Original title: 中国法院知识产权司法保护状况 (2015年) Zhōngguó Fǎyuàn Zhīshì Chǎnquán Sīfǎ Bǎohù Zhuàngkuàng (2015 Nián)], 14 December 2018, (http://ipc.court.gov.cn/zh-cn/news/view-61.html, accessed: 6 March 2021) [in Chinese].

The United States Trade Representative "2019 Special 301 Report", April 2019, (https://ustr.gov/sites/default/files/2019_Special_301_Report.pdf, accessed: 6 March 2021) [in English].

The United States Trade Representative "Findings of the Investigation into China's Acts, Policies, and Practices related to Technology Transfer, Intellectual Property, and Innovation under Section 301 of the Trade Act of 1974", 22 March 2018, (https://ustr.gov/sites/default/files/Section%20301%20FINAL.PDF, accessed: 6 March 2021) [in English].

The United States Trade Representative, "Section 301 Investigation Fact Sheet", June 2018 (ustr.gov: https://ustr.gov/about-us/policy-offices/press-office/fact-sheets/2018/june/section-301-investigation-fact-sheet, accessed: 6 March 2021) [in English].

Trade Act of 1974 of the United States of America (U.S. Trade Act of 1974), 1974 - enacted 3 January 1975, 19 U.S.C. ch. 12 §§2101 et seq. [in English].

Transparency International, "Corruption Perceptions Index 2020" (transparency.org: https://www.transparency.org/en/cpi/2020/index/nzl, accessed: 16 March 2021) [in English].

Tsoi, Annie, "Principle Impact of Copyright Law Amendments", *China Law & Practice* (May 2010) [in English].

U.S. and China "Economic And Trade Agreement Between The Government Of The United States Of America And The Government Of The People's Republic Of China", 15 January 2020, (https://ustr.gov/sites/default/files/files/agreements/phase%20one%20agreement/Economic_And_Trade_Agreement_Between_The_United_States_And_China_Text.pdf, accessed: 6 March 2021) [in English].

U.S. Copyright Act (U.S. Copyright Act), 1995 - 19 Oct 1979, 17 U.S.C. §§ 101 et seq. [in English].

Understanding on Rules and Procedures Governing the Settlement of Disputes (DSU), 1994 - 15 April 1994, 869 UNTS 401; 33 I.L.M. 1226 (Annex 2 of the Marrakesh Agreement establishing the World Trade Organization, signed in Marrakesh, Morocco on 15 April 1994 , 33 I.L.M. 1125) [in English].

UN Educational, Scientific and Cultural Organization (UNESCO) *Universal Copyright Convention* (UCC), 1952 - 6 Sept 1952, revised 24 July 1971, effective 10 July 1974, U.N.T.S. No. 13444, vol. 943, pp. 178-325 (https://www.refworld.org/docid/3ddb88377.html, accessed: 5 March 2021) [in English].

Urheberrechtsgesetz Deutschland (German Copyright Act) (UrhG (Germany)), 1965 - 9 September 1965 (Federal Law Gazette I, p. 1273), as last amended by Article 1 of the Act of 28 November 2018 (Federal Law Gazette I, p. 2014), [in German].

Wan Hui Da Intellectual Property Agency (Chao Feng and Paul Ranjard), "Final draft of proposed PRC Copyright Law amendment released by NCAC", 7 January 2013 (Lexology: https://www.lexology.com/library/detail.aspx?g=eb127dd5-03cc-43ed-b0ba-4c3b6974e9b8, accessed: 6 March 2021) [in English].

Wan, Yong, "Copyright Damages in China", *Journal, Copyright Society of the USA* 61 (2013-2014): 517-544 [in English].

Wang, Chenguang, "Law-making functions of the Chinese courts: Judicial activism in a county or rapid social changes", *Frontiers of Law in China* 1, 4 (2006): 524-549 [in English].

Wang, Lina, "Intellectual Property Protection in China", *International Information & Library Review* 36, 3 (2004): 253-261 [in English].

Wei, Zhi, *Der Urheberrechtsschutz in China mit Hinweisen auf das Deutsche Recht* [Translated title: Copyright protection in China with references to German law], Rechtswissenschaftliche Forschung und Entwicklung, Band 462, München: Verlag V. Florentz, 1994 [in German].

WIPO, "Basic Proposal for the Substantive Provisions of the Treaty on Certain Questions Concerning the Protection of Literary and Artistic Works to be Considered by the Diplomatic Conference (Document CRNR/DC/4, 30 August 1996) " In *Diplomatic Conference on Certain Copyright and Neighbouring Rights Questions* Geneva 1996.

WIPO, "China - Legal Information" (WIPO: http://www.wipo.int/members/en/details.jsp?country_id=38, accessed: 6 March 2021) [in English].

WIPO, "Copyright - What is copyright?" (WIPO: http://www.wipo.int/copyright/en/, accessed: 6 March 2021) [in English].

WIPO, "Implications of the TRIPS Agreement on Treaties Administered by WIPO", 2012 - WIPO Publication No. 464 (E) (WIPO: http://www.wipo.int/edocs/pubdocs/en/intproperty/464/wipo_pub_464.pdf, accessed: 6 March 2021) [in English].

WIPO, *Introduction to Intellectual Property: Theory and Practice*, London: Kluwer Law International 1997 [in English].

WIPO, "Main Provisions and Benefits of the Beijing Treaty in Audiovisual Performances (2012)", 2016 (WIPO: http://www.wipo.int/edocs/pubdocs/en/wipo_pub_beijing_flyer.pdf, accessed: 6 March 2021) [in English].

WIPO, "Other IP Treaties - IP-related Multilateral Treaties < Contracting Parties/Signatories < Universal Copyright Convention 1952" (WIPO: http://www.wipo.int/wipolex/en/other_treaties/parties.jsp?treaty_id=208&group_id=22, accessed: 6 March 2021) [in English].

WIPO, "What is Intellectual Property?" (WIPO: http://www.wipo.int/about-ip/en/index.html, accessed: 6 March 2021) [in English].

WIPO, "WIPO-Administered Treaties - Contracting Parties > Berne Convention" (WIPO: http://www.wipo.int/treaties/en/ShowResults.jsp?treaty_id=15, accessed: 6 March 2021) [in English].

WIPO, "WIPO-Administered Treaties - Contracting Parties > Rome Convention" (WIPO: http://www.wipo.int/treaties/en/ShowResults.jsp?treaty_id=17, accessed: 6 March 2021) [in English].

WIPO Copyright Treaty (WCT), 1996 - adopted in Geneva on 20 December 1996; entry into force on 6 March 2002, S. Treaty Doc. No. 105-17 (1997); 36 ILM 65 (1997) (provided by WIPO: http://www.wipo.int/treaties/en/text.jsp?file_id=295166, accessed: 5 March 2021) [in English].

WIPO Performances and Phonograms Treaty (WPPT), 1996 - adopted in Geneva on 20 December 1996; entry into force on 20 May 2002, S. Treaty Doc. No. 105-17, 36 ILM 76 (1997) (provided by WIPO: http://www.wipo.int/treaties/en/text.jsp?file_id=295578, accessed: 5 March 2021) [in English].

WTO "Accession of the People's Republic of China", Protocol WT/L/432 [in English].

WTO "China - Certain Measures Concerning the Protection of Intellectual Property Rights - Request for Consultations by the United States", 2018, WT/DS542/1 (18-1799) 1-2 (https://docs.wto.org/dol2fe/Pages/SS/directdoc.aspx?filename=q:/WT/DS/542-1.pdf&Open=True, accessed: 6 March 2021) [in English].

WTO "China - Measures Affecting the Protection and Enforcement of Intellectual Property Rights - Report of the Panel", 2009, WT/DS362/R (09-0240) 1-135 (http://www.wto.org/english/tratop_e/dispu_e/362r_e.pdf, accessed: 6 March 2021) [in English].

Xin, Zhiming, "Developed country status is still some distance away", 5 March 2020 (Chinadaily: http://global.chinadaily.com.cn/a/202003/05/WS5e605c3ba31012821727c7bd.html, accessed: 6 March 2021) [in English].

Xinhua, "China issues guideline for enhancing IPR protection", 24 November 2019 (gov.cn: http://english.www.gov.cn/policies/latestreleases/201911/24/content_WS5dda789bc6d0bcf8c4c17bd4.html, accessed: 6 March 2021) [in English].

Xinhua, "China to step up IPR trials to stimulate innovation", 12 March 2017 (ShanghaiDaily: http://www.shanghaidaily.com/nation/China-to-step-up-IPR-trials-to-stimulate-innovation/shdaily.shtml, accessed: 6 March 2021) [in English].

Xue, Hong, "A User-Unfriendly Draft: 3rd Revision of the Chinese Copyright Law", *Journal of International Commercial and Technology Law* 7, 4 (2012): 350-354 [in English].

Xue, Hong, "One Step Ahead, Two Steps Back: Reverse Engineering the Second Draft for the Third Revision of the Chinese Copyright Law", *American University International Law Journal* 28, 1 (2013): 295-309 [in English].

Yang, Deli, "The Development of Intellectual Property in China", *World Patent Information* 25, 2 (2003): 131-142 [in English].

Yang, Xiaonan, "Legislative Interpretations by the Standing Committee of the National People's Congress in China", *Hong Kong Law Journal* 38, 1 (2008): 255-285 [in English].

Yang, Zhiwen, "A Commentary on the Selection of Judges in China: From the Perspective of Judicial Professionalization", *US-China Law Review* 14 (2017): 251-269 [in English].

Yu, Peter K., "Piracy, Prejudice, and Perspectives: An Attempt to Use Shakespeare to Reconfigure the U.S.-China Intellectual Property Debate", *Boston University International Law Journal* 19, 1 (2001): 1-87 [in English].

Yu, Peter K., "The TRIPS Enforcement Dispute", *Nebraska Law Review* 89, 4 (2010): 1046-1131 [in English].

Yu, Xun, *Schadensersatzanspruch im Urheberrecht - Eine vergleichende Betrachtung des chinesischen und deutschen Rechts* [Translated title: Compensation Claims in Copyright Law - A Comparative View of Chinese and German Law], Reihe Rechtswissenschaft, 1. Auflage, Göttingen: Sierke Verlag, 2005 [in German].

Yufeng, Li, and Ng, Catherine W., "Understanding the Great Qing Copyright Law of 1910", *Journal of the Copyright*

Society of the U.S.A. 56 (2008-2009): 767-788 [in English].

Zhang, Jinfan, *The Tradition and Modern Transition of Chinese Law*, Heidelberg: Springer-Verlag Berlin, 2014 [in English].

Zhang, Naigen, "Intellectual Property Law Enforcement in China: Trade Issues, Policies and Practices", *Fordham Intellectual Property, Media and Entertainment Law Journal* 8, 1 (1997): 63-82 [in English].

Zhang, Naigen, "Intellectual Property Law in China: Basic Policy and New Developments", *Annual Survey of International & Comparative Law* 4, 1 (1997): 1-17 [in English].

Zhang, Yue, "China to enhance IPR protection to improve business climate, boost tech innovation", 17 July 2019 (gov.cn: http://english.www.gov.cn/premier/news/201907/17/content_WS5d2fdfb2c6d00d362f668704.html, accessed: 6 March 2021) [in English].

Deutsches und internationales Wirtschaftsrecht

hrsg. von Prof. Dr. Dr. h.c. Marian Paschke (Universität Hamburg)

Lin Li
Die Wesentliche Vertragsverletzung
Vergleichende Betrachtung der Rechtslage nach CISG, CESL, VG und BGB
Die Regelungen der wesentlichen Vertragsverletzung haben maßgeblichen Anteil an der Risikozuordnung und am Ausmaß der Risikotragung im Vertragsrecht. Die vorliegende Untersuchung widmet sich der vergleichenden Betrachtung der wesentlichen Vertragsverletzung zwischen zwei nationalen Vertragsrechtsregimen (BGB und VG) sowie zwei internationalen Regelwerken (CISG und CESL). Der Rechtsvergleich wird hierbei anhand von konkreten Fällen und deren Behandlung in den jeweiligen Rechtsordnungen durchgeführt und mündet im Vorschlag eines relativ „vollständigen und gerechten Systems der wesentlichen Vertragsverletzung".
Bd. 61, 2020, 308 S., 44,90 €, gb., ISBN 978-3-643-91279-4

Bernadette Lorenzen
Schranken für die rechtliche Bewertung innerhalb der schiedsgutachterlichen Tätigkeit
Gewährleistung der Privatautonomie im Spannungsverhältnis zur verfahrensrechtlichen Stellung des Schiedsgutachters
Schiedsgutachter bewerten Sachverhalte in der Praxis vielfach nicht nur im Hinblick auf tatsächliche Umstände, sondern auch aus rechtlicher Perspektive. Die rechtliche Bewertung durch den Schiedsgutachter bewegt sich allerdings im Spannungsfeld zwischen der Privatautonomie einerseits und der verfahrensrechtlichen Stellung des Schiedsgutachters andererseits. Basierend auf einer ausführlichen Analyse der dogmatischen Grundlage der schiedsgutachterlichen Tätigkeit gelangt die Verfasserin zu einer neuen rechtlichen Einordnung der Funktion, des Aufgabenbereichs sowie der Kompetenzen des Schiedsgutachters und setzt neue Schranken für die rechtliche Bewertung durch den Schiedsgutachter.
Bd. 60, 2020, 192 S., 44,90 €, gb., ISBN 978-3-643-14306-8

Indira Benten Patury
Die Entwicklung des Rohstoffsektors in Südamerika
Eine Untersuchung unter besonderer Berücksichtigung von Nachhaltigkeitspostulaten
Die Dissertation beinhaltet eine Darstellung der Rechtslage des nichtenergetischen Rohstoffsektors in den Ländern Südamerikas. Dabei wird der nachhaltigen Entwicklung besondere Aufmerksamkeit gewidmet. Umwelt-, Arbeitnehmer- und Menschenrechte sowie der Klimaschutz werden intensiv beleuchtet. Zudem erfolgt eine Analyse der Rohstoffspekulation und der möglichen Regulierung von Rohstoffmärkten. Die Arbeit stellt die zu geringe Leistungsfähigkeit der Rechtssysteme südamerikanischer Länder heraus, um aktuelle Herausforderungen im Rahmen des Rohstoffabbaus zu bewältigen. Dies wird im Verlauf der Arbeit anhand konkreter Beispiele dargelegt und diskutiert.
Bd. 59, 2021, ca. 240 S., ca. 44,90 €, gb., ISBN 978-3-643-13884-2

Johannes Lange
Die Neuordnung der energetischen Modernisierung im Recht der Wohnraummiete
Zur Umsetzung klima- und umweltpolitischer Ziele mit den Mitteln des privaten Vertragsrechts
Die Arbeit befasst sich mit den Regelungen über die energetische Modernisierung von Wohnraum nach dem Mietrechtsänderungsgesetz 2013. Neben den technischen, wirtschaftlichen und steuerlichen Gesichtspunkten, stehen insbesondere die sich aus der neuen Rechtslage für die modernisierungsrechtlichen Vorschriften der §§ 555b ff. BGB ergebenen Folgen und Fragestellungen im Fokus. Zugleich wird am Beispiel der energetischen Modernisierung aufgezeigt, dass der Gesetzgeber in zunehmenden Maße auf das private Vertragsrecht zur Umsetzung klima- und umweltpolitischer Ziele Einfluss nimmt.
Bd. 58, 2018, ca. 396 S., ca. 49,90 €, gb., ISBN 978-3-643-13634-3

LIT Verlag Berlin – Münster – Wien – Zürich – London
Auslieferung Deutschland / Österreich / Schweiz: siehe Impressumsseite

Martina Mittendorf
Compliance Management System als Haftungsbegrenzungsinstrument in der mittelständischen Wirtschaft
Die Arbeit verbindet interdisziplinär die Fachgebiete der Betriebswirtschaft und Rechtswissenschaft, indem geprüft wird, ob die Implementierung eines Management Systems zur Einhaltung von Compliance-Verpflichtungen eine haftungsbegrenzende Wirkung entfalten kann.
Um darüber hinaus in Erfahrung zu bringen, ob mittelständische Unternehmen für ihre Unternehmensgröße die Einrichtung von Compliance Management Systemen als ein taugliches Instrument ansehen, wurde eine Umfrage an Unternehmen dieser Größenordnung im Wirtschaftsraum Hamburg gerichtet und ausgewertet.
Bd. 57, 2017, 320 S., 39,90 €, gb., ISBN 978-3-643-13521-6

Cheng Shi
Rechtliche Rahmenbedingungen für die Entwicklung der Handelsbeziehungen zwischen China und der EU im Rohstoffsektor
Die Arbeit befasst sich mit dem juristischen Handelsbedingungen zwischen China und der EU im Rohstoffsektor. Sie beleuchtet die Entwicklung dieser Handelsbeziehungen und deren WTO-rechtlichen Rahmen bei Rechtsstreitigkeiten. Der Fokus liegt dabei auf den Rechtsgrundsätzen, die bei bilateralen Verträgen der EU mit der Volksrepublik China zu beachten sind, und vor allem auf die europäischen Rechtsgrundlagen ausgerichtet sind.
Bd. 56, 2016, 396 S., 59,90 €, gb., ISBN 978-3-643-13436-3

Bongseock Seo
Der Vergleich des BGB-Systems nach koreanischem und deutschem Recht anhand der subektiven Rechte und Ansprüche
Bd. 55, 2014, 64 S., 24,90 €, gb., ISBN 978-3-643-12514-9

Nele Julie Todsen
Grenzen gebührenfinanzierter Telemedien
Eine kritische Bewertung des Drei-Stufen-Tests mit besonderm Blick auf das Wettbewerbsverhältnis zur Presse
Die Arbeit befasst sich mit dem Spannungsverhältnis von gebühren- zu privatwirtschaftlich finanzierten Telemedien auf dem Medienmarkt „Internet“. Sie schildert den sogenannten Beihilfekompromiss und untersucht, ob der Drei-Stufen-Test ein geeignetes Vehikel ist, die Online-Präsenz der öffentlich-rechtlichen Sender mit den europarechtlichen Vorgaben kompatibel zu machen. Weiter beleuchtet die Arbeit kritisch, ob der Rundfunkrat in der Lage ist, bei der Durchführung des Drei-Stufen-Tests unbefangen die entscheidenden Abgrenzungen zu ziehen. Die Arbeit wirft dazu einen Blick auf die Handhabung in Großbritannien, wo externe Gremien im Rahmen des Public Value Tests über die Zulässigkeit öffentlich-rechtlicher Telemedien entscheiden.
Bd. 54, 2013, 288 S., 29,90 €, gb., ISBN 978-3-643-12082-3

Kristin Bartel
Wettbewerbsprobleme auf dem deutschen Energiemarkt durch Unternehmenszusammenschlüsse
Entflechtung als Mittel der Marktöffnung
Auf dem deutschen Elektrizitäts- und Gasmarkt bestehen ausgeprägte horizontale, vertikale und konglomerate Unternehmensverflechtungen. Obwohl der Liberalisierungsprozess des Energiemarktes vor über 10 Jahren begonnen hat, bestehen diese vermachteten Marktstrukturen fort oder haben sich noch verstärkt. Die Ursachen hierfür werden von der Autorin eingehend analysiert. Daneben geht die Untersuchung der Frage nach, inwieweit Entflechtungsregelungen zu einer Belebung des Wettbewerbs führen können. Der britische Energiemarkt dient dabei als Vergleich.
Bd. 53, 2011, 696 S., 94,90 €, br., ISBN 978-3-643-11256-9

LIT Verlag Berlin – Münster – Wien – Zürich – London
Auslieferung Deutschland / Österreich / Schweiz: siehe Impressumsseite

Constantin Sapunov
Verhaltenspflichten von Wertpapierdienstleistungsunternehmen gegenüber Emittenten bei IPO's
Bd. 52, 2013, 392 S., 39,90 €, gb., ISBN 978-3-643-10864-7

Antonia Papadelli
Beweislastverteilung bei der privaten Durchsetzung des Kartellrechts
Eine rechtsvergleichende Studie
Die Bekämpfung von kartellrechtswidrigen Geschäftspraktiken anhand von privatrechtlichen Anspruchsgrundlagen steht in unmittelbarem Zusammenhang mit dem einzelstaatlichen Beweisrecht. Die Verfasserin untersucht die Einführung von einschlägigen Erleichterungen in der deutschen, französischen und griechischen Rechtsordnung und lotet die Regelungsdivergenzen bei der privaten Kartellrechtsanwendung in Europa aus, die auf die verschiedenartige Beurteilung von gleichen Sachverhalten je nach den anwendbaren nationalen Beweismechanismen hinauslaufen. Im Ergebnis erscheint die Einführung von einheitlichen beweislastrechtlichen Begünstigungen auf EU-Ebene als unerlässlich.
Bd. 51, 2011, 448 S., 59,90 €, gb., ISBN 978-3-643-90055-5

LIT Verlag Berlin – Münster – Wien – Zürich – London
Auslieferung Deutschland / Österreich / Schweiz: siehe Impressumsseite